Beginner's Guide to iOS® 10 App Development Using Swift™ 3

Xcode, Swift and App Design Fundamentals

Serhan Yamacli

Manchester Academic
Publishers

Beginner's Guide to iOS 10 App Development Using Swift 3 – Second Edition

This book is dedicated to Dilek and Yusuf Arda...

Table of Contents

Chapter 1

INTRODUCTION

Welcome to your guide to iOS® 10 app development.

This compact book aims to teach app development for iOS devices using Swift™ programming language. You don't need to have app development experience to learn the concepts and projects presented in this book. I'll assume that you have no knowledge on programming and app development. I'll try to explain every bit of app development process with plain words and will try to make things easy to understand. This book will take you as a beginner and at the end of the book; you'll be able to create your very own apps that are ready to run on actual devices and also ready to be sold at the App Store®. By the way, I'd like to remind you that a single book cannot make you an expert on a subject. However, this book will teach you a lot and you'll have a solid background to learn more afterwards.

As you might have heard, iOS apps have been developed using a programming language called Objective-C® for a long time. However, Apple recently introduced a new programming language: Swift. They announced Swift in the World Wide Developer Conference (WWDC) in 2014. In that year, first version of Swift was released. After some important modifications, Swift 2 came around and finally Swift 3 is released in September 2016. Swift was a proprietary project in the beginning but now it is open source and a lot of developers contribute to this promising language. Swift has a more active community compared to Objective-C by September 2016 therefore your investment on learning Swift is a good choice.

As you follow this book, you'll go through the following steps:

1. Using Xcode® integrated development environment

2. Coding in Swift programming language

3. Designing user interfaces for your apps

4. Developing real world apps that will teach a lot in practice

5. Utilizing internal devices like GPS in your own apps

I'll not introduce complicated subjects until I'm sure that you understand the basics because it is very easy to get lost while learning a new programming language. You'll not be in such a situation with this book. I'll try to teach new concepts in the simplest way possible. Please don't forget that learning a programming language is a non-stop process, it never ends and this book will help you to get started easily.

Now, you know the aims and the method of this book. Let's set up Xcode 8 integrated development environment on our Mac®. By the way it is worth noting that the development environment we will use can only be installed on a Mac.

Chapter 2

SETTING UP YOUR DEVELOPMENT ENVIRONMENT

In my opinion, one of the good things about Apple products is that their version number usually increases periodically making it easy to track. For example, the release years of iPhone® series follow this pattern: iPhone 5 in 2012, iPhone 5s in 2013, iPhone 6 in 2014, iPhone 6s in 2015 and iPhone 7 in 2016. Similar patterns are also observed in most of their software versions. In our case, Xcode versions are important.

2.1. Xcode Development Environment

Xcode is an integrated development environment (IDE) for developing native software that runs on Apple devices. It means that if you want to develop native apps for iOS devices, for Macs, for Apple TV® and for Apple Watch®, you do this using the software called Xcode. Xcode is developed by Apple and it is free to download and use. However, it is worth noting that Xcode can be installed and ran only on a Mac. Therefore, you need a Mac in order to install Xcode and start developing iOS apps.

Xcode has several versions each corresponding to the year it is released. For example, Xcode 6 was made available in 2014. Then, in 2015 Xcode 7 came and Xcode 8 is released in 2016. You may say "why are we so interested in this version thing?" It is because the appropriate version of Xcode is required to develop apps for specific iOS versions. Moreover, each Xcode version is bundled by different Swift versions.

2.2. Swift Programming Language

Swift is a programming language that is used to develop apps for iOS®, Mac OS®, watchOS® and tvOS™ (and for Linux® recently). Xcode is bundled with Swift therefore you don't have to separately download anything related to Swift. Swift has gone through important changes while evolving from the first version of Swift (Swift 1) to Swift 3. A code you have written in the Swift 1 or Swift 2 probably will not be valid in Swift 3. This is called as "code incompatibility".

Xcode 8 has the updated Swift 3 language inside. Xcode 8 supports also Swift 2 however it is of course a good idea to develop in Swift 3 for continuity.

2.3. Installation of Xcode

How to install Xcode? Xcode 8 can be downloaded from the App Store on your Mac. Just go there and search for 'Xcode' (without quotes). It will show Xcode ready to be downloaded as shown in Figure 2.1 (All figures shown in this book can be viewed in colour and in full resolution on the book's website: www.ios-swift.net). Just click "Get" as shown inside the smallest rectangle in Figure 2.1 then it'll be downloaded and installed automatically in a while depending on your Internet connection speed (1 min~20 mins). As you can see from Figure 2.1, your Mac OS version should be at least 10.11.5 to install Xcode 8 (shown inside the rectangle at the bottom). Moreover, this download page shows that Xcode 8 includes Swift 3 and iOS 10 SDK (Software Development Kit) meaning that in Xcode 8, you can use Swift 3 to develop iOS 10 apps (shown inside the big rectangle). After successful installation, launch Xcode by clicking on its icon in the Launcher and then the welcome screen shown in Figure 2.2 should appear. As you can see from this figure, my Xcode's version is 8.1.

2.4. Setting up Signing Identities

In Xcode, you will develop iOS apps however, in order to build them (making the executable) for running on simulators or real iOS devices, **you need to sign the app**. Signing is a proof which shows that the app cannot be modified by anybody other than you hence assuring users that the app is from a trustable developer. Therefore, signing is essential and have to be done for every app you develop in Xcode. The good news is that once you set up code signing in Xcode, you can easily sign all your apps.

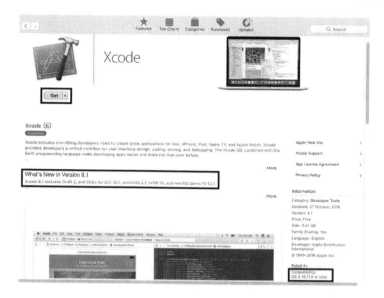

Figure 2.1. Xcode 8 download screen in the Mac App Store (full resolution colour images on the book's website: www.ios-swift.net)

Figure 2.2. Xcode welcome screen

If you want to develop apps in Xcode and try these apps on simulators or on your own devices, you just need a usual Apple ID for code signing. This process is free. However, if you want to sell/distribute your apps on the iOS App Store, you need to enrol in the Apple Developer Program which currently starts from $99 per year. Details of the Apple Developer Program can be found on their official site: https://developer.apple.com/support/purchase-activation/. Since you're just beginning iOS development, you may continue without enrolling in developer program for now. You can always do it later when you are ready to sell your apps.

Setting up code signing is simple: just go to the Xcode menu as shown in Figure 2.3 and click on the "Preferences..." button.

Figure 2.3. Xcode menu

When you click on the "Preferences..." button, you'll see a window as in Figure 2.4 which shows a very detailed set of preferences regarding Xcode's general settings. Click on the "Accounts" tab shown by the arrow. Then you'll see the window shown in Figure 2.5. Click on the plus sign (+) indicated by the arrow and then you can add your Apple ID. After you enter your own Apple ID and password in this window, click "Sign In" button as shown in Figure 2.6.

Figure 2.4. Preferences window of Xcode

After you add your Apple ID and password to Xcode, you'll see the window shown in Figure 2.7. In this window, click "View Details..." button as shown by the arrow.

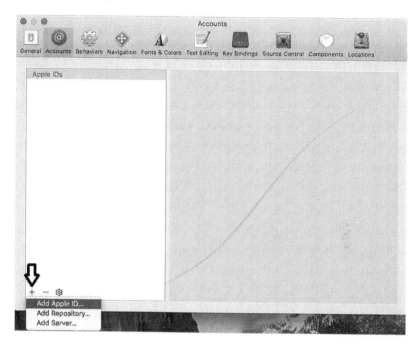

Figure 2.5. Adding a new Apple ID in the Accounts window

Figure 2.6. Adding your Apple ID to sign your apps

Click on the "Create" button for iOS Development as shown by the small arrow in Figure 2.8. It may take a little time. Then click "Done" as indicated by the big arrow. You can now close the "Accounts" window. If you did all these without a mistake, you did successfully set up your Xcode environment with the signing identity.

2.5. Viewing Installed Simulators and Devices

There is one step remaining to develop and test our first app. That is: setting up (or viewing) simulators in Xcode 8. Simulators are programs that mimic the behaviour of real devices. Therefore, you don't need to have all possible devices to test your app, you can use their simulators. The good news is that simulators of most devices are already installed by default when you install Xcode 8. To view the installed simulators, select Window → Devices from the Xcode's main menu as in Figure 2.9.

Figure 2.7. "View Details..." menu to add an app developer profile

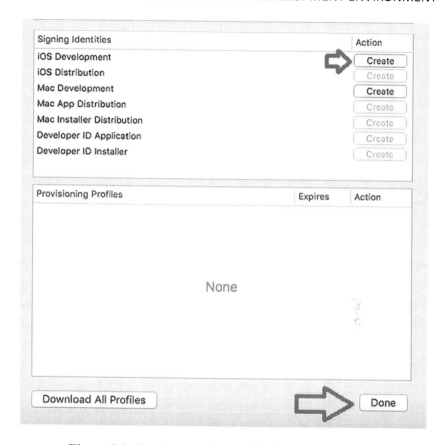

Figure 2.8. Creating signing profile for your Apple ID

Figure 2.9. Viewing device simulators already installed in Xcode

Xcode will show available devices and simulators as in Figure 2.10. Devices list shows the real hardware connected to your Mac. At the bottom of the devices, default simulators already installed in the Xcode are shown inside the rectangle in Figure 2.10. In my Xcode 8, simulators of all up-to-date devices are already installed. The iOS versions of these simulators are also shown just below the device names. All simulators have iOS 10 by default. If you want to add more simulators like a simulator for iPhone 4s, you can click on the plus button as shown by the arrow in Figure 2.10 and go to the related menu. After reviewing the installed simulators, we are now ready to develop our "Hello World" app in the next chapter.

Figure 2.10. Default device simulators in Xcode

Chapter 3

TEST DRIVE: THE HELLO WORLD APP

3.1. General Procedure for Developing an App

A good convention to start learning a programming language and a development environment is to try a "Hello World" example. It is just displaying the "Hello World" expression on the screen. OK, I know it is not an app that you'd be proud of showing to your family or friends but its usefulness stems from testing whether your programming environment is working properly and to see if you're ready to go for real projects. In our very first iOS 10 project, we will write "Hello, World!" in the middle of our device screen in any colour and font we like. We will test it on simulators but if you have access to an iOS device, you can test your "Hello World" app on it too.

Before we start building our first app, I'd like to point out general steps of app development:

1. Creating the Xcode project,

2. Setting up the User Interface (UI) of the app,

3. Connecting the UI components such as buttons, labels, textboxes, etc. to the Swift code,

4. Coding in Swift – the actual programming part

5. Building the project: this means creating the executable (file that actually runs on device or simulator). This is not difficult as it sounds; Xcode does the entire job with a single click,

6. Trying the app on a simulator,

7. Running the app on a real iOS device (optional),

8. Publishing the app on the iOS App Store (optional).

3.2. Creating a New Xcode Project

When you start Xcode, it gives you three choices as shown in Figure 3.1: i) Get started with a playground, ii) Create a new Xcode project and iii) Check out an existing project. Xcode offers a good method for learning Swift language using a concept called "playground" and we will go through this in detail in the next chapter. Now, we will develop our first project therefore let's choose to create a new project in Xcode (Second option in Figure 3.1 as shown by the arrow.). The last alternative is for opening an existing project but since this is your first project, this option does not apply.

Figure 3.1. Creating a new Xcode project for our first app

After you select "Create a new Xcode project", Xcode asks you what type of application you will create. Xcode is not only used for iOS development, it can also be used for developing Mac OS, watchOS and tvOS apps. For our iOS app, we need to select the iOS option from the top (shown inside the ellipse) and then a "Single View Application" (shown by the rectangle) as in Figure 3.2. "Single View Application" means that you will create an app which has only one screen (one page) and you won't use tabs to change screens, etc. Since our aim is to simply write "Hello, World!" in the middle of the screen, "Single View Application" does the job. After then please click "Next" (shown by the arrow).

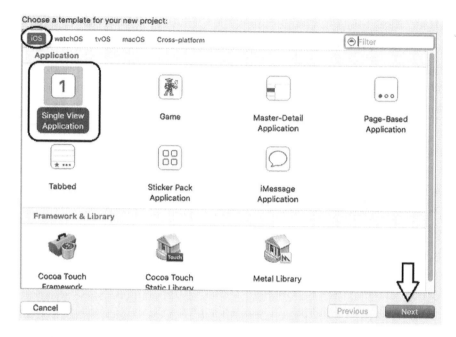

Figure 3.2. Creating a "Single View App"

3.3. Project Settings

Xcode now shows an options dialog box as in Figure 3.3. It asks for the "Product Name" (indicated by number 1). This will be the name of your app. We can fill in "Hello World" as shown in the figure. Of course you can give any name you like but it is a good practice to name your projects in such a way that you can guess what it does by just simply checking its name a few months later.

Next, the development team is selected by the drop down box (click the blue arrow at number 2). You'll see your name here since you set up signing before. It will automatically be available in the drop down box menu.

Then, you can enter an organization name (shown by number 3). This is optional; you may leave the organization name blank.

Next, the organization identifier is needed (shown by number 4). This is an essential information you should enter. It is generally in the form of com.yourname (like a reversed web address). Organization identifier is used to generate the "Bundle Identifier" shown beneath the organization identifier. This is used to distinguish among developers when you upload your app to the App Store. "Bundle Identifier" is automatically generated so you don't have to worry about it.

You can select between Objective-C (foregoing language) and Swift (new language) in the selection box shown in number 5. You are heading up for learning Swift so please select Swift there.

Finally, you can select the device families you want your apps to run on (shown by number 6). You can select iPhone, iPad or Universal. You don't have a specific screen size, etc. in this project so it is OK to select "Universal".

If you were patient enough to read until here, click next and then select the place where you want to save your Xcode project on your Mac as shown in Figure 3.4. I selected my Desktop but anywhere you like is OK. Then click "Create" as shown by the arrow in Figure 3.4.

Now you have created your project files and Xcode main screen appears as in Figure 3.5. In this window, you can view and change general properties of your project (section inside the ellipse). I'll not dive deep here and the defaults are OK for now. You don't need to change these settings for this project.

3.4. Default Files of a New Project
At the left pane lies the list of the files and folders of your project (inside the rectangle in Figure 3.5). When you created your project, these files are automatically generated and saved at the location you indicated in Figure 3.4. File type is specified by the file extension as you probably know. I'd like to bring your attention towards the default files included in your project:

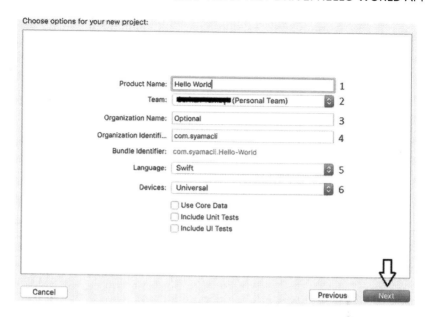

Figure 3.3. Setting options for your first project

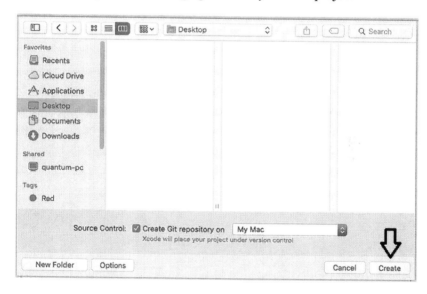

Figure 3.4. Selecting the place to save your Xcode project

1. Some files in your project have the extension of .swift and these files are Swift files. You write your Swift code in these files and make your app to do what it is supposed to do. AppDelegate.swift file determines how our app will talk to iOS while **ViewController.swift** is your main code file that will determine the behaviour of your controller (app) screen.

2. Some files have the extension of .storyboard. These files store the information regarding the user interface of your app such as where a button should be or what colour your screen background will be. Launchscreen.storyboard holds information that will be shown to the user while the app is being loaded (splash screen). **Main.storyboard** contains the layout of the main screen of your app.

3. There is a file called Assets.xcasseets. This file holds data, images, etc. that will be used by the app such as an app icon or a background image for your app.

4. There is another file called info.plist. This is a **property list** file and it contains the configuration data of the finalized executable such as copyright info, release date of the app or the device capabilities required to install the app.

You can view the contents of these files by single-clicking on them. When you click on files with the extension of .swift, Xcode shows an editor in the middle pane in which you can write Swift code inside. This editor has syntax highlighting and auto-completion properties that are really useful during coding. The ViewController.swift file is shown in Figure 3.6 as an example. Similarly when you click on the Main.storyboard as in Figure 3.7, Xcode shows an empty device screen in which you can place visual components like textboxes, buttons, etc.

In short, you design the user interface of your app in .storyboard files while you write the required code in .swift files.

3.5. Adding a Label Object

Let's see how you'll write "Hello, World" on the app screen. Firstly, single-click on the Main.storyboard file on the left pane of Xcode and the main app layout will be displayed as in Figure 3.7. Here you can see that the selected device size is iPhone SE as shown inside the small rectangle at the bottom. If you click on the "iPhone SE" text there, you can switch

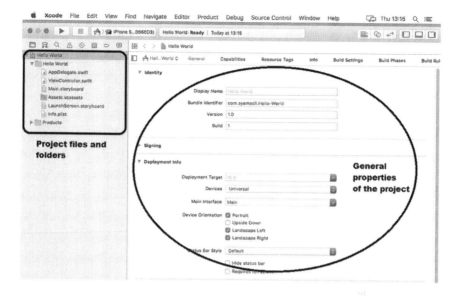

Figure 3.5 General properties of the project in Xcode

Figure 3.6. The "ViewController.swift" file of our app

among all iOS device sizes such as iPhone 7, iPhone 7s plus, etc. In the bigger rectangle at the right bottom in this Figure, the so-called "object library" is shown. All available user interface objects that you can use in your app are shown in the object library. If you cannot see the object library, make sure that the "component menu selector" shown by the arrow (a circle with a small square inside) is selected.

"Label" objects are used to display text on the app screen. Xcode is very user-friendly, it shows small explanations of all components that you can use on the layout. You can find the component called "Label" manually from that menu or you can search for it by writing "Label" in the small search box just beneath that components menu. When you find the

"Label" component, you can drag it and drop on the screen. I mean left-click on the label component, hold down the mouse button, drag it on the screen where you want to place it and then release the mouse button. If you try to place the "Label" in the middle of the screen, Xcode will help you by showing horizontal and vertical guiding lines as shown in Figure 3.8.

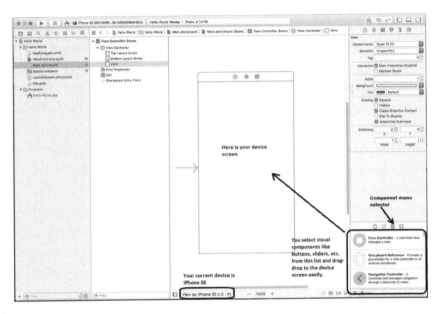

Figure 3.7. The "Main.storyboard" file of the project

After placing the "Label" component, it will be automatically selected. If not, single-click on it and it will be selected. Now, we can set the properties of this component. As you can see from Figure 3.9, the attributes of the selected "Label" component are shown in the right pane of Xcode. Please note that since a component has vast number of properties in Xcode, Xcode groups these properties for ease of view. In order to change the text properties of the "Label", select the "Attributes" group by clicking the fancy icon shown inside the small rectangle at top right in Figure 3.9. In this case, we are ready to change the text written inside the "Label" object. When you place a "Label" object on the screen, it automatically sets its text as "Label".

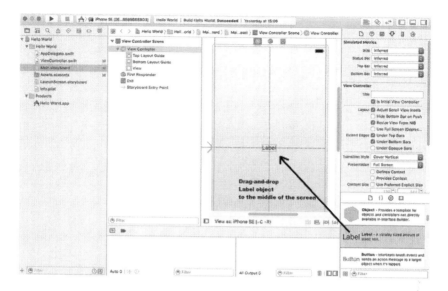

Figure 3.8. Placing a "Label" component on the screen

Figure 3.9. Changing the attributes of the "Label" object

We will now change its text to "Hello, World!". You can change the text from the second box in the right pane shown in Figure 3.9. It is "Label" by default; replace that text with "Hello, World!" (without quotation marks) or whatever you like to write on the app screen. After you change the text, hit Return on the keyboard. Now, the text should be changed as "Hello, World!" on the screen. If the text is too long compared to the Label's length, it may not be shown completely. In this case, you can **drag one of the edges** of the Label component to fit the text inside it. In other words, stretch out the Label object so that you fit the text inside. Then, reposition the Label component in the middle of the screen with the help of guiding lines as before.

This process is summarized in Figure 3.10. The final screen layout of your app should be the one shown in the right image of Figure 3.10.

Since we don't want our first app to do something interactive, we don't need to write single line of code for now. Of course we'll do a lot of coding in the upcoming projects but for now, we don't need to do coding.

Figure 3.10. Final touches to our first app

3.6. Building the Project and Running on a Simulator

Your first app is now ready to be built in Xcode and run on a simulator or an actual device. This is easy in Xcode. Firstly, you have to select a simulator or device to run your app on. You can do this by clicking on the device or simulator name located at the left top of your Xcode window as shown in Figure 3.11. An iPhone SE simulator is selected in this example but you can select any simulator you want or download more simulators which are also given as a choice in the selection menu (explained in detail in Chapter 2).

After selecting the simulator as shown inside the rectangle, the only thing you need to do is to press the "Run" button shown inside the circle in Figure 3.11. When you click the "Run" button, Xcode builds the project (makes the executable file), the device simulator starts running and boots like a real device. Note that this make take a while depending on your computer speed. After the simulator boots, it automatically installs the app you created and runs it as shown in Figure 3.12. **If you see the simulator screen shown in this figure, congratulations. You've successfully created your first iOS 10 app.**

Figure 3.11. Selecting a simulator or device to run your first app

In order to change anything in your app, you can press the "Stop" button which is next to the "Play" button in Xcode. After stopping the app, the simulator won't shut down completely but it will stop running your app. Then you can make any modification you want in your app such as changing the position of the Label component or the text you've written inside it. After changes, restart the simulator again by the "Run" button. As you can see from your very first project, Xcode provides a user-friendly interface and vast number of possibilities for transforming your ideas into real iOS apps.

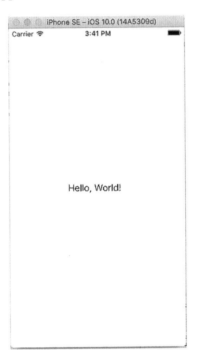

Figure 3.12. Simulator screen showing our "Hello, World!" app

3.7. Running on a Real Device

It is also easy to try your app on a real iOS device. In order to do that, you just need to connect your device to your Mac using the lightning cable. Xcode will automatically detect and show it in the available devices as shown in Figure 3.13. I connected my iPhone but you can run the app on any compatible iOS device. Note that, you can run your apps on a device connected to your Mac but you cannot distribute it for installing on other devices, you need to join Apple Developer Program for that.

Figure 3.13. Selecting a real device in Xcode

After selecting the device, hit the "Run" button to install the app on the device. Xcode will give an error as shown in Figure 3.14. It says that you should allow running apps from this developer on your device. As the error box says, navigate to General → Device Management and click "trust the developer profile" on the device. After that, you can run your apps on your device.

Figure 3.14. Error dialog in Xcode about running the app on a real device

After allowing on your device, hit the "Run" button in Xcode again to run it. If you see the "Hello, World!" text on the real device, excellent. You now know how to install apps on real iOS devices. Running an app on an actual device is sometimes essential since some operations like SMS sending can only be done on real devices.

Final note: If the iOS version on your device is lower than iOS 10, then Xcode will issue an error and won't run the app on the device. In order to solve this, you should either update the device OS to iOS 10 or change the iOS version of your app to match the iOS version of your device. For example, if you're using a device with iOS 9.3, you can make your app compatible with iOS 9.3 from the main project menu as shown in Figure 3.15.

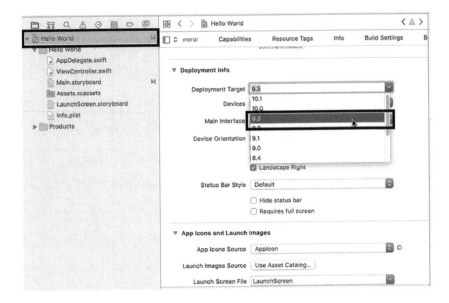

Figure 3.15. Changing the iOS compatibility of the app in Xcode

Chapter 4

SWIFT BASICS

4.1. Introduction to Playgrounds

We have created our first app. Great. But as you may have noticed, we didn't have any interaction with it. It just writes a text on the screen and that's it. In order to make an app to do something, we need to tell it what to do. And we need to tell it exactly.

As an old saying states: "Computers are actually rather stupid". This is because: **if you're telling a computer to do a task, then you need to tell it in exact terms. The operation principles of computers are different than those of humans.** Let's try to explain this by an example: imagine that you're going home after a tiring workday and your wife is already at home. You want to have a pizza for the dinner and ring her for baking a frozen pizza. A usual form of conversation would be like the following:

You – Hi darling, hope you're OK.

Your wife – Thanks, a bit tired. You?

You – Me too. And also hungry as a wolf. Didn't have a bit since lunch. Could you bake a pizza for me? There should be some frozen pizzas in the fridge.

Your wife – Of course, I'll. See you in a while, bye.

You – Thanks, bye.

Then, she'll find the pizza wherever it is in the fridge, unpack it, set the timer, power on the microwave and bake it. That's it. However, if you had a robot wife with a computer brain, the dialog would be more like this:

You – Hi darling, hope you're OK.

Robot wife – I'm OK, just charged. You OK? (not in a romantic tone!)

You – Thanks. I'm tired and hungry. Could you bake a pizza for me please, I guess there are some in the fridge.

Robot wife – Where are the pizzas in fridge, what type of pizza do you want: margherita, pizza with egg, etc., do you want it crispy? When do you want it to be ready?....

You – Stop, stop please. I'll drive to a restaurant.

Robot wife – I don't understand, you are nonsense....

Well, any programmable digital device is more or less the same. **You have to tell exact things to them.** You do this by using programming languages. There are a lot of different programming languages used to develop software for different platforms. You can check the widely used programming languages and their rankings at the TIOBE index website: http://www.tiobe.com/tiobe-index/. It is sometimes difficult to choose which programming language to use. There is not a universally excellent/complete programming language; they have strong and weak sides. On the other hand, another good thing about Apple is that they design both software and hardware in such a way that you don't get confused. The same is valid for their programming languages.

The main programming language for Mac OS and iOS devices had been Objective-C before Swift came into play. Objective-C can still be used to create apps. However, Swift is the newer technology and its popularity is constantly rising. Moreover, Swift took over Objective-C in the TIOBE index in September 2016.

Apple developed Swift and introduced it in 2014 WWDC (World Wide Developers Conference). Swift was a proprietary language then, but in

2015 Apple made it open-source software. You can view the evolution of Swift on its official website: https://swift.org.

Important changes were made in Swift since its introduction. Swift 2 came in 2015 and in September 2016, the third version of Swift, Swift 3, is released. Please note that these major versions are not compatible with each other.

In this chapter, you will learn the basics of Swift 3. It is worth noting that learning everything of a programming language is almost impossible nowadays but learning its logic and the syntax is the first step. You can improve your knowledge easily once you grasp the basics.

In the previous chapter, you learned that it is possible to write Swift code inside the files with the extension ".swift" in an Xcode project. You can then build the project to try on a simulator or a device. In this case, you will need to do the modify-build-run cycle each time you change something in the Swift code. Since this is a time consuming process for learning a new programming language, Xcode offers something better to replace this cycle: Swift Playgrounds. In Swift Playgrounds, you can see the output of your code in real time as you type without the need of the modify-build-run cycle.

We will use playgrounds in this chapter since our aim is not creating an app now, we'll focus on the syntax and the logic of Swift 3. In order to do this, we need to create a new playground file. We can do this by selecting the "Get started with a playground" button that appears when you run Xcode first time as pointed out by the arrow in Figure 4.1 or you can select File → New → Playground from the top toolbar of Xcode. It will ask you for a file name, you can give any name you want and the platform will be iOS, which is the default one. Xcode will also ask you for a place on your Mac to save the new playground file; it is also up to you. When created, the default Xcode playground looks like in Figure 4.2.

Figure 4.1. Creating a new playground file to try Swift code

Figure 4.2. The default playground just after we create it

As you can see from Figure 4.2, Xcode places three default lines of code when you create a new playground. The first line is:

```
//: Playground - noun: a place where people can play
```
Code 4.1

This is a comment line. It defines what a playground is. In fact, this is not an actual code. It is a comment for you to read and get an idea about what's going on in these code lines. Xcode ignores comment lines when it builds an app from your code. Comments exist in almost all programming languages and their aim is to make people understand the code easier. In Swift, a comment can be a single line as above or several lines if you need. For a single line comment, // is used. Xcode will consider that all the text written after // is a part of the comment and will ignore whatever you write after // in that line.

The next line is:

```
import UIKit
```
Code 4.2

This line is used to import a library called UIKit. There are loads of libraries in iOS software development kit (SDK) and they provide ready to use functions that help us to develop apps. Libraries should be imported in our Swift code before we can use the functions or classes belonging to those libraries. The keyword **import** enables us to include libraries in our code.

In the above line, a framework called **UIKit** is imported. Xcode automatically places this line of code on top of playground files because UIKit contains the main framework for the user interface.

The last line is

```
var str = "Hello, playground"
```
Code 4.3

In this line, a variable named "str" is defined. Variables are entities that hold information. You can think them as boxes that you put and get data into and from them. There are several types of boxes sorry; types of variables exist in Swift.

One of the widely used variable types is the **string. A string holds a group of characters.** For example, the word "example" is a string since it is composed of characters "e", "x", "a", "m", "p", "l", "e". Similarly, the following is also a string: "Swift 3" since it is composed of the following characters: "S", "w", "i", "f", "t", " ", "3". Note that the space between "t" and "3" is also counted as a character. In our playground, a variable called "str" is created and it holds the string of "Hello, playground". This is a simple line but also an important line. It shows the basic structure of variable declaration in Swift. You'll see various variable types in the next subsection.

It is important to note that Swift keywords such as **var** and **import** are automatically coloured in Xcode to increase the readability of the code.

The unique property of a playground is that it shows the contents of variables immediately in the right pane. For example, consider the output of the playground file as shown inside the rectangle in Figure 4.2. In that output, Xcode says that: "The variable you created has this value: "Hello, playground" ". In other words, Xcode shows the content of the newly created variable. This makes it easy for us to follow the variable across our code. If you change the value of the variable "str" to something else later, Xcode will also show that next to the related code line.

We'll learn more on variables in the following subsection.

4.2. Variables in Swift

As just stated, variables can be thought as boxes that hold data. Firstly, you create these boxes: this is called "declaration of variables". You can insert the data which will be held by the variable during the declaration or later, it is up to you.

Just as real world boxes that can be used to hold different things like a sugar box, a match box or a component box, **variables in Swift also have different types**. For example, if you want to store a numeric data (a number) in a variable, the type of the variable should be Integer. If you don't specify the variable type, Xcode will automatically guess its type. Let's explain this on a simple example. Please consider the following code line:

```
var myNumber = 3
```
Code 4.4

In this line, we declare a variable called "myNumber" using the keyword **var** and assign the number 3 to this variable using the assignment operator: = (the equal sign). Xcode automatically colours the value that will be assigned to the variable. In this code, we made both **a declaration and an assignment**. We declared the variable name and assigned 3. Since this is an integer value (a whole number that doesn't have fractional part), Xcode will automatically set the type of this variable as Integer (shortly: Int). If you want to be in full control of the type of your variable (which is a good practice in programming), then you can explicitly specify its type during declaration as follows:

```
var myNumber: Int = 3
```
Code 4.5

In this code, you tell Xcode that your variable will have the type **Int** (Integer) and you want to assign the value 3 to this variable during declaration as sketched in Figure 4.3.

Another way of declaring the variable "myNumber" and **then** assigning its value is as follows:

```
var myNumber: Int
//Some other code here...
myNumber = 3
```
Code 4.6

In the first line, we declared the variable myNumber first but didn't assign a value. Because of this, Xcode cannot guess the type of the variable therefore we are required to define the type of the variable. Otherwise, Xcode will issue an error. After the declaration of the variable, we may have some other code. And then we assigned the value 3 to your variable in the third line. Declaring a variable and assigning its value later may be useful when its value will be calculated in the code.

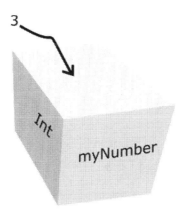

Figure 4.3. Assigning 3 to the variable "myNumber"

When we create the variable "myNumber" and assign its value, the playground shows the value in the right pane as in Figure 4.4.

Figure 4.4. Declaration and assignment of a variable

It is worth repeating that the equal sign, **=**, is called as the "assignment operator" in Swift. It assigns the value at its right to the variable placed at its left. In the above example, the value 3 is assigned to the variable named "myNumber".

Another widely used variable type in Swift is the **string** as stated before. Strings are anything composed of characters. Assigning the word "Hello" to a string variable is shown below:

```
var myString: String = "Hello"
```
Code 4.7

Note that the value we want to assign is written inside quotation marks. This is a rule for assigning a string.

The code shown below may confuse you a bit:

```
var myNewString: String = "3"
```
Code 4.8

In this code, we assigned "3" to "myNewString". The "3" here is not a number. It is a string because it is written in quotation marks. Anything inside quotation marks will be treated as a string by Swift. Let's have a look at the output of our playground file in Figure 4.5.

Note that, playground output shows "3" inside quotation marks. This means that it uses this variable as a string.

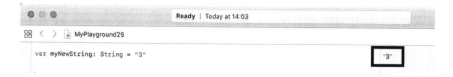

Figure 4.5. Declaration of a string

If you define an integer and try to assign a string value to it as in Code 4.9, you get an error:

```
var myWrongNumber: Int = "3"
```
Code 4.9

Xcode shows the erroneous code line as in Figure 4.6. It places an exclamation mark at the left of the wrong code (indicated by the arrow in the figure). If you single-click on the exclamation mark, Xcode shows further explanation about what's wrong with your code as shown inside the rectangle in Figure 4.6.

Figure 4.6. Wrong assignment to an integer variable

Other frequently used variable types are the **double** and **float**. They hold decimal numbers and very useful if you need to store any sort of number having decimal point such as 3,14 or 27,6935.

The difference between **double** and **float** types is the number of decimal digits they can hold. You can see their difference by trying Code 4.10 in the playground.

```
var myDouble: Double = 3.12345678901234567890
var myFloat: Float = 3.12345678901234567890
```
Code 4.10

In the above code, we are trying to assign a decimal number with 20 decimal digits to a double and float variable. Let's check what Xcode gets from these assignments:

41

Figure 4.7. Double and float assignments in Xcode

It can easily be seen that Xcode takes 15 decimal digits for the **double** type and 6 digits for the **float** type (see the output of the playground file above). Considering that iOS devices have big amount of RAMs, it is better to define decimal numbers in **double** type. If you don't specify the type of a decimal assignment, Xcode automatically treats it as a **double** type variable anyway.

Another useful and widely used variable type is the **boolean**. This variable type takes two values only: `true` or `false`. You can think it as a yes-no question like "Is the screen background red?". The answer can only be "yes" or "no". Instead of the words "yes" and "no", Swift uses `true` and `false`.

Assignment of a boolean variable is also simple as shown below:

```
var myBoolean: Bool = true
```
Code 4.11

You'll see the importance of Boolean variables when you start to code apps that have complex logic inside.

We have studied simple variable types so far. These types are called as "primitive" types since they are used for storing single data at a time whether it is an integer, string, etc. In Swift, as in other programming languages, there are also complex variable types that hold groups of data. Arrays, dictionaries and sets are the widely used ones among complex types and these will be covered here.

Arrays store multiple values of the same type in an ordered fashion. A typical array can be illustrated as in Figure 4.8.

Index	Value
0	"Tea"
1	"Coffee"
2	"Sandwich"
3	"Chocolate"
4	"Pizza"

Figure 4.8. Contents of a typical array

Array elements have indices so that you can access them, delete them or replace them. Indices of arrays always start with 0 and increase one by one. In order to declare the array shown above, we use the following code:

```
var myArray: [String] = ["Tea", "Coffee", "Sandwich",
"Chocolate", "Pizza"]
```
Code 4.12

We can access each element in our array using the following template: myArray[index]. The following code accesses first and fourth elements of the array we just formed:

```
myArray[0]    //First element
myArray[3]    //Fourth element
```
Code 4.13

We can change any element of our array using a simple assignment as follows:

```
myArray[3]  = "Cola"
```
Code 4.14

The 4th element of our array is changed from "Chocolate" to "Cola" by this code. After this line, if we just write the name of your array in the playground, it will show our array as ["Tea", "Coffee", "Sandwich", "Cola", "Pizza"].

We can remove any element using the following pattern:

```
myArray.remove( at: 3)
```
Code 4.15

This line removes the element at the 4th position. After this modification, our array has the following structure: **["Tea", "Coffee", "Sandwich", "Pizza"]**.

We can append a new element to our array as follows:

```
myArray.append("IceTea")
```
Code 4.16

After this line, our array owns **"IceTea"** as its last element: **["Tea", "Coffee", "Sandwich", "Pizza", "IceTea"]**. All of these operations and their results are shown below:

Figure 4.9. Basic array operations in Swift

Finally, let's see how we can define an empty array:

```
var myIntArray = [Int] ()
```
Code 4.17

Arrays are really useful while dealing with chunks of data of the same type. For example if we want to log (save) our geolocation data read from GPS by regular time intervals, we can use an array consisting of **double** type elements.

Another useful complex variable type is the "dictionary". Dictionaries hold elements as a **key-value pair**. Let's form a dictionary of the exam results of a student. His points were as follows: Maths: 8, Physics: 9, Chemistry: 7, Programming: 10. We can illustrate these results as in Figure 4.10 which shows a dictionary structure. The **keys** are the strings that are names of the lectures and the **values** are the exam points the student got.

Key	Value
Maths	8
Physics	9
Chemistry	7
Programming	10

Figure 4.10. Exam results of a student

We can define a dictionary from this table as follows:

```
var examResults = ["Maths" : 8 , "Physics" : 9,
"Chemistry" : 7, "Programming" : 10]
```
Code 4.18

After defining the dictionary, we can query (ask) the value corresponding to a key. If we write "examResults["Physics"]" in the playground, Xcode will output the value for the "Physics" key as shown below:

Figure 4.11. Declaring and querying a dictionary in Swift

Replacing the value in a dictionary is very similar to changing the elements of an array. The following code changes the value of "Physics" to 10.

```
examResults["Physics"] = 10
```
Code 4.19

We can also remove a key-value pair as shown in Code 4.19. Please note the form of the method we need to apply is: **removeValue(forKey : (the key of the entry to be removed))**.

```
examResults.removeValue(forKey : "Chemistry")
```
Code 4.20

After all these changes, if we just write the name of the dictionary (examResults) in our playground, Xcode will show the contents of our dictionary as shown below:

Figure 4.12. Basic dictionary operations

The third important complex variable type is the "set". Sets have two unique properties: i) they hold data of the same type without an order; ii) an element can only be added to a set only once. In other words, the same value can only appear once in a set. Let's create a set of strings as an example. We can create a set of fruits and then insert a new element as shown below:

```
var fruits: Set<String> = ["Strawberry", "Banana",
"Peach", "Apricot"]
fruits.insert("Mango")
```
Code 4.21

If we just write "fruits" (name of the set) in the playground, Xcode will show the contents of the set in the right pane as: {"Mango", "Banana", "Apricot", "Strawberry", "Peach"}.

We can think sets as a magic bag. When we throw in an element that already exists, one of them vanishes. Let's try to insert the element "Banana" again to the set as below:

```
fruits.insert("Banana")
```
Code 4.22

Xcode will not issue a warning or an error but if we again check the contents of "fruits" set, Xcode will show {"Mango", "Banana", "Apricot", "Strawberry", "Peach"}, which is the same as before adding "Banana" the second time. Hence, only one instance of an element can exist inside a set. Sets are useful for checking if one of several conditions is met in a complex app. The playground page of basic set operations is given below:

Figure 4.13. Creating and manipulating a set in Swift

In summary, we have learned following variable types that are widely used in Swift:

1. Primitive types: integer, string, double, float, boolean.

2. Complex types: array, dictionary, set.

Warning: Swift is case-sensitive, "myNumber" is not the same as "mynumber", so be careful about naming and calling your variables.

Apart from regular variables, there are two related concepts: "optionals" and "constants".

"Optionals" are the variables that may not contain data. It may seem awkward at first glance but it is true and sometimes very useful. We define an optional but we may or may not place a value in it. We can think of optionals as an empty box. If we ask its value before assigning a value, Swift will show its value as "nil" meaning nothing or empty. If we place a value inside an optional and then ask its content, Swift will return whatever it contains as a regular variable.

A real-world example is the middle name. Not everybody should have a middle name. Some people have and some not. If we need variables to hold initial name, middle name and surname as strings in Swift, **we could try** to do this by the following code:

```
var initialName: String = "John"
var middleName: String
var surname: String = "Smith"
print(initialName)
print(middleName)
print(surname)
```
Code 4.23

Xcode will give an error in this code because the variable "middleName" is declared but not assigned a value before trying to print it on the 5th line.

If we define the "middleName" variable as an optional, Xcode will not issue an error. Optionals are declared with a question mark (?) at the end of the declaration as shown in Code 4.24. The optional "middleName" is defined but not assigned a value. In this case, Swift automatically sets its value to "nil". Xcode shows "nil" when we try to print the value of "middleName" as shown in Figure 4.14.

```
var initialName: String = "John"
var middleName: String?
var surname: String = "Smith"
print(initialName)
print(middleName)
print(surname)
```
Code 4.24

After we assign a value to an optional (also called as wrapping the optional) as in Code 4.25, we can then print its value by unwrapping it (reading its value). **An exclamation mark (!) is used for reading the value of an optional as given in Code 4.25.** The Xcode output for this code is also shown in Figure 4.15.

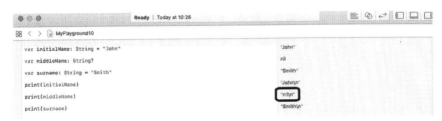

Figure 4.14. Printing the value of an empty optional

```
var initialName: String = "John"
var middleName: String?
var surname: String = "Smith"
print(initialName)
middleName = "Doe"      //optional wrapped
print(middleName!)      //optional unwrapped
print(surname)
```
Code 4.25

Figure 4.15. Wrapping and unwrapping an optional

Another important keyword in Swift is the **let** keyword. We can define **constants** (data that will be assigned once and will not change ever in your code) using **let**. We just use **let** instead of **var** keyword for defining a constant; type definition and assignment process are the same as regular variables as shown the following code:

```
let SPEED_LIMIT_MWAY = 70   // speed limit = 70 mph for
                            // all motorways
let SPEED_LIMIT_RA = 30     // speed limit = 30 mph for
                            //restricted areas
print("Speed limit in motorways
is: \(SPEED_LIMIT_MWAY), speed limit in roads with
traffic lights is \(SPEED_LIMIT_RA)")
```
Code 4.26

In this code, **print()** function prints the string inside the parentheses in the right pane of the playground. It is a very handy function to track your code. Please note that numeric values are printed using the **\()** operator inside the **print()** function. Constant declaration in the playground is also shown in Figure 4.16.

Some programmers use all capital letters to define constants so that they will remember these are constants in their code as we did for our example here.

If we try to re-assign a value to a constant, Swift will throw an error which is shown in Figure 4.17. Hence, we have to be extra careful when using constants. **Assign once and never assign again, don't ever try** ☺.

Figure 4.16. Defining constants in Swift

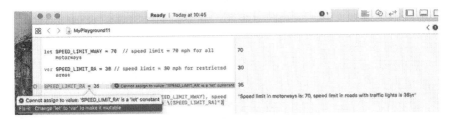

Figure 4.17. Trying to change the value of a constant

The next subject is the logical decision making structures in Swift, let's have a coffee break and then continue with if-else statements.

4.3. Logical Decision Making Statements in Swift

Logical decision making is one of the main concepts in programming languages, like in real-world problems. In daily life, we make a lot of logical decisions such as:

- "**If** their pizza is tasty, I'll order again next week, **else** I'll not order from them again".

- "**If** it's sunny I'll go for a walk, **else** I'll stay home".

Just like in daily life, an if-else statements basically checks if a condition is met or not in a programming language. If the condition is met, the code inside the **if block** is executed. If the condition isn't met, then the code in the **else block** is executed. Hence, if we wanted to tell the above sunny – not sunny example to the computer, we would do it like this:

if it's sunny {

      I'll go for a walk

}

else {

I'll stay home

}

Let's see how we can check if two numbers are equal in Swift using an if-else statement:

```swift
var myNumber1 = 3
var myNumber2 = 3
if (myNumber1 == myNumber2) {
    print("These numbers are equal.")
}
else {
    print("These numbers aren't equal.")
}
```
Code 4.27

In this code, two variables, **myNumber1** and **myNumber2**, are defined. Both variables are assigned the value of 3 during declaration. Then, an **if** statement checks if **myNumber1** is equal to **myNumber2**. The operator **==** checks if these contents of these variables are equal. If they are equal, the condition of the **if** statement is met therefore the code inside the **if block** is executed. If they are not equal, then the code inside the **else block** is executed. Note that these blocks are specified by curly braces. Since the two numbers are equal, the code inside the **if block** will be executed as you shown below:

Figure 4.18. If-else statement example in Swift

If we change one of the numbers to something different than 3, then the code inside the **else block** will be executed. This is also shown below:

Figure 4.19. If-else statement in Swift when the condition isn't met

We can also use several if-else statements in a nested form as in Code 4.28. In this code, the conditions are checked from top to down. If a condition is met, then the code inside its block is executed and the program ends. If none of the conditions are true, then it means that **myNumber1** is lower than **myNumber2** and the statement in the final **else** block is executed. **In other words, the statements in the last else block is executed if none of the conditions above it are met.** The screenshot of this nested code in the playground is given in Figure 4.20.

```
var myNumber1 = 1
var myNumber2 = 3
if (myNumber1 == myNumber2) {
    print("These numbers are equal.")
}
else if (myNumber1 > myNumber2){
    print("myNumber1 is greater than myNumber2.")
}
else {
    print("myNumber1 is lower than myNumber2.")
}
```

Code 4.28

Figure 4.20. Nested if-else statements in Swift

Nested if-else statements may become confusing as more and more conditions are added. In order to check several conditions easier, **switch-case** statements are used. Switch-case statements function similar to nested if-else blocks but they are less error-prone for coding multiple numbers of conditions. A switch-case example is given in Code 4.29. The variable to be checked is written next to the **switch** keyword. In this example, the content of the variable "temperature" is checked. In each **case** statement, the "temperature" variable is checked against their condition. For example, in the first **case** statement, temperature is checked if it meets the condition of "-40..<0". In Swift 3, the statement **a..<b** means: "between a and b (a is included, b is not included in the comparison)". Hence, if temperature is between -40 and 0, then the statement inside the "case -40..<0:" condition is executed which is **print("It's very cold.")**. Each **case** statement is checked one by one from top to down. If none of the conditions inside the given case statements are met, then the code inside the **default** block is executed.

```
var temperature = 22
switch temperature {
case -40..<0:
    print("It's very cold.")
case 0..<15:
    print("It's cold.")
case 15..<30:
    print("It's nice")
case 30..<40:
    print("It's hot")
default:
    print("It's either too cold or too hot.")
}
```
Code 4.29

In Swift, switch cases must be "exhaustive" meaning that you have to cover all possibilities regarding the switched variable. Since it is usually difficult to cover all values for data types except the Boolean, the inclusion of a default case is almost mandatory. In the code above, the temperature variable is assigned 22. This value is between 15 and 30 therefore the condition of the third **case** statement is satisfied. In this case, the program outputs the text "It's nice." as shown below:

Figure 4.21. Switch-case statement in Swift

If we change the temperature, then the program will check it again and output a different text accordingly as in Figure 4.22.

Figure 4.22. Switch-case: another condition is met

We'll use decision making statements extensively. Let's now move on to another important subject: loops.

4.4. Loops in Swift

Performing the same operation in a repeated manner is a frequently needed concept in programming. We do these repetitions using loops. Without loops, programming would be almost impossible. For example, let's try to find the sum of numbers from 1 to 20. Without loops, we would do this as follows:

```
var sum = 0
sum = sum + 1
sum = sum + 2
sum = sum + 3
.... (15 more lines of code here)
sum = sum + 18
sum = sum + 19
sum = sum + 20
```

Code 4.30

Please note that there are 15 more lines of code in the place shown by dots (shortened above). Therefore, this simple task takes 21 lines of code. And it's error prone. Remember that we want to do things with shortest code possible to prevent errors. Below, we'll see how we can obtain the sum of these numbers with loops in a shorter and more elegant way.

There are two main looping methods in Swift. First of them is the loop structure using the **for** keyword. The basic structure of the **for** loop is given below:

```
for (sweep elements) {
    (code to be repeated)
}
```
Code 4.31

In this snippet, the **(code to be repeated)** is repeated again and again as long as the there's a remaining element in the **(sweep elements)**. In order to explain this in a better way, let's calculate the sum of the numbers from 1 to 20 using the **for** loop as in Code 4.32. In this code, the expression **1...20** is a range structure. In each iteration of the **for loop**, the loop variable called **counter** takes one value from the range **1...20**. In this way, the counter takes the values of **1, 2, 3, 4, ..., 18, 19, 20** one by one. In each iteration (i.e. for each value of the **counter** variable), the expression inside the loop: **sum = sum + counter** is executed. Since the declared variable **sum** is initialized to zero before the loop, the expression inside the loop adds the numbers from 1 to 20 and stores the sum in the variable **sum**. In the end, the expression **print(sum)** just outputs the sum variable in the playground as in Figure 4.23.

```
var sum = 0
for counter in 1...20 {
    sum = sum + counter
}
print(sum)
```
Code 4.32

As it is seen from Figure 4.23, the sum of the numbers from 1 to 20 is calculated as 210.

Figure 4.23. **for** loop in Swift

Note: As it is stated above, the expression **start_num...end_num** means that all the numbers from **start_num** to **end_num** will be included in the loop. If it is **1...5**, the for loop will be repeated for **1, 2, 3, 4, 5**. It is also possible to not to include the **end_num**. If we write the loop sweep as **1..<5**, it means that 5 is not included and the loop variable will take the values of **1, 2, 3 and 4**.

We can use other variable types as the loop variable, not just numbers. For example, let's to access the elements of an array using a **for** loop as shown in the following code:

```
var myArray: [Character] = ["S", "w", "i", "f", "t"]
for myChar in myArray {
    print(myChar)
}
```
Code 4.33

In this code, we have defined an array of characters composed of the letters of the word "Swift". Then we access the elements of this array with a **for** loop. We print its characters one by one as we sweep them. We can see the output of the print statement at the bottom of the playground as below:

Figure 4.24. Accessing array elements using a **for** loop

The other looping structure in Swift is the **while** loop. It is very similar to the **for** loop. The main difference of the **while** loop is as that the incrementing method of the loop variable is specified inside the loop therefore it provides a bit more flexibility. The calculation of the sum of numbers from 1 to 20 using a **while** loop is shown in Code 4.34. In this code, the loop variable is also defined as a separate variable: **counter** before the loop begins. The **while** loop will be executed as long as **counter < 21** condition is satisfied. When **counter** becomes equal or greater than 21, the loop will quit. In order to increment the loop variable, the expression **counter = counter+1** is added inside the loop.

```
var counter = 0
var sum = 0
while counter < 21 {
    counter = counter + 1
    sum = sum + counter
}
print(sum)
```
Code 4.34

If we don't change the loop variable inside the loop, the loop continues forever making it an **infinite loop** which is a big trouble in programming. When a program goes into an infinite loop, it probably won't respond to user intervention and will crash a while later. Hence, always remember to change the loop variable in a **while** loop in such a way that your loop will quit after a finite number of executions.

The result of the **while** loop of is shown in the following figure:

Figure 4.25. **while** loop in Swift

The advantage of a **while** loop is that the increment of the loop variable can easily be controlled by the programmer. For example, if we wanted to increment the loop variable by 2 (which means calculating the sum of the odd numbers in the range of 1...20), we could just change the loop variable as **counter=counter+2**. In this case, the loop will add odd numbers in the range of 1-20 (1, 3, 5, ..., 17, 19) as in Figure 4.26.

Figure 4.26. Adding odd numbers with a **while** loop

In addition to the regular usage of the **for** and **while** loops as shown above, there are two Swift commands that provide further control of loops. These are **break** and **continue** keywords.

These commands are generally used together with an **if** statement. The **break** command breaks the loop, in other words the program quits the current loop before the loop condition expires. On the other hand the **continue** keyword makes the loop continue, i.e., the loop doesn't execute statements inside the loop block for the current value of the loop variable but continues with the next iteration.

4.5. Functions in Swift

Functions enable us to write programs with reduced number of repetitions. In other words, we can put the repeating code in function blocks. Let's clarify this by an example. Consider the code shown below that prints the elements of a character string using a **for** loop:

```
var myCharArray: [Character] = ["F", "u", "n", "c"]
for myChar in myCharArray {
    print(myChar)
}
```
Code 4.35

If we wanted to print the contents of the array ["F", "u", "n", "c"] 3 times, we would use Code 4.36. As the number of times we want to print increases, the code length increases proportionally. The number of total code lines would reach hundreds easily for a middle sized program with a lot of repetitions.

```
var myCharArray: [Character] = ["F", "u", "n", "c"]
for myChar in myCharArray {
    print(myChar)
}
for myChar in myCharArray {
    print(myChar)
}
for myChar in myCharArray {
    print(myChar)
}
```
Code 4.36

We can shorten this process by placing the repeating code inside a function. A function is defined with the **func** keyword in Swift as shown in Code 4.37. In this code, we defined a function called **repeatMyLoop**: this is the name of our function. The contents of a function are written inside curly braces. The array definition and the **for** loop for printing the elements of the array are placed inside this function.

```
func repeatMyLoop () {
var myCharArray: [Character] = ["F", "u", "n", "c"]
    for myChar in myCharArray {
        print(myChar)
                        }
                }
```
Code 4.37

When we write this function in the playground, nothing shows at the output as seen in Figure 4.27 because **we defined the function but didn't call it**. Our function just stays there ready to be called. A function executes when it is called.

We call the function by shouting his name, sorry writing its name as shown in Figure 4.28. In this example, we have called the function **repeatMyLoop()** 3 times and it did its duty: created the array and printed its elements. Once we define a function, we can call it as many times as we want.

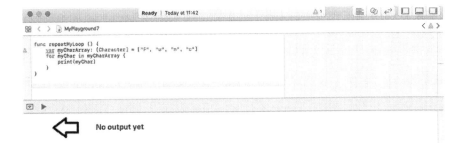

Figure 4.27. Function definition in Swift

As you may have noticed, the function is defined and called with regular parentheses. In the above example, inside of these parentheses is empty. We can define **parameters (inputs, arguments)** in these parentheses and use these parameters inside the function. In other words, we can pass any variable to a function as an input.

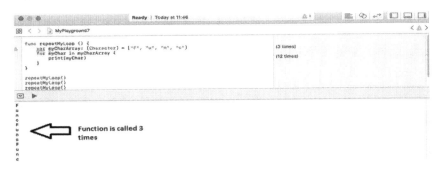

Figure 4.28. Calling our function 3 times

As an example, let's define a function that takes the raw price (price before tax) of a product and prints the selling price (price after tax). We can take the tax fixed at 8% for now. The function definition is as follows:

```swift
func printTaxed (priceBeforeTax: Double) {
    var priceAfterTax: Double = priceBeforeTax * 1.08
    print(priceAfterTax)
}
```

Code 4.38

In this definition, the function takes the variable **priceBeforeTax** as the input and this input is expected in Double type. Then, it calculates the taxed price inside by multiplying the **priceBeforeTax** by 1.08 (since the tax is 8%, price after tax = price before tax + 0.08*price before tax = 1.08*price before tax). The taxed price is stored in the variable called **priceAfterTax**. Finally, this variable is printed. We can calculate the taxed price of three different products easily by calling this function and giving the prices of items as inputs to the function as follows:

Figure 4.29. Passing inputs to a function

A function can take any number of parameters, not just one. In our example, we can also specify the tax rate since tax rate may be different for different products. In this case, we simply specify two inputs separated by a comma as shown below:

```
func printTaxed (priceBeforeTax: Double, taxRate: Double)
{
    var priceAfterTax: Double = priceBeforeTax *
(1+taxRate/100)
    print(priceAfterTax)
}
printTaxed(priceBeforeTax: 100, taxRate: 8)
printTaxed(priceBeforeTax: 52, taxRate: 8)
printTaxed(priceBeforeTax: 20, taxRate: 10)
```
Code 4.39

In this code, the formula priceAfterTax = priceBeforeTax * (1+taxRate/100) is used since the **taxRate** is considered as a percentage. In function calls, both the prices before taxes and tax rates should be provided as inputs.

Assume that we want to calculate the selling prices for three products. Two of these products have the prices of 100 and 52 with the tax rate of 8% while one product has the price of 20 and the tax rate of 10%. We can do these calculations using our function as follows:

Figure 4.30. Functions with multiple parameters (inputs)

Functions in Swift do not only accept inputs (function parameters, arguments) but they can also have outputs that can be assigned to other variables in the main code. Let's get the selling price as an output from our new function **getTaxed** as shown below:

```
func getTaxed (priceBeforeTax: Double, taxRate: Double)
-> Double {
    var priceAfterTax: Double = priceBeforeTax *
(1+taxRate/100)
    return priceAfterTax
}
print(getTaxed(priceBeforeTax: 100, taxRate: 8))
```
Code 4.40

In this function, the output of the function is a Double type therefore the function definition is closed with **a -> Double** expression. The function outputs the **priceAfterTax** variable with the **return** keyword. Therefore, this function accepts 2 Double type variables as inputs and it outputs a new Double type variable. This is shown in Figure 4.31.

We can use the output of our function in any way Swift allows. For example, we can print it as shown in Code 4.40 and Figure 4.32 or assign the output to another variable.

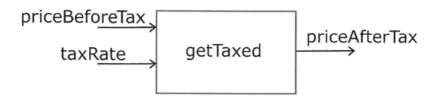

Figure 4.31. Our function's input and output structure

Figure 4.32. Printing the output of our new function "getTaxed"

As you have learned in this subsection, functions provide us a good way of shortening our code and making it compact. They are also important to share code among developers. If you can find a ready-coded function on the Internet, you can easily use it in your app. Hence, functions provide a good way of sharing code among developers. As stated before, iOS SDK has a lot of ready functions. You'll see how convenient it is to use SDK functions for developing interactive apps in the following chapters.

4.6. Classes, Objects and Inheritance in Swift

Classes and objects play an important role in "object-oriented" programming languages like Swift. Classes can be thought as template containers that have empty properties of the objects created using them. The relation of class and object concepts are as follows:

1. Firstly, a **class** that contains variables and functions is defined

2. This **class** definition is used to define **one or more objects**.

We can consider a car example to understand classes better. There are different cars having specific properties like colour, number of doors, brand, model year, etc. Car (as a concept) as can be considered as a class and each real car having specific properties can be thought as objects belonging to the car class. This is shown in Figure 4.33.

Let's create a car class in Swift as an example. Classes are defined similar to functions but without any parameters as in Code 4.41.

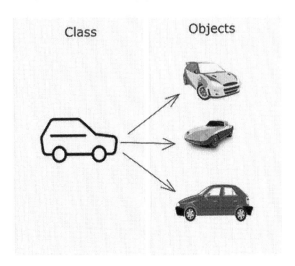

Figure 4.33. Class-object concept

```
class Car  {
    var colour: String

    init (colour: String) {
        self.colour = colour
    }
func askColour () -> String {
    return self.colour
    }
}
```
Code 4.41

This is a class definition example. This class has three main sections inside.

➢ First section is the definition of a variable called "colour". As you may have noticed, it isn't assigned a value since each instance of a "Car" object will have different colour property.

➤ The second section has a special function called **init**. It is used to set variables inside a class when creating an object. In this case, an object created using this class will have to be defined with a colour property and the **init** function will set the colour variable of the class to the passed colour data.

➤ Finally, this class has a function called "askColour". It returns the value of the colour variable when called.

Two objects named "myCar" and "yourCar" are created using the "Car" class below:

```
var myCar = Car(colour: "red")
var yourCar = Car(colour: "white")
```
Code 4.42

Please pay attention to object definitions. They are created similar to a variable however they are **instances** of the "Car" class. In the above code, "myCar" object is created having the red colour and the object named "yourCar" is created with white colour. Since there is a method in the class for asking their colour, **we can apply that method on these objects** to extract their respective colours:

```
print(myCar.askColour())
print(yourCar.askColour())
```
Code 4.43

Playground output of the class-object example is given in the following figure.

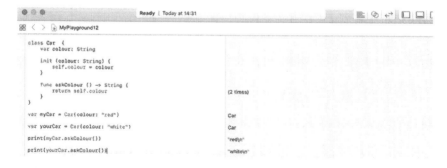

Figure 4.34. Class and object definitions in the playground

There's an important concept related to classes: **inheritance**. If a new class (class$_2$) inherits from an existing class (class$_1$), it means that class$_2$ takes variables and methods of class$_1$. As an example, let's define a new class inheriting from our existing Car class:

```
class hatchbackCar: Car {
    var length = "short"
}
```
Code 4.44

In the above code, the new class "hatchbackCar" **inherits** all the variables and methods of its **parent class** "Car". New classes inherit properties of a parent class with the following form: "class newClass: parentClass". Hence in the above code, "hatchbackCar" has the variable "colour" from its parent class while it additionally has the "length" variable. We can define a new object "myNewCar" from the new class and ask for its variables as in Code 4.45.

```
var myNewCar = hatchbackCar(colour: "black")
print(myNewCar.askColour())
print(myNewCar.length)
```
Code 4.45

The output of the playground is shown in the following figure:

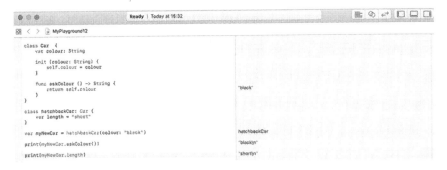

Figure 4.35. Printing the inherited and the specific properties of the new object

If you don't feel comfortable with classes, objects and inheritance for now, don't worry. You'll learn more about them when you use them in actual app development.

Well, I think this much of Swift basics is enough for starting to develop our iOS apps. Swift is, of course, a very extensive programming language and has much more to learn about it but this is a beginner's book and I think you're good to continue to app development.

The good news is that the boring stuff ends here and the fun stuff is beginning: developing apps that actually do something. In the next chapters, there will be a lot of hands on Swift coding which will make your apps to interact with the user such as changing screen colour by pushing a button and sending an SMS within your own app, etc. Let's get a coffee and relax for some time before continuing to the next chapter.

Chapter 5

iOS APP #1: DISCO LIGHTS

5.1. Creating the Project

We'll develop a **disco lights app** in our first Swift coded project. You'll see how we can interact with our app using a button and connecting this button to our code.

Our aim is to develop an app in which the screen background colour is changed in a disco light fashion. Each time we click a button, we want the background of the screen to take the following colours in a sequential order: red, orange, yellow, green, blue, cyan, purple and white.

Firstly, open Xcode and select "Create a new Xcode project" as shown in Figure 5.1. If your Xcode is already open, then select File → New → Project to create a new project.

Figure 5.1. Creating a new Xcode project

Since we'll just develop a single screen app, select the "Single View Application" in the dialog window shown in Figure 5.2. Click "Next" afterwards.

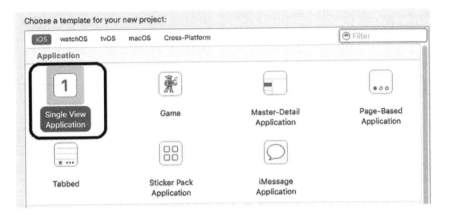

Figure 5.2. Selecting the single view app

Xcode will then ask for the main project parameters as in Figure 5.3. I named the project as "disco-lights" but you can give any name you want. On the other hand, you need to select a team as indicated by the arrow in the figure. If you cannot see an account to select, it means that you haven't set up code signing yet. In this case, please review Chapter 2 to set up code signing and continue after.

After naming your project and selecting the team, you're ready to save your project files, for that click "Next". In the next screen, Xcode just asks where to save the new project as shown in Figure 5.4. I selected my desktop but again you can select any place on your Mac to save.

5.2. Project Settings

After saving the project, Xcode opens it and shows the detailed project settings as in Figure 5.5. In this window, perhaps the most critical part is the so-called "Deployment info" section. The "deployment target" is the iOS version we'll develop our app for. Since we want to invest in the newest devices and technologies, it's better to develop for iOS 10, which Xcode 8 selects automatically as you can see in Figure 5.5. The other important setting is the "Devices" which is just below the iOS version box.

Figure 5.3. Basic project settings

The default is "Universal" and it's OK for us. It means that our app will run on all iOS devices having iOS 10 or later. In summary, there's no need to change anything in the detailed project settings window of Figure 5.5 for now.

We have reviewed the files that are automatically generated in an Xcode 8 project in Chapter 3. These files are shown in the left pane of the Xcode window as in Figure 5.6.

Figure 5.4. Saving your project files

Figure 5.5. Detailed project settings in Xcode 8

In this design, we will place a button in the middle of the device screen. When we click on it, the screen background will take the colours we listed before. In order to place a button on the screen, select the file "Main.storyboard" and the device screen will appear in the main Xcode window as shown in Figure 5.7. I selected an iPhone SE screen size manually. If you want to select a different device, click on the "View as..." text at the bottom left and select the device. After selecting the device you want, click on the "View as..." text again to close the device selection menu.

Figure 5.6. Files in our project

5.3. Adding a Button

We now have an empty screen. We need to place a button to click on. For this, find the "Button" component from the object library, then drag and drop it on the empty device screen as shown in Figure 5.8. If you try to place the button in the middle, Xcode will automatically show guiding lines in horizontal and vertical axes as shown in the figure, which helps you to drop the button component just in the middle. If you couldn't drop the button in the middle, don't worry. Xcode has advanced positioning methods. I'll now show you how to position it as you wish. Please see Figure 5.9 where I dropped the button somewhere in the screen and I now want to position it in the middle.

Figure 5.7. Main Xcode window showing the device screen

5.4. Adding Positioning Constraints

In Figure 5.9, I selected the button by single-clicking on it and then if I click on the two-rectangle shaped button shown by the arrow, I reach a popup menu where I can do some positioning operations regarding the selected component (button in this case). The popup menu is shown in Figure 5.10.

Figure 5.8. Placing a button component on the device screen

Figure 5.9. Positioning a component

We want to align our button horizontally and vertically on the screen (screen is the container here), therefore we need to tick the boxes to the left of the "Horizontally in Container" and "Vertically in Container" texts as shown inside the rectangle. After then, click on the "Add 2 Constraints" button (shown by the arrow in Figure 5.10) to add these constraints to our design. Our design now looks like Figure 5.11.

Figure 5.10. Alignment menu

The added constraints now appear in the design tree as shown in the rectangular box in Figure 5.11. However, the button position didn't change yet. For viewing the results of the newly added constraints, press the button shown inside the rectangle in Figure 5.12 to update frames.

After you update frames, your screen should look like Figure 5.13 i.e. the button should be positioned in the middle of the screen. If not, try the steps above again to make sure you applied all the steps correctly.

Figure 5.11. Our design after adding constraints

Figure 5.12. Updating frames

Figure 5.13. Device screen after updating frames

5.5. Editing Button Attributes

Now, let's change some properties of the button component. For this, select it by a single-click and then press the "Show attributes inspector" button as shown inside the rectangle in Figure 5.14.

I'll change the text of the button from "Button" to "Change!" in the box shown by the arrow in Figure 5.14. I'll also change the font size to 20 from the menu shown by the ellipse in the figure. After these changes, the user interface looks like Figure 5.15. Note that you may need to drag the edges of the button if you cannot see the text "Change!" at full length.

5.6. Connecting Button to the Code

We're now ready to write our code in Swift. In order to connect the button (or any component that may exist in our user interface) to our code, we need to open the "Assistant editor" of Xcode. To do this, select the double-circle as shown inside the box in Figure 5.16. Note that this button group lies at the top right of the main Xcode window.

Figure 5.14. Changing the attributes of the button component

Figure 5.15. Finalized screen setup

Figure 5.16. Switching to the "Assistant editor"

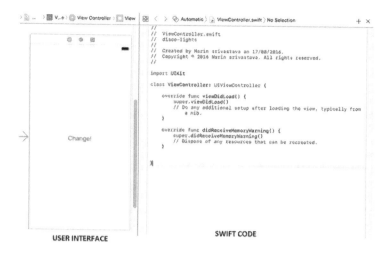

Figure 5.17. Assistant editor

When the assistant editor opens, the Xcode main screen looks as in Figure 5.17. Xcode shows the user interface (screen) and the Swift code related to this screen together. It is useful to check what's already there in the Swift code. The code automatically generated by Xcode is shown in Code 5.1. In this code, the first line imports the user interface kit, which is needed for all user interface functions. And then a class definition comes: **class ViewController: UIViewController**.The "ViewController" class is the main class of our user interface. As you can see, it inherits the methods and variables of the class "UIViewController". And then two methods are generated: **viewDidLoad()** and **didReceiveMemoryWarning()**. These are general methods that check the proper loading and the memory problems related to the user interface.

```
import UIKit
class ViewController: UIViewController {
    override func viewDidLoad() {
        super.viewDidLoad()
        }
    override func didReceiveMemoryWarning() {
        super.didReceiveMemoryWarning()
    }
}
```
Code 5.1

Whatever we'll design will execute inside the main class: "ViewController". We need to keep this in mind.

The "ViewController" class is the main class however it doesn't know about the components placed on the user interface until we tell. **We need to connect the components of the user interface (the button in this example) to the code.** In order to do this, Xcode offers an easy method. Just single-click on the button and select it. Then, hold down the Ctrl key on the keyboard and drag the button to the Swift code as shown in Figure 5.18. Xcode will show a connection line. You can drop the line anywhere in the main class. When you drop it (i.e., stop clicking the left mouse button and release the Ctrl key), Xcode will ask you about the connection you want to make. This dialog box is shown in Figure 5.19. In this dialog box, the connection type is important. "Outlet" type is used for static components such as a text label while the "Action" type is used for components that cause an action in your app. In our example, the button will trigger the colour changes hence it will cause an action. Thus, we'll select the "Action" type for the connection as shown in Figure 5.19.

Then we need to type a name for the connection. It can be anything you want but it's of course a good practice to give a meaningful name. I named it as "changeColours". After setting the connection's type and name, click "connect" in this dialog box and then the connection will be completed. The connection appears as an @IBAction function in Swift code as shown inside the rectangle box in Figure 5.20. This function is also shown in Code 5.2.

```
@IBAction func changeColours(_ sender: AnyObject) {
    }
```
Code 5.2

5.7. Writing the Swift Code of the App

We'll write button's actions inside its function shown in Code 5.2. We want the screen background colour to take the mentioned colours in a sequence but for now, let's start with a simple code that will show if our button and the connection work properly. Let's change the screen background colour to red when the button is clicked. In order to do user interface related actions in Xcode and Swift, we will use the `self` keyword, which refers to the current view.

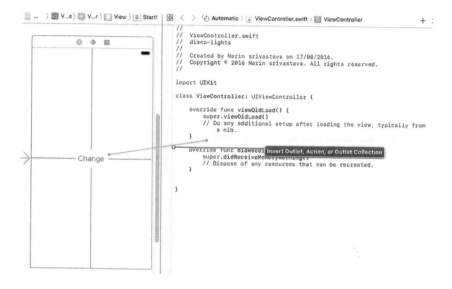

Figure 5.18. Connecting the user interface to the code

Figure 5.19. Xcode dialog for connection

Figure 5.20. The established connection in the code

We will change the current screen's (self's) view's (its appearance) background colour to the user interface colour of red. Let's translate this statement to Swift language:

```
self.view.backgroundColor = UIColor.red
```
Code 5.3

This code changes the background colour to red. We'll insert this code in the button's **@IBAction** function and then the whole ViewController.swift code should look like below:

```
import UIKit
class ViewController: UIViewController {
    override func viewDidLoad() {
        super.viewDidLoad()
        }
    @IBAction func changeColours(_ sender: AnyObject) {
        self.view.backgroundColor = UIColor.red
    }
    override func didReceiveMemoryWarning() {
        super.didReceiveMemoryWarning()
            }
}
```
Code 5.4

Let's run our app in the simulator. For that please press the "Run" button at the top of Xcode (as explained in Chapter 3, Figure 3.11). After then, the simulator will start with our app loaded as shown in Figure 5.21.

Figure 5.21. User interface of our app when it first starts

Now, it's the great moment. Click on the "Change!" button and hopefully the screen background colour will change to red as shown in Figure 5.22. Note that clicking the button again will have no effect since the background is red and the code we have written inside the button's **IBAction** won't do anything different. Let's improve our code so that it will change the background colour to red, orange, yellow, green, blue, cyan, purple and then white again as we click on the button.

There are various ways to do this but I'll define an array which holds the colour values that the background colour will take as follows:

```
let colours: [UIColor] = [UIColor.red, UIColor.orange,
UIColor.yellow, UIColor.green, UIColor.cyan,
UIColor.blue, UIColor.white]
```
Code 5.5

Figure 5.22. Background colour changes to red after clicking the button (full resolution colour figures online at: www.ios-swift.net)

The type of the elements of this array is **UIColor** as you can see. The reason of defining this array is that we can easily sweep the array elements as we click on the "Change!" button. We can modify button's **IBAction** function as in Code 5.6 that will change the background colour by taking elements from the **colours** array.

```
var i = 0
@IBAction func changeColours(_ sender: AnyObject){
        self.view.backgroundColor = colours[i]
        i += 1
        if ( i == colours.count ) {
            i = 0
        }
    }
```
Code 5.6

Here is the explanation of this code:

➢ The line **self.view.backgroundColor = colours[i]** changes the background colour according to current array element **colours[i]**.
➢ Note the variable declaration before the button code. This variable, "i", holds the array index and initialized to 0. Hence at the start, **colours [i] = colours [0] =UIColor.red**.

➤ Each time the button is pressed, this index variable is incremented by 1 with the code i += 1.

➤ However, we have a problem. The **colours** array has 7 elements. Remember that the array index starts with 0 hence the elements of the **colours** array have the following indices: 0, 1, 2, 3, 4, 5, 6. When we click the button for 7 times, then the variable i will have the value of 7 and our app will crash since the expression **colours[7]** is invalid, it can take the values up to **colours[6]**.

➤ In order to prevent this, we have added an **if** statement that checks if the index variable reaches the element count of the **colours** array: **if (i == colours.count) {i = 0}**. (The expression **colours.count** returns the number of elements of the **colours** array, 7 for our case). If the index variable i reaches the number of array elements, it is reset to 0.

➤ In short: when the variable i reaches the maximum value it can take, it is reset to 0 so that we can start sweeping the colours array from the beginning.

The complete code of the ViewController.swift file is shown below:

```swift
import UIKit
class ViewController: UIViewController {
    let colours: [UIColor] = [UIColor.red,
        UIColor.orange, UIColor.yellow, UIColor.green,
        UIColor.cyan, UIColor.blue, UIColor.white]
    var i = 0
    override func viewDidLoad() {
        super.viewDidLoad()
    }
    @IBAction func changeColours(_ sender: AnyObject) {
        self.view.backgroundColor = colours[i]
        i += 1
        if ( i >= colours.count ) {
            i = 0
        }
    }
    override func didReceiveMemoryWarning() {
        super.didReceiveMemoryWarning()
    }
}
}
```

Code 5.7

5.8. Building and Running the App

Let's run our disco-lights app. Run the project in a simulator and click on the "Change!" button a lot of times. The screen should take the colours of red, orange, yellow, green, cyan, blue, white, red, orange, yellow, green, cyan, blue, white, red, orange, yellow, green, cyan, blue, white, red, orange, yellow, green, cyan, blue, white, red, orange, yellow, green, cyan, blue, white, red, orange, yellow, green, cyan, blue, white etc. **Sorry, just checking white, red, orange, yellow, green, cyan, blue, white is enough...** I have shown different colours I obtained as I clicked the "Change!" button in Figure 5.23.

You can install this app on your real device as explained in the last pages of Chapter 3. I verified that this app runs on real devices (iPhone SE, iPad Mini and iPad Air 2) as expected. You can of course install and run this app on any iOS device.

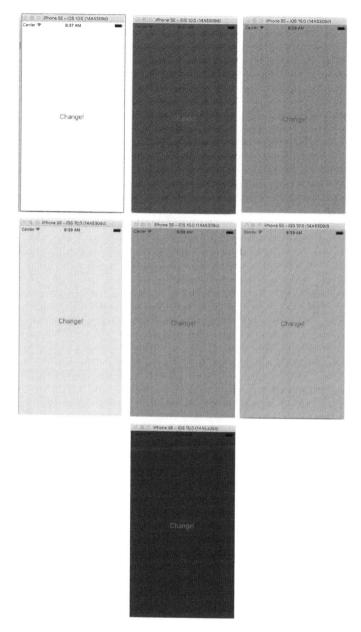

Figure 5.23. Different screen colours obtained as the "Change!" button is clicked (colour figure on the book's website: www.ios-swift.net)

Chapter 6

iOS APP # 2: BODY MASS INDEX CALCULATOR

6.1. General Information

Body mass index (BMI) is a figure of merit that is used for assessing the thickness-thinness of a person. BMI is defined as the ratio of the mass and height-squared with the formula below:

$$BMI = \frac{mass\,(kg)}{(height\,(m))^2}$$

After the calculation of the BMI, the following table is the used for assessing the weight category:

Weight category	from BMI	to BMI
Very severely underweight	0	15
Severely underweight	15	16
Underweight	16	18.5
Normal (healthy weight)	18.5	25
Overweight	25	30
Obese Class I (Moderately obese)	30	35
Obese Class II (Severely obese)	35	40
Obese Class III (Very severely obese)	40	-

Table 6.1. Weight categories
(source: https://en.wikipedia.org/wiki/Body_mass_index)

In this chapter, we'll develop a BMI calculator app and learn to use user inputs, make calculations inside our code and display results to the user.

In order to calculate the BMI in our app, we obviously need weight and height inputs. Our Swift code will calculate the BMI using the formula above and then it will decide the category according to Table 6.1. First of all, let's create the user interface of our app. In Xcode, create a new project called "BMI Calculator" and save it anywhere you want on your Mac. (I'll not repeat myself about these things, these were explained in detail in the previous chapters).

Firstly, let's place a UI component called "Label" to the user interface as shown in Figure 6.1. "Label" is a static text, the user cannot edit it but the app can change the text written in the Label. Please place the label in the middle of the screen with the help of the guiding lines as we did in the previous chapter. After placing the "Label", please select it and then change its text to "BMI Calculator" as shown by the upper arrow in Figure 6.1. Drag the edge of the label box to fit the text inside as we did before. **I have placed numbers in Figure 6.1 to indicate the order of the operations.**

Figure 6.1. Adding a "Label" component

6.2. Adding and Positioning the Labels

After editing the text, select the label component and align it in horizontal and vertical axes as shown in Figure 6.2: tick the boxes shown and then click "Add Constraints".

Figure 6.2. Aligning the label component horizontally and vertically

Now, select "Update Frames" as shown in Figure 6.3 and then the label box should be aligned in the middle of the screen.

Figure 6.3. Updating frames

We'll place other components on the screen so we don't need the title "BMI Calculator" to lie in the middle vertically. Therefore, we'll move it up a bit. To do this, select the y-constraint (1) as shown in Figure 6.4, which will display the constraints attributes section (2).

Figure 6.4. Selecting the y-axis constraints

Change the "Constant" value (shown by (3) in Figure 6.4) from 0 to -200 and then hit return on the keyboard. The "BMI Calculator" label will move up 200 units as shown in Figure 6.5.

Similarly, we will place four more label components as shown in Figure 6.6. These are labels for: weight, height, BMI and the category.

Figure 6.5. The label component at its desired place
(200 units above the vertical middle)

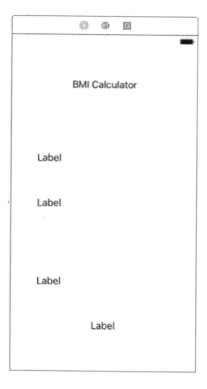

Figure 6.6. Adding four more labels to the user interface

We can now change the texts of these labels as: "Enter your weight (kg):", "Enter your height (m):", "Your BMI result:", "Category appears here!" as shown in Figure 6.7.

Alignment plays a central role in app design as we explained before. We need to align the objects in the user interface so that they will appear as expected for different screen sizes. Until now, we only aligned the title label "BMI Calculator". We need to align the new 4 labels too. However, instead of aligning them with horizontal and vertical guide lines, it is more practical to align them relative to each other. In other words, we'll first align "Enter your weight" label relative to the "BMI Calculator" label. And then we'll position the next label "Enter your height" relative to the "Enter your weight" label and so on. Let's align the "Enter your weight" label relative to the "BMI Calculator" label. First, select the "Enter your weight" label and then click on the "Pin" button shown inside the small rectangle in Figure 6.8.

Figure 6.7. Label texts in the user interface

Figure 6.8. Selecting the "Pin" menu

The "Pin" menu enables us to set various parameters of the selected component such as width and height as shown in Figure 6.9. There are also settings for the "Spacing to the nearest neighbour" shown inside the big rectangle in Figure 6.9. This part will help us position the components relative to each other or relative to the edges.

Figure 6.9. The "Pin" menu

It is worth noting that Xcode asks us to provide both height, width, and 2 spacing constraints to complete the positioning of the label, if there's a missing constraint then Xcode won't update the frame.

We can specify the width and height values of the "Enter your weight" label as 180 and 20 respectively as shown in the dialog box in Figure 6.10 (of course you can use any value as long as the text fits inside). Then, we'll specify its distance to the "nearest neighbour above" as 70 units. We can also specify its distance to the device's left edge as 5 units. The spacing section looks as shown below with these values:

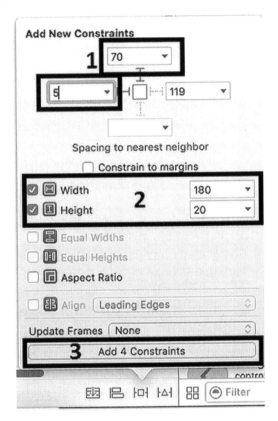

Figure 6.10. Setting the constraints of "Enter your weight" label

These four constraints are enough to represent the dimensions and the spacing of this label. After you clicking on "Add 4 Constraints" button, you can see that these constraints are now included in the scene explorer as in Figure 6.11.

After you update frames, your screen should look like Figure 6.12. It is good to summarize what we did up to here using Figure 6.12: We set the fixed position constraints of the "BMI Calculator" label (shown by rectangle 1) and then we set the relative constraints of the "Enter your weight" label (shown by rectangle 2). We still need to position remaining three labels shown inside ellipses in Figure 6.12.

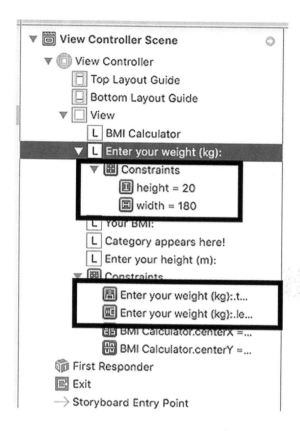

Figure 6.11. Newly added constraints shown in the scene explorer

It is worth noting that we also need to add text fields (boxes that we can input text) to enter the weight and height values and for displaying the BMI result. In addition, we have to include a button to calculate the BMI. The textboxes to enter the weight and the height will be next to their labels and the BMI result textbox will be next to the "Your BMI:" label. I'll put the "Calculate" button between the "Enter your weight" section and the "Your BMI" section but note that these are only personal choices, you can position your components as you wish and it'll be true as long as the components do not overlap. Anyway, let's align the "Enter your height", "Your BMI" and "Category" labels using the positioning and width/height values shown in Figures 6.13, 6.14 and 6.15, respectively.

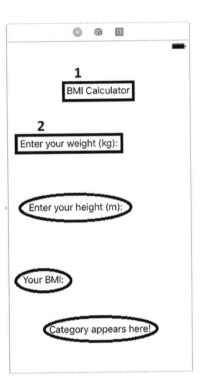

Figure 6.12. Device screen after updating frames

Figure 6.13. Constraints for the "Enter your height" label

Figure 6.14. Constraints for the "Your BMI" label

Figure 6.15. Constraints for the "Category" label

Note that, there are 3 constraints set from the "Pin" menu for the "Category" label in Figure 6.15. Since it won't have any other component next to it (since it'll show words like "normal" which is the result), I decided to align it in the middle horizontally. I did it from the "Alignment" menu as in Figure 6.16 (we did it before, you may remember). After updating frames, we obtain the device screen shown in Figure 6.17.

6.3. Adding the Text Fields and the Button

We'll now place "text fields" that will enable us to input the weight and height information. Text fields can also be used for displaying text hence we'll use it also for displaying the calculated BMI next to the label "Your BMI:". In the component menu of Xcode, just search for "text" and then drag and drop three "Text Fields": next to the weight (1), height (2) and BMI labels (3) as shown in as shown in Figure 6.18.

Figure 6.16. Horizontal alignment of the "Category" label

Figure 6.17. Final view of the label components in our screen

Figure 6.18. Adding text fields to the user interface

Finally, let's insert the button that will trigger the BMI calculation in between the height input and BMI output sections as shown in Figure 6.19. And then we will proceed for the final touches to position the newly added components.

We are now ready to set the positions of the new components on the device screen:

➢ Text field of weight: Select the text field next to the weight label. Then, using the "Pin" menu, set the constraints of its position and size as in Figure 6.20. **Make sure that the "Enter your weight" label is selected as the relative element for the left constraint as shown in Figure 6.20.**

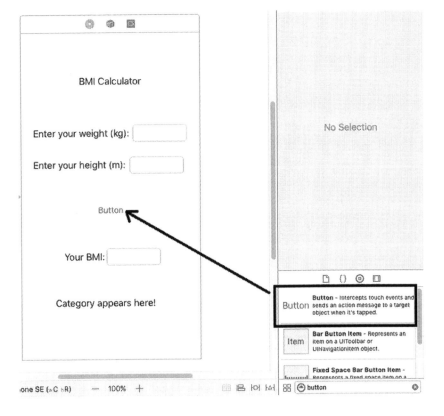

Figure 6.19. Adding the last component: the button

➢ Text field of height: We set constraints of this text field as shown in Figure 6.21. Note that our aim is to position this text box next to the height label.

➢ Button: I have increased the font size of the button to 25 and also changed its text to "Calculate my BMI!". The constraints for this button are given in Figure 6.22.

Figure 6.20. Adding constraints for the weight input text field

Figure 6.21. Constraints for the height input text field

Figure 6.22. Constraints for the button

Note that we have added only three constraints here because it'd be better to align it horizontally with the "Align" menu as shown in Figure 6.23.

Figure 6.23. Aligning the button horizontally in the container

➤ Your BMI label: The following constraints are appropriate for this component:

Figure 6.24. Constraints for the "Your BMI" label

Figure 6.25. Constraints for the BMI display text field

➢ BMI text field: Since this component is supposed to be next to the "Your BMI" label, the settings shown in Figure 6.25 do the job.

➢ The category label: We'll add three constraints for that and then align it horizontally similar to the one we did for the button. The constraints for the category label are as in Figure 6.26 while its horizontal positioning can be made as shown before in Figure 6.23.

Figure 6.26. Adding constraints for the "Category" label

Before moving on to writing the code for our app, I changed the colours of the title and the category labels. You can also change their properties as you like. In addition, since I'll not enter any value into the BMI text field but only read the value calculated by the app, I made this text field disabled for text inputs. For this, select this text field and then deselect the "user interaction enabled" box as shown in Figure 6.27 from the right pane of Xcode.

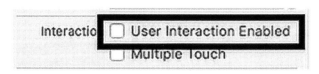

Figure 6.27. The user interaction option in Xcode

After these alignment and editing operations, the user interface looks like Figure 6.28.

Figure 6.28. The appearance of the user interface

6.4. Connecting the Objects to the Code

As we did in the previous app, we'll now connect the interactive elements to the Swift code. Weight, height and BMI text fields, the "Calculate my BMI!" button and the "Category appears here!" labels are interactive, they'll either provide input to the calculation or they'll display the results of the calculation. **We'll set the connection type of the "Calculate my BMI!" button as an IBAction and all other elements as IBOutlets.** After these connections, the ViewController.swift file will look like below:

```
import UIKit
class ViewController: UIViewController {

        override func viewDidLoad() {
        super.viewDidLoad()
        // Do any additional setup after loading the
view, typically from a nib.
    }
```

```
    @IBOutlet weak var weightInput: UITextField!
    @IBOutlet weak var heightInput: UITextField!
    @IBOutlet weak var BMIOutput: UITextField!
    @IBOutlet weak var categoryOutput: UILabel!
    @IBAction func calcBMI(_ sender: AnyObject)
{

    }
    override func didReceiveMemoryWarning() {
        super.didReceiveMemoryWarning()
        // Dispose of any resources that can be
recreated.
    }
}
```

Code 6.1 (cont'd from the previous page)

6.5. Developing the Main Code of the App

We'll pull the values entered in the weight and height text input boxes, perform the BMI calculation according to the equation given before, show the resulting BMI value in the BMI text field and then check the BMI category according to the BMI table using switch-case statements.

1. Firstly, let's read the weight and height values from the text fields. It's better to take these values when the button is pressed therefore we'll write this code inside the button's function **@IBAction func calcBMI(_ sender: AnyObject)** as in Code 6.2.

```
@IBAction func calcBMI(_ sender: AnyObject) {
if let heightStr = heightInput.text {
 if heightStr == "" {
   return
 }
 else {
   if let weightStr = weightInput.text {
     if weightStr == "" {
       return
     }
     else {
         if let heightNum = Double(heightStr)  {
         if let weightNum = Double(weightStr)  {
                     } }
             }
}}
```

Code 6.2

As you can see from Code 6.2, the string entered in the weight and height text fields are taken by the **heightInput.text** and **weightInput.text** structures: if let heightStr = heightInput.text and if let weightStr = weightInput.text statements assign the text inputs to the **heightStr** and **weightStr** constants. The nested if-else structures are used to control if values are actually entered in these text fields by checking **if heightStr == "" and if weightStr == ""** conditions. If any of these conditions is true (meaning that nothing is entered in one or both text fields), a **return** statement is executed and the program exits doing nothing other. In the end, **if let heightNum = Double(heightStr)** and **if let weightNum = Double(weightStr)** statements are used to convert the string values of **heightStr** and **weightStr** to Double type and then assign them to **heightNum** and **weightNum** variables. The **if** statements are used here since we're not sure if the texts entered into height and weight fields can be converted to Double type (the user may enter a non-numerical text and that cannot be converted to Double type). **If these texts are convertible to Double type then we will have the numerical values of height and weight stored in heightNum and weightNum constants.**

2. The BMI is calculated according to the equation given in the beginning of this chapter using the code shown in Code 6.3. Note that a constant named BMI is created and then the result of the calculation is assigned to it in the first line. In the second line, numerical BMI is converted to String type and it is assigned to the text of the BMIOutput label.

```
let BMI: Double = (weightNum) / (heightNum * heightNum)
BMIOutput.text = String(BMI)
```
Code 6.3

3. Finally, the switch-case statements are employed to check the calculated BMI value according to Table 6.1 as in Code 6.4. In each of the cases, the text of the **categoryOutput** is set accordingly.

```
switch BMI {
    case 1..<15:
        categoryOutput.text = "Very severely underweight"
    case 15...16:
```

```
    categoryOutput.text = "Severely underweight"
  case 16..<18.5:
    categoryOutput.text = "Underweight"
  case 18.5..<25:
    categoryOutput.text = "Normal"
  case 25..<30:
    categoryOutput.text = "Overweight"
  case 30..<35:
    categoryOutput.text = "Moderately obese"
  case 35..<40:
    categoryOutput.text = "Severely obese"
  case 40..<60:
    categoryOutput.text = "Very severely obese"
  default:
    return
}
```

Code 6.4 (cont'd from the previous page)

Combining all of these codes, the complete ViewController.swift file of our app is obtained as the following (**you can download these codes from the book's website:** www.ios-swift.net):

```
import UIKit

class ViewController: UIViewController {

    @IBOutlet weak var weightInput: UITextField!
    @IBOutlet weak var heightInput: UITextField!
    @IBOutlet weak var BMIOutput: UITextField!
    @IBOutlet weak var categoryOutput: UILabel!

    override func viewDidLoad() {
    super.viewDidLoad()
    // Do any additional setup after loading the
view, typically from a nib.

    }
    @IBAction func calcBMI(_ sender: AnyObject) {
    if let heightStr = heightInput.text {
        if heightStr == "" {
        return
        }
        else {
            if let weightStr = weightInput.text {
                if weightStr == "" {
```

```
                            return
                        }
                        else {
if let heightNum = Double(heightStr) {
if let weightNum = Double(weightStr) {
let BMI: Double = (weightNum) / (heightNum * heightNum)
BMIOutput.text = String(BMI)

switch BMI {
  case 1..<15:
    categoryOutput.text = "Very severely underweight"
  case 15...16:
    categoryOutput.text = "Severely underweight"
  case 16..<18.5:
    categoryOutput.text = "Underweight"
  case 18.5..<25:
    categoryOutput.text = "Normal"
  case 25..<30:
    categoryOutput.text = "Overweight"
  case 30..<35:
    categoryOutput.text = "Moderately obese"
  case 35..<40:
    categoryOutput.text = "Severely obese"
  case 40..<60:
    categoryOutput.text = "Very severely obese"
  default:
    return
        }
} }
                    }
                  }
                }
              }


      }
      override func didReceiveMemoryWarning() {
          super.didReceiveMemoryWarning()
          // Dispose of any resources that can be
recreated.
      }
}
```

Code 6.5 (cont'd from the previous pages)

6.6. Building and Running the App

Let's now try our app in the simulator. Just hit the "Run" button in Xcode and you should see the user interface shown in Figure 6.29.

Enter weight and height values (in kg and metres) and then tap the "Calculate my BMI!" button. If you followed all steps correctly, you should see the BMI value and the BMI category on your app screen as in Figure 6.30.

6.7. Final Notes

Note 1. You can set the keyboard type that will pop up on a real device while entering the height and weight values by selecting the respective text field and then setting the "keyboard type" from the attributes menu in Xcode as shown in Figure 6.31. It's better to select "Numbers and punctuation" in our app since we don't want the user to enter any text.

Figure 6.29. The user interface of the BMI calculator app

Note 2. The text field that shows the BMI index cannot accommodate the all the digits as you can see from Figure 6.30. You can either increase the width of the text field or set the text with `BMIOutput.text = String(Int(BMI))` which will just show the integer part of the BMI.

iPhone SE – iOS 10.0 (14A5309d)

Carrier 📶   7:42 AM

BMI Calculator

Enter your weight (kg):   89

Enter your height (m):   1.85

Calculate my BMI!

Your BMI: 26.00438…

Overweight

Figure 6.30. Our BMI calculator app in action

Note 3. In the simulator, the keyboard may not show up by default. In order to switch the keyboard, you can select/deselect Hardware → Keyboard → Connect Hardware Keyboard from the Simulator menu while the simulator is the active window.

Figure 6.31. Changing the popup keyboard type

Note 4. I have verified that the BMI calculator app runs on real devices as expected (installing on a real device was explained in the last pages of Chapter 3). However there's a problem with devices having moderate screens. After entering height and weight info, the keyboard does not disappear and the user cannot click on the button and see her/his BMI result. In order to make the keyboard disappear after clicking on the "Return" key, you can use a method called **textFieldShouldReturn**. In order to use this method, we need to add the **UITextFieldDelegate** class to extend our ViewController class. We can use this method as shown in Code 6.6.

```
func textFieldShouldReturn(_ textField: UITextField) -
> Bool {
        self.weightInput.resignFirstResponder()
        self.heightInput.resignFirstResponder()
        return true
}
```
Code 6.6

When the user enters the height and weight info and taps the "Return" key on the real device, this method is called and it makes the keyboard to disappear. The whole ViewController.swift file with this method and its class added is shown below:

```swift
import UIKit

class ViewController: UIViewController, UITextFieldDelega
te {

        @IBOutlet weak var weightInput: UITextField!
        @IBOutlet weak var heightInput: UITextField!
        @IBOutlet weak var BMIOutput: UITextField!
        @IBOutlet weak var categoryOutput: UILabel!

        override func viewDidLoad() {
        super.viewDidLoad()
           self.weightInput.delegate = self
           self.heightInput.delegate = self
    }
@IBAction func calcBMI(_ sender: AnyObject) {
        if let heightStr = heightInput.text {
            if heightStr == "" {
               return
            }
        else {
          if let weightStr = weightInput.text {
          if weightStr == "" {
          return
          }
          else {
if let heightNum = Double(heightStr) {
  if let weightNum = Double(weightStr) {
    let BMI: Double = (weightNum) / (heightNum *heightNum)
    BMIOutput.text = String(BMI)
     switch BMI {
       case 1..<15:
         categoryOutput.text = "Very severely underweight"
       case 15...16:
         categoryOutput.text = "Severely underweight"
       case 16..<18.5:
         categoryOutput.text = "Underweight"
       case 18.5..<25:
          categoryOutput.text = "Normal"
       case 25..<30:
```

```
         categoryOutput.text = "Overweight"
      case 30..<35:
         categoryOutput.text = "Moderately obese"
      case 35..<40:
          categoryOutput.text = "Severely obese"
      case 40..<60:
         categoryOutput.text = "Very severely obese"
      default:
         return
                              }
                            }
   }
                       }
                    }
                 }
             }
}
   func textFieldShouldReturn(_ textField: UITextField) -
> Bool {
         self.weightInput.resignFirstResponder()
         self.heightInput.resignFirstResponder()
         return true
      }

      override func didReceiveMemoryWarning() {
         super.didReceiveMemoryWarning()
         // Dispose of any resources that can be
   recreated.
      }
}
```

Code 6.7 (cont'd from the previous pages)

Note 5. Don't worry if the app categorizes you obese, it does me too (the values shown in Figure 6.30 are not mine ☺). I'm trying to do exercises and eat food with lower calories to decrease my BMI. (Sorry, this monologue made me hungry. See you in the next chapter later after having a big meal!).

Chapter 7

iOS APP # 3: SIMPLE DIE ROLLER

7.1. Creating the Project and Adding an Image View Object

In this chapter we will develop a die rolling app. We'll learn how to use images in the user interface and also the basic random number generation procedure in Swift. When we hit a rolling button, the app will choose a number between 1 and 6 randomly, show the result as a number in a label and also display a die image showing the outcome.

Please create a new project and save it on your computer. First of all, let's design the user interface. We need an image view component which is used to display an image or an animation of images. While the Main.storyboard file is selected in Xcode, find the Image View object in the object library and add it by drag and drop operation somewhere in the user interface as shown in Figure 7.1.

Let's align the image view on the screen and set its height and width values. Select the image view with a single-click, and then check the horizontal and vertical alignment in the "Align" menu. We'll add a button and a label below the image view therefore it is better to position the image view a bit above the vertical centre. For that, set the vertical alignment value to -100 as shown in Figure 7.2.

Since we'll show a die face in this image view, it's better to have a square shape. In order to set the height and width values of the image view, single-click to select it and then in the "Pin" menu set the height and width values you like. I set them to 128 as in Figure 7.3. After the position and dimension settings, image view appears on the Main.storyboard file as shown in Figure 7.4.

Figure 7.1. Adding an image view

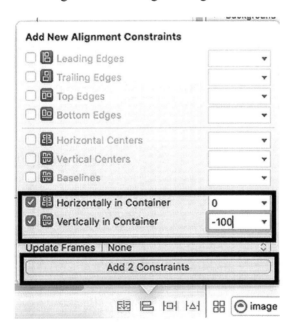

Figure 7.2. Adding alignment constraints for the image view

Figure 7.3. Setting the dimensions of the image view

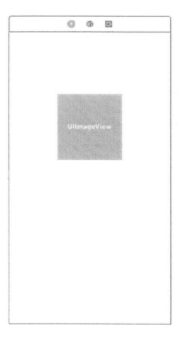

Figure 7.4. Image view after the position and dimension settings

Now, we shall add a label component to show the outcome of the die roll as a text. Find the label component from the object library and then drag and drop to add it somewhere below the image view in the device screen as shown in Figure 7.5. This label will show the outcome as a number but before the rolling, it may show any default text you can set in the label text box shown by the ellipse in Figure 7.5. I set it as "Waiting...". I also set the text alignment as centred.

Figure 7.5. Adding a label component to show the rolling outcome as a number

Let's set the position and size constraints for the label component. I set the height and width to 25 and 128, respectively as shown in Figure 7.6.

The positioning constraints of the label will be set as "align horizontally in the container" from the "Align" menu as given in Figure 7.7 and 50 units below the nearest component above it with the "Pin" menu as shown in Figure 7.8.

Figure 7.6. Width and height constraints for the label

Figure 7.7. Alignment of the label horizontally

Figure 7.8. Setting the vertical constraint for the label

After these constraints, we have the label positioned 50 units below the image view component and aligned in the middle horizontally as shown below:

Figure 7.9. Image view and label components after alignment

Finally we need to add a button which will perform the die roll. Find the button component from the object library and drag and drop it somewhere below the label component as shown in Figure 7.10. After adding the button, you can set its text to something related to what it will do. I set its text to "Roll!" and changed its font size to 25.

Figure 7.10. Adding the button

Now it's time for setting its dimension and alignment constraints. From the "Pin" menu, I set its height to 30, height to 80 and its distance to the component above it (the label) to 50 units as shown in Figure 7.11.

Figure 7.11. Adding height, width and vertical constraints of the button

After aligning its horizontal position to the middle from the "Align" menu as shown in Figure 7.12, we are ready to update the frame as in Figure 7.13. Remember that these buttons are located at the bottom right of the middle pane of Xcode.

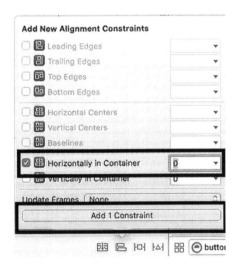

Figure 7.12. Setting the horizontal alignment of the button

"Update Frames" button

Figure 7.13. Updating frames in the user interface

After updating frames, the user interface should look like Figure 7.14. This is not the best user interface I know, but it'll do the job. You can do more artwork on it if you wish.

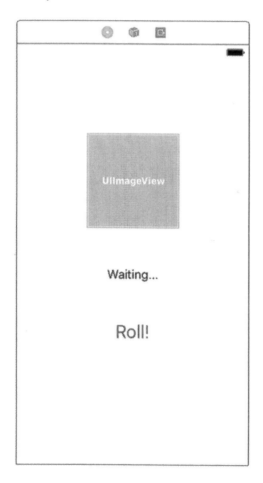

Figure 7.14. Final view of the device screen

7.2. Adding Images to the Project

We want to generate a random number in the range of 1 to 6 and then show the corresponding die image in the UIImageView object. Therefore we need the images of die faces from 1 to 6. I downloaded royalty-free die face images from the Internet and you can access them from this book's website www.ios-swift.net. These images are shown in Figure 7.15 together with their filenames.

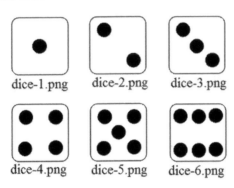

dice-1.png   dice-2.png   dice-3.png

dice-4.png   dice-5.png   dice-6.png

Figure 7.15. Die face images used in our app

As explained in Chapter 2, the file Assets.xcassets stores the images and similar data files that are used in the app. We open this file by single-clicking it inside the Xcode and then we are presented with an empty file as shown in Figure 7.16.

Figure 7.16. Empty "assets file"

In order to add images, right-click in the middle area and select "New Image Set" as shown in Figure 7.17.

Figure 7.17. Creating a new image set

A new image set is now created. Click once on the "Image" text as shown in Figure 7.18 and it will be highlighted. Change its name to something meaningful such that you can easily access it from your code later (don't forget to hit return on your keyboard after renaming it). I named it as "dice-1".

Figure 7.18. Renaming the image set

As you can see, there are three sizes for the new image set. If you insert only one image at 1x, then your app will use it everywhere you reference the image set name. Since there will be only one size for dice face images in our app, inserting an image only to 1x is OK.

In order to insert an image, drag it and drop to the 1x frame from the Finder of your Mac as shown in Figure 7.19.

Figure 7.19. Inserting an image to the image dataset by drag and drop

Please repeat, "creating an image dataset, renaming it and inserting its image" procedure for each die face image. I have also added an image to display when the app first starts before any rolling operation. You can find it as "dice-general.png" on the book's website: www.ios-swift.net. After adding all these, you should have the assets file shown below:

Figure 7.20. Assets file after adding all die face images

After adding these images, you can set the default image of the image view object of the user interface by selecting the Main.storyboard file in Xcode and then clicking on the image view object as shown in Figure 7.21. Please select dice-general from the drop-down box as indicated by the arrow.

Figure 7.21. Setting the default image of the image view

You may have noted that there's an empty "AppIcon" image set in the assets file. If you insert an image there, it will be your app's icon that will be shown to the user on a real device.

7.3. Connecting UI Objects to the Code

We'll do the usual connecting procedure for the components of our user interface using the "Assistant editor" as explained in detail before. The connections of the image view and the label components will be of type **IBOutlet** while the connection type of the button will be **IBAction**. I named their connection names as "dieImage", "dieResult" and "rollDie", respectively. After the connections, the ViewController.swift file looks like below:

```swift
import UIKit

class ViewController: UIViewController {

    override func viewDidLoad() {
        super.viewDidLoad()
    }

    @IBOutlet weak var dieImage: UIImageView!
    @IBOutlet weak var dieResult: UILabel!
    @IBAction func rollDie(_ sender: AnyObject) {
    }
    override func didReceiveMemoryWarning() {
```

```
            super.didReceiveMemoryWarning()
    }
}
```

Code 7.1 (cont'd from the previous page)

We'll write our main code inside the rollDie button's function since our app is not supposed to do anything until the user taps this button.

7.4. Randomness Function in Swift

Each time the user clicks on the "Roll!" button, the app has to generate a random number between 1 and 6. In Swift 3, we can generate random numbers with the built-in function **arc4random_uniform(x)** where x is an integer and the return value of this function is a random number between 0 and x-1. Therefore, in order to generate a random number between 1 and 6, we can employ this function as **arc4random_uniform(6) + 1**. Adding this code line to the ViewController.swift file and also including the usual label text setting, we have the code below:

```
import UIKit

class ViewController: UIViewController {

    override func viewDidLoad() {
        super.viewDidLoad()
    }
    @IBOutlet weak var dieImage: UIImageView!
    @IBOutlet weak var dieResult: UILabel!
    @IBAction func rollDie(_ sender: AnyObject) {
        let randomNumber = arc4random_uniform(6) + 1
        self.dieResult.text = String(randomNumber)
    }
    override func didReceiveMemoryWarning() {
        super.didReceiveMemoryWarning()
    }
}
```

Code 7.2

7.5. Updating Images in the Code

Note that, the keyword **self** is used to access the **dieResult** label in Code 7.2 since we're accessing the label located in the storyboard related to this ViewController class. Now, we need to change the die image according to the generated random number. We can use if-else or switch-case statements. Since here are 6 possibilities, it is better to utilize a switch-case structure. In each of the cases, we can set the image with the code **self.dieImage.image = UIImage(named: "imageName")** where imageName is the image set's name we created in the assets file before. Incorporating the switch-case statements, the final code of our app can be given as below:

```
import UIKit
class ViewController: UIViewController {

    override func viewDidLoad() {
        super.viewDidLoad()
    }

@IBOutlet weak var dieImage: UIImageView!
@IBOutlet weak var dieResult: UILabel!
@IBAction func rollDie(_ sender: AnyObject) {
let randomNumber = arc4random_uniform(6) + 1
self.dieResult.text = String(randomNumber)
switch randomNumber {
case 1:
 self.dieImage.image = UIImage(named: "dice-1")"
case 2:
 self.dieImage.image = UIImage(named: "dice-2")"
case 3:
 self.dieImage.image = UIImage(named: "dice-3")"
case 4:
 self.dieImage.image = UIImage(named: "dice-4")"
case 5:
 self.dieImage.image = UIImage(named: "dice-5")"
case 6:
 self.dieImage.image = UIImage(named: "dice-6")"
default:
 return
        }
    }

    override func didReceiveMemoryWarning() {
        super.didReceiveMemoryWarning()
    }
}
```

Code 7.3

7.6. Building and Running the App

Let's run our die roller app by hitting the "Run" button in Xcode. The user interface shown in Figure 7.22 appears. Each time we click the "Roll!" button, the app should show a different number with the corresponding die face image as in Figure 7.23.

It is worth noting that random numbers are not only used for fun apps but also in everyday cryptographic processes like online credit card transactions, etc. Hence there are much more sophisticated random number generation functions in Swift, also with the incorporation of external libraries. However for simple randomness like in our die rolling game, `arc4random_uniform` function seems adequate. You can check its randomness by consecutively clicking on the "Roll!" button and observing if you obtain the same number a lot or if the numbers show a pattern such that you can guess the next number. However, please keep in mind that accurate testing of randomness requires complex tools.

Figure 7.22. The user interface of the die rolling app when it's first run

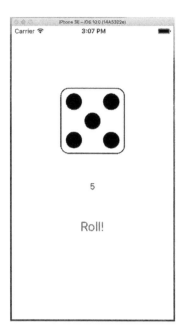

Figure 7.23. Die rolling app showing 5 after one of the rollings

Final note: You can try to change the die rolling game to a food rolling game: change the die face images with pizza, burger, kebabs, etc. and roll to see what you'll order before you continue to the next chapter where we will develop our 4th app: the exercise calorie calculator.

Chapter 8

iOS APP # 4: EXERCISE CALORIE CALCULATOR

8.1. General Information

We have developed single view apps until now. However, tabbed apps also have a significant place in mobile development. In this chapter we will develop a tabbed app. This app will be a simple exercise calorie calculator that will be used to calculate the calories burned during a physical exercise. The app will have 3 tabs. In the first tab, the user will enter the constants: age, weight and gender information; in the second tab, exercise parameters will be entered: average heart rate and workout time. Finally, the burned calories will be calculated and displayed in the third tab. In this chapter, we'll learn how we can pass small data between tabs using global variables.

We'll use the following formulas for calculating the calories burned utilizing the input from the user (taken from: http://fitnowtraining.com/2012/01/formula-for-calories-burned/):

For women:

$$Burned\ calories = \left[\begin{array}{l} (Age\ x\ 0.074) - (Weight\ x\ 0.05741) \\ + (Heart\ rate\ x\ 0.04472) - 20.4022 \end{array} \right] x\ Exer.\ time / 4.184$$

For men:

$$Burned\ calories = \left[\begin{array}{l} (Age\ x\ 0.2017) - (Weight\ x\ 0.09036) \\ + (Heart\ rate\ x\ 0.06309) - 55.0969 \end{array} \right] x\ Exer.\ time / 4.184$$

Don't worry if equations make you dizzy, we won't go deep into how these equations are obtained or what we can do with them mathematically. We'll just use them in our app and I'll show you how we can easily implement these calculations in our Swift code.

8.2. Creating a Tabbed App

Start Xcode, select "Create a new Xcode project" and then choose the tabbed application as shown in Figure 8.1. Give a name to your project and save the project to the disk as usual.

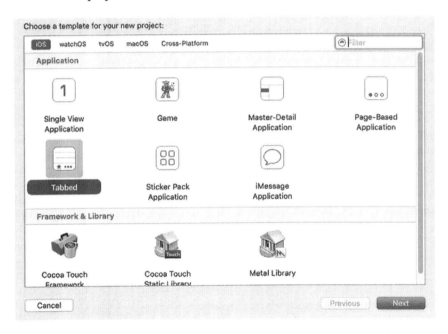

Figure 8.1. Creating a tabbed application in Xcode

Xcode creates two view controllers and their corresponding Swift files by default when a tabbed app is created as shown in Figure 8.2.

8.3. Adding More Tabs

For this project, we need 3 tabs therefore we need to add one more view controller and its tab. To do this, select the Main.storyboard file. Then find the "View Controller" object from the object library and drag and drop it to somewhere empty in the storyboard viewer as shown in Figure 8.3.

Figure 8.2. Tabbed app with 2 view controllers

After the drag and drop operation, the newly created empty view controller is shown in the storyboard as in Figure 8.4.

In order to be able to open the new view controller from the tab menu, we need to attach a tab bar item to it. Find the tab bar item from the object library and then drag-drop on the newly added empty view controller as in Figure 8.5.

Figure 8.3. Drag and drop of a new view controller to the scene

Figure 8.4. Newly added view controller in the storyboard

Figure 8.5. Adding a tab bar item to the new view controller

8.4. Connecting the New Tab to the Navigator

After adding the tab bar item, our view controller is ready to be a component of the tabbed app. However, the main tab bar controller shown by the grey screen in the storyboard doesn't know about the newly added view controller yet. We need to make a connection between the two. In fact as you may have noticed before, the view controllers are shown as connected to the tab view controller by big arrows as shown inside the ellipses in Figure 8.5. In order to connect the main tab bar controller to the new view controller, **hold down the control key** and then drag and drop a line from the greyed tab bar controller to the new empty view controller as in Figure 8.6. After dropping, Xcode will present you a menu as shown in Figure 8.7.

In the menu of Figure 8.7, select the "view controllers" option and then your new view controller will be connected to the tab bar controller as shown in Figure 8.8.

Figure 8.6. Connecting the tab bar controller and the new view controller

Figure 8.7. Connecting the new view controller using the "view controllers" option

Figure 8.8. The new view controller after the connection

8.5. Connecting a New Class to the New Tab

Note that, the tab bar controller now shows the tab symbol of the new view controller as shown inside the circle in Figure 8.8. As you know there should be a Swift file corresponding to each view controller. However our new view controller doesn't have one yet. Let's create its class by right clicking on the file explorer as in Figure 8.9 and selecting "New File". In the next menu, **select "Swift File"** and give it a name accordingly like **ThirdViewController** as in Figures 8.10 and 8.11, respectively. After these steps, Xcode file explorer should look like Figure 8.12 where the new file is shown inside the rectangle.

Figure 8.9. Adding a new file to the project

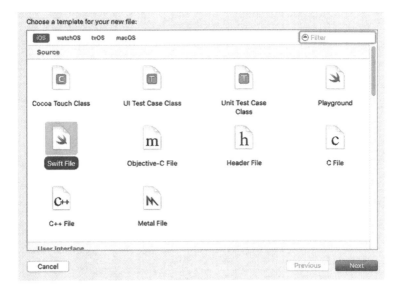

Figure 8.10. Selecting the file type

Figure 8.11. Naming the new file

Figure 8.12. Xcode file explorer after adding the new file

Now we have a new Swift file but it is empty as you can see by clicking on it. In order to connect the new view controller to this file, we need to create a new class in it. The easy way is copying the contents of one of the existing Swift files like FirstViewController.swift and then pasting it inside the new ThirdViewController.swift file. And then, let's change the name of the class to ThirdViewController. The content of the ThirdViewController file will be as shown below:

```
import UIKit
class ThirdViewController: UIViewController {

    override func viewDidLoad() {
        super.viewDidLoad()
    }
    override func didReceiveMemoryWarning() {
        super.didReceiveMemoryWarning()
    }
}
```
Code 8.1

Now we need to attach the new view controller to the ThirdViewController.swift file we just created. For that, select Main.storyboard from the file explorer and the view controllers will be displayed. Select the new view controller **by clicking on the yellow circle called "Item"** as shown in Figure 8.13.

When the view controller is selected, find and select the "ThirdViewController" class from the "Identity inspector" tab at the right frame of Xcode as shown in Figure 8.14.

Let's run the project in the simulator to see what our app looks like at this stage. Hit the play button on Xcode and you should see the user interface shown in Figure 8.15.

Figure 8.13. Selecting the new view controller

Figure 8.14. Attaching the ThirdViewController class to the view controller

Figure 8.15. App's user interface at this stage

As you click on the tabs located at the bottom, you can navigate through the first, second and the newly added third view. However there's a problem: the last view's icon is missing, there's only one plain "Item" text for it. We can easily change the tab bar items to an image set already existing in Xcode or a custom image from an image set we can create. Let's set the icon for the third tab as the circle (first image existing in the assets file by default) and set its text as "Calculate calories" as we aimed in this project using the "Bar Item" menu from the right frame of Xcode as in Figure 8.16. I also changed the titles of the first and second tabs as "Enter personal info" and "Enter exercise info" with the same method. If we hit the play button in Xcode, our app's screens for different tabs should be as in Figure 8.17.

Figure 8.16. Setting the bar item's title and image

As you can see from Figure 8.17, the tabs of our app work perfectly. Now it's time for the usual interface design and coding. Currently our app's first two views have the default texts as set by Xcode and the third view has nothing in it, just a blank screen.

8.6. Adding a Segmented Control Object

We will enter text fields for the age and weight information. We can easily do this using our experience from previous chapters. Since I explained the text fields and labels in detail before, I won't do the same here in order not to make things boring for you. The only new component I added is a "Segmented Control" for selecting the gender info. A segmented control behaves as a two section button and it is easy to get its value in Swift. In order to add the segmented control, find it from the object library in Xcode as in Figure 8.18 and drag and drop on the screen. You can set its constraints as usual.

Figure 8.17. The app's different tabs

Figure 8.18. Adding a segmented control

Segmented control has two sections by default and they are named as "First" and "Second". Our gender info will also have two values: male and female hence we don't need to change the number of sections but the names. Select each section of the segmented control and then on the top right pane of Xcode, change the names to female and male, respectively as shown below:

Figure 8.19. Setting properties of the segmented control

Finally, add a button below the segmented control to save the personal information. After these changes, the screen for the first tab looks like

Figure 8.20 (note that your screen layout may look significantly different as I didn't give the details about the positioning of the components).

Similarly, we need to add labels and text fields for the exercise time and the average heart rate in the second tab's view. I have designed a similar layout as shown in Figure 8.21 but you can design it as you like as long as it can take the needed information from the user.

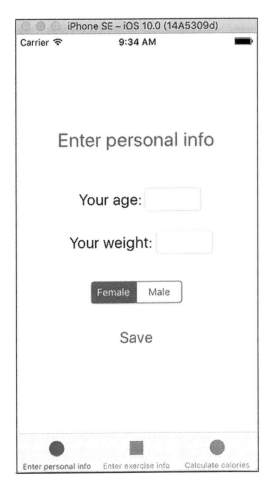

Figure 8.20. The storyboard of the first view

In the third tab we will just have a button to calculate the calories burned and a label to show the result. I designed it like in Figure 8.22. I know it looks plain, you can do some make up on it if you wish.

Figure 8.21. Layout of the second tab

8.7. Connecting UI Elements to the Code

We'll connect each view's components to their own classes located in FirstViewController.swift, SecondViewController.swift and ThirdViewController.swift for the first, second and the third tabs, respectively. We'll use **IBOutlet** for label, text fields and the segmented control and **IBAction** for the buttons and the segmented control of the first tab. Note that we need to add both an outlet and an action for the segmented control to take its value and get a trigger when the user taps on it. After the usual connections using the assistant editor of Xcode, the Swift files for all three tabs are as shown in Code 8.2, 8.3 and 8.4.

Figure 8.22. The third tab's view

```
import UIKit
class FirstViewController: UIViewController {
    override func viewDidLoad() {
        super.viewDidLoad()
    }
@IBOutlet weak var yourAge: UITextField!
@IBOutlet weak var yourWeight: UILabel!
@IBOutlet weak var segmentedControl: UISegmentedControl!
@IBAction func genderButton(_ sender: AnyObject)
    }
@IBAction func savePersonalInfo(_ sender: AnyObject) {
    }
override func didReceiveMemoryWarning() {
  super.didReceiveMemoryWarning()
    }
}
```

Code 8.2

```swift
import UIKit

class SecondViewController: UIViewController {

    override func viewDidLoad() {
        super.viewDidLoad()
    }

    @IBOutlet weak var exerciseTime: UITextField!
    @IBOutlet weak var avgHeartRate: UITextField!
    @IBAction func saveExerciseInfo(_ sender: AnyObject)
{
    }

    override func didReceiveMemoryWarning() {
        super.didReceiveMemoryWarning()
    }
}
```

Code 8.3

```swift
import UIKit
class ThirdViewController: UIViewController {
    override func viewDidLoad() {
        super.viewDidLoad()
    }
    @IBOutlet weak var calories: UILabel!

    @IBAction func calcCalories(_ sender: AnyObject) {
    }
    override func didReceiveMemoryWarning() {
        super.didReceiveMemoryWarning()
    }
}
```

Code 8.4

8.8. Developing the Main Code

Now we are ready to write the actual code for calculating the calories burned. Since we need to pass data from the first and second tabs to the third tab for calculation (the calculation will take place when the user clicks the "Click to calculate calories burned" button in the third tab), we will define the variables that will contain the age, weight, gender, exercise time and heart rate information as global variables. Global variables are the variables that can be accessed from any code line in the project. Some programmers dislike using global variables since they may easily cause errors in big projects however there's no problem using global variables in our small project here. The ViewController.swift files after adding the global variables and the related calculation code are given in Code 8.5, Code 8.6 and Code 8.7, for the first, second and third views respectively. Note that we define global variables before the class definitions so that their scope won't be limited to that class.

```swift
import UIKit

var userAge: Double?
var userWeight: Double?
var userGender: String = "Female"
class FirstViewController: UIViewController {
    override func viewDidLoad() {
        super.viewDidLoad()
    }
@IBOutlet weak var yourAge: UITextField!
@IBOutlet weak var yourWeight: UITextField!
@IBOutlet weak var segmentedControl: UISegmentedControl!
@IBAction func genderButton(_ sender: AnyObject) {
  switch segmentedControl.selectedSegmentIndex {
    case 0:
      userGender = "Female"
    case 1:
      userGender = "Male"
    default:
      return
          }
}
@IBAction func savePersonalInfo(_ sender: AnyObject) {
        userWeight = Double(yourWeight.text!)
        userAge = Double(yourAge.text!)
    }
    override func didReceiveMemoryWarning() {
        super.didReceiveMemoryWarning()
    }
}
```
Code 8.5

Note that in Code 8.5, the "Save" button enables the variables "userWeight" and "userAge" to be set by the values entered in the respective text fields. On the other hand, the segmented control's action outlet sets the **userGender** variable to "Female" or "Male". Note that when one of the two sections (female and male) of the segmented control is clicked, the state of the segmented control is read by the method **selectSegmentIndex** which is applied on the outlet variable **segmentedControl**. The segment indices start with 0 and increase one by one. Since we have female at index 0 and male at index 1 in our example, case 0 will correspond to the female user while case 1 will indicate a male user. If the user is female, she will not click on the segmented control since it is set to female when the app starts. In order to cover this situation, **userGender** variable is set to "Female" at the start of the code by default.

```
import UIKit
var userExerciseTime: Double?
var userHeartRate: Double?
class SecondViewController: UIViewController {
    override func viewDidLoad() {
        super.viewDidLoad()
    }
    @IBOutlet weak var exerciseTime: UITextField!
    @IBOutlet weak var avgHeartRate: UITextField!
    @IBAction func saveExerciseInfo(_ sender: AnyObject)
{
        userExerciseTime = Double(exerciseTime.text!)
        userHeartRate = Double(avgHeartRate.text!)
    }
    override func didReceiveMemoryWarning() {
        super.didReceiveMemoryWarning()
            }
}
```
Code 8.6

The listing of the SecondViewController is given in Code 8.6. It just takes the values of the text fields "exerciseTime" and "avgHeartRate", converts them to Double type (since we'll do maths with them in the third tab) and stores them in the global variables named **userExerciseTime** and **userHeartRate** when the "Save" button is clicked.

```
import UIKit

var caloriesBurned: Double?
class ThirdViewController: UIViewController {

    override func viewDidLoad() {
        super.viewDidLoad()
    }

    @IBOutlet weak var calories: UILabel!

    @IBAction func calcCalories(_ sender: AnyObject) {
switch userGender {
    case "Female":
        caloriesBurned = ((userAge!*0.074)-
        (userWeight!*0.05741)+(userHeartRate!*0.4472)-
        20.4022)*userExerciseTime!/4.184
    case "Male":
        caloriesBurned = ((userAge!*0.2017)-
        (userWeight!*0.09036)+(userHeartRate!*0.6309)-
        55.0969)*userExerciseTime!/4.184
    default:
        return
        }
        calories.text = String(Int(caloriesBurned!))
    }

    override func didReceiveMemoryWarning() {
        super.didReceiveMemoryWarning()
    }
}
```
Code 8.7

Code of the ThirdViewController is given in Code 8.7. When the "Click to calculate!" button is pressed, the burned calories are calculated in the switch-case statement depending on the gender (remember than burned calories are calculated using different formulas for male and female as given at the beginning of this chapter). The result is then displayed by the **caloriesBurned** label. It is also important to remember to unwrap optionals with (!) as you can see in this code listing.

8.9. Running the App

We have completed coding phase of our exercise calculator app. Let's run it on the simulator by pressing the "Run" button in Xcode. The screen shown in Figure 8.23 appears, which is the first tab for entering personal info. I entered the values shown in the figure and then clicked the save button. **Note that the formulas and our app use pounds as the weight unit.** Then, in the second tab, I entered the exercise info given in Figure 8.24 and again clicked the save button. Finally, in the third view of Figure 8.25, I clicked the button to calculate and the app gave the result of 154 calories. It's for 1 hour of exercise. **I verified the result by calculating the formula manually. The number is correct, just 154 calories!** Considering that an average sized burger has around 250 calories according to calorielab.com, I feel depressed now and will take a break to have a coffee before the next chapter where we will develop an app that uses GPS and map services.

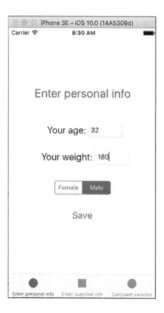

Figure 8.23. Entering personal info in the first view

Figure 8.24. Entering exercise info in the second view

Figure 8.25. Calories calculated by our app

Note: The app runs well on a real device; however as in the BMI Calculator app, the keyboard does not disappear after entering values. In order to make the keyboard disappear, we'll do the same trick we did in the BMI Calculator app (please see Note 4 in Chapter 6). The codes for the FirstViewController.swift and SecondviewController.swift files are

shown in Code 8.8 and Code 8.9, respectively after adding the keyboard
hiding method **textFieldShouldReturn**. When you update your code
according to these, the keyboard should hide on a real device when the
user clicks the "Return" button after entering her/his personal and
exercise info. Remember that complete project files are available for
download on the book's website: www.ios-swift.net.

```
import UIKit

var userAge: Double?
var userWeight: Double?
var userGender: String = "Female"

class FirstViewController: UIViewController, UITextFieldD
elegate {

    override func viewDidLoad() {
        super.viewDidLoad()
        self.yourAge.delegate = self
        self.yourWeight.delegate = self
    }
@IBOutlet weak var yourAge: UITextField!
@IBOutlet weak var yourWeight: UITextField!
@IBOutlet weak var segmentedControl: UISegmentedControl!
@IBAction func genderButton(_ sender: AnyObject) {
        switch segmentedControl.selectedSegmentIndex {
        case 0:
            userGender = "Female"
        case 1:
            userGender = "Male"
        default:
            return
        }
    }
@IBAction func savePersonalInfo(_ sender: AnyObject) {

    userWeight = Double(yourWeight.text!)
    userAge = Double(yourAge.text!)
    }
func textFieldShouldReturn(_ textField: UITextField) -
> Bool {
        self.yourWeight.resignFirstResponder()
        self.yourAge.resignFirstResponder()
        return true
```

```
    }

    override func didReceiveMemoryWarning() {
        super.didReceiveMemoryWarning()
    }
}
```

Code 8.8 (cont'd from the previous page)

```
import UIKit

var userExerciseTime: Double?
var userHeartRate: Double?

class SecondViewController: UIViewController, UITextField
Delegate {
override func viewDidLoad() {
        super.viewDidLoad()
        self.exerciseTime.delegate = self
        self.avgHeartRate.delegate = self
    }

@IBOutlet weak var exerciseTime: UITextField!
@IBOutlet weak var avgHeartRate: UITextField!
@IBAction func saveExerciseInfo(_ sender: AnyObject) {

        userExerciseTime = Double(exerciseTime.text!)
        userHeartRate = Double(avgHeartRate.text!)
    }

func textFieldShouldReturn(_ textField: UITextField) -> Bool {
        self.exerciseTime.resignFirstResponder()
        self.avgHeartRate.resignFirstResponder()
        return true
    }

    override func didReceiveMemoryWarning() {
        super.didReceiveMemoryWarning()
    }
}
```

Code 8.9

Chapter 9

iOS APP # 5: SHOW MY LOCATION: USING GPS AND MAPS

9.1. Creating the Project and Adding a Map Kit View

Geolocation and navigation apps are popular in all mobile platforms. Considering this, most mobile devices especially smartphones include components called GPS receivers. These receivers take microwave band radio signals from global positioning satellites that move in specified orbits around the earth. These GPS signals are extremely weak but thanks to the electronics tech, amplifier and processing circuits in smartphones can utilize these signals for location services.

Anyway, let's start developing our 5th app: Show My Location. In this chapter, you'll learn to use maps and geolocation data from GPS in your apps. It sounds easy but there are some confusing tricks to use the GPS receiver; don't worry I'll show all of them in a while.

In this app, we aim to show our location on the map while displaying the coordinate info just beneath the map in real time.

Let's start with creating a new project and saving it on the disk as usual. From the object library, place a label to show the title of your app and then find the object called "Map Kit View" and drag and drop it on the storyboard as in Figure 9.1.

A Map Kit View shows a map on the screen together with the annotations and other info we can place on the map. Most of the properties of the map are set programmatically.

We will show real time the latitude, longitude and altitude values besides the map in our app therefore I have added the required labels and text fields for these too as in Figure 9.2.

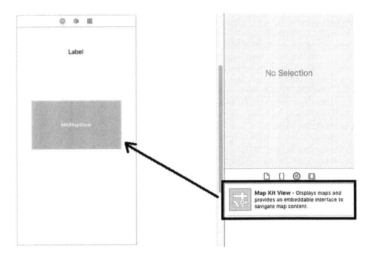

Figure 9.1. Adding a Map Kit View to the storyboard

Figure 9.2. The layout template of the view

9.2. Adding the Constraints

We now have to edit the labels in the view and add constraints so that the components will not free float on the screen.

> **For the title label:** I have set the title's font size to 25 with the heavy option (remember that we do all these by selecting the component and then using the Attributes menu in the top right pane in Xcode). I centred the text inside the label and set the font colour as brown. Then I centred it horizontally with the "Align" menu as shown in Figure 9.3. Its distance to the top edge is set as 20 units while the width and height are given the values of 250 and 30 units, respectively from the "Pin" menu. These constraint settings are also given in Figure 9.4.

Figure 9.3. Centring the title label horizontally

> **The map:** Again, please align it horizontally from the "Align" menu as above and you can set the constraints as: distance to the nearest component above: 10 units, width and height: 300 units from the "Pin" menu. These settings are shown in Figure 9.5.

➢ **The labels and the text fields below the map:** I changed the text of the label just below the map as "Your coordinates" since we'll show the numerical coordinate info at this section. Its font size is set as 20 units and the text is centred. It is horizontally aligned and then the following constraints are added: distance to the component above: 25 units, width: 200 units, height: 25 units. These are shown in Figure 9.6.

Figure 9.4. Setting the constraints for the title label

Three labels and associated three text fields are about the user's latitude, longitude and altitude. Hence the labels' texts are changed as "Latitude", "Longitude" and "Altitude" from top to down.

Figure 9.5. Constraints for the map component

Figure 9.6. Constraints for the label just below the map

➢ **Constraints for the "Latitude" label** are set as follows: Distances to the nearest top and left components: 18 and 40 units; width and height are 100 and 21 units, respectively. These are shown in Figure 9.7.

Figure 9.7. Constraints for the "Latitude" label

➢ **Text field next to the latitude label:** The distance to the nearest component to the left (the "Latitude" label) is 0 and width and height are 120 and 30 units, respectively, as in Figure 9.8. In order to align the "Latitude" label and the text field next to it vertically, please hold down the Command key on your keyboard, select the "Latitude" label and its text field. Then from the "Pin" menu, select Align → Vertical centres and click "Add Constraint" button. If you update frames now, you should see that the label and its text field will be aligned vertically (on the same horizontal line).

➢ **The longitude label:** This is the label at the second row at the bottom section. Its constraints are set as follows: distances to the top and left components as 12 and 40 units; width and height as 100 and 21 units, respectively. These settings are shown in Figure 9.10.

➢ **Longitude text field:** The 3 constraints for the longitude text field are defined as: distance to the left item: 0, width: 120 and height 30 units as in Figure 9.11. The vertical axes of the longitude label and longitude text field are aligned as we did for the latitude components before. Hence, both label and the text field for the longitude are completely positioned.

Figure 9.8. Constraints for the latitude text field

➢ **Altitude label and the text field:** The settings for these components are the same as the longitude label and component, respectively. After completing all the constraints, the main view of your app should look like Figure 9.12.

Figure 9.9. Aligning the vertical centres of the "Latitude" label and its text view from the "Pin" menu

Note that if you run the project at this stage, it will crash because we haven't added the required code to handle the map. I'll show it in a short while.

Figure 9.10. Settings for the "Longitude" label

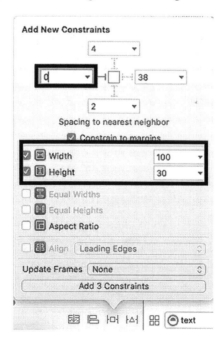

Figure 9.11. Settings for the longitude text field

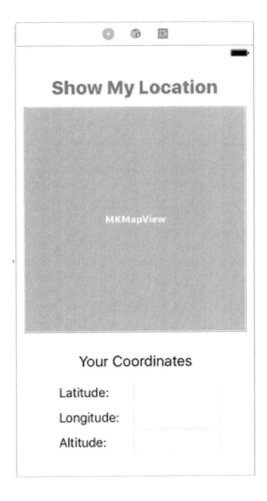

Figure 9.12. Finalized storyboard of our app

9.3. Adding Required Permissions

We'll set the properties of the map kit now. Let's start with setting the permissions for GPS and location services so that our app can use the GPS receiver on a real device. For this, single-click the Info.plist file on Xcode and then in the "Required Device Capabilities" tab, click the plus button as shown in Figure 9.13.

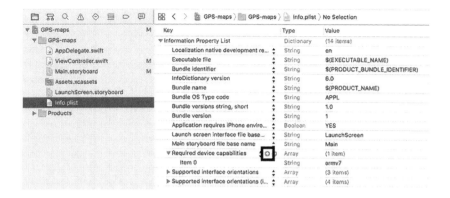

Figure 9.13. Adding the required device capabilities

Please add the text "gps" and then hit enter in the field which opens after the plus button is clicked. Do the same operation and write "location-services" this time. After these 2 steps, your Info.plist file should look like below:

Figure 9.14. Info.plist file after adding the required device capabilities

In the next step, click on the plus button next to the "Information Property List" in Info.plist file and then select "Privacy-Location When In Use Usage Description" as in Figure 9.15.

Figure 9.15. Adding the location services popup info

After adding this property, we can set a text in the "Value" section that will be shown to the user in the GPS usage permission dialog box. I added the text "This app needs GPS signals to run." as shown below:

Figure 9.16. Finalized Info.plist file

9.4. Adding the Map Kit Library

We have added the required permissions. We can now add the library of map-related functions that already exists in Xcode. For this, select the main project tab in the left pane and then click on the "Build Phases" tab in the main pane; select the "Link Binary with Libraries" section and then click on the plus button. The order of this operation is shown in Figure 9.17.

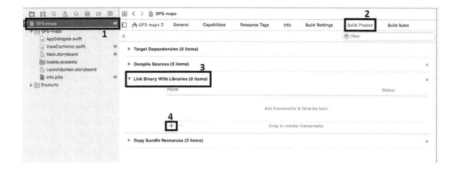

Figure 9.17. Steps to add a library to the project

When you click on the plus button, a menu appears where you can select built-in libraries. In the search box type "map", click on the MapKit.framework and then click on the "Add" button to add the map library to the project as shown in Figure 9.18.

9.5. Connecting the Map Kit View to the Code

It's now time to connect the storyboard components to the ViewController.swift file. We have done this several times so I don't expect a problem. We need to connect the map and the 3 text field to the code since the remaining storyboard components are the labels that won't change when the app runs. Please connect the 3 text fields and the map as outlets. You can connect the map to the code as usual. The ViewController.swift file after connecting these objects is as shown as below:

```
import UIKit
class ViewController: UIViewController {
    override func viewDidLoad() {
        super.viewDidLoad()
    }
    @IBOutlet weak var myMap: MKMapView!
    @IBOutlet weak var myLatitude: UITextField!
    @IBOutlet weak var myLongitude: UITextField!
    @IBOutlet weak var myAltitude: UITextField!
    override func didReceiveMemoryWarning() {
        super.didReceiveMemoryWarning()
    }
}}
```
Code 9.1

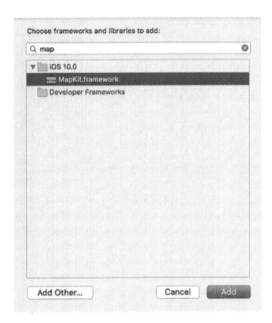

Figure 9.18. Adding the map library to the project

Xcode will show an error at the map outlet line. It is because we have included the MapKit Framework in the project however we didn't import it in our code yet. Hence, before the class definition (just after the **import UIKit** line), add the following line and the error will be gone:

```
import MapKit
```
Code 9.2

9.6. Main Code

We made the component connections and added the map library in the code. We can now write our main code for the operation of the GPS and location services to pinpoint our position on the map, give our coordinates in degrees and the altitude in metres.

First of all, in order to use the map related functions we need to extend our ViewController class with a class called **CLLocationManagerDelegate** by adding it in the class definition as in Code 9.3.

```
class ViewController: UIViewController, CLLocationManagerDelegate
```
Code 9.3

Note that we added the newly added class name after a comma. By inheriting from this class, we can use everything included in **CLLocationManagerDelegate** in our code.

We need three Double type variables that will hold the latitude, longitude and altitude information. We can define optionals for this just after the class definition as in Code 9.4.

```
var latitude: Double?
var longitude: Double?
var altitude: Double?
```
Code 9.4

Then we define an instance of **CLLocationManager** that will hold all information regarding the location as follows:

```
let locationManager = CLLocationManager()
```
Code 9.5

The **locationManager** object should start tracking the location as soon as the app loads. Therefore we need to place the initial operations regarding the start of the location tracking in the **viewDidLoad()** function. In this way the app will ask for location tracking and start tracking when the app first fires before any user intervention. We do this as in Code 9.6.

```
override func viewDidLoad() {
        super.viewDidLoad()
        locationManager.delegate = self
        locationManager.requestWhenInUseAuthorization()
        locationManager.startUpdatingLocation()
    }
```
Code 9.6

This code will ask for user permission to track location and then start updating the location info. Next, we will use one of the built-in instance methods for checking if the GPS authorization status is changed. This function is shown in Code 9.7. If the GPS is enabled, it will print "GPS allowed." text in the Xcode terminal and will start showing your location on the map; otherwise it will print "GPS not allowed." in the Xcode terminal and will exit when you run the app in the simulator.

```
func locationManager(_ manager: CLLocationManager,
didChangeAuthorization status: CLAuthorizationStatus)
{
        if status == .authorizedWhenInUse {
            print("GPS allowed.")
            myMap.showsUserLocation = true
        }
        else {
            print("GPS not allowed.")
            return
        }}
```
Code 9.7

Finally, we will use another instance method to update the position info (latitude, longitude and altitude) written in the respective text fields. This method is shown in Code 9.8.

```
func locationManager(_ manager: CLLocationManager,
didUpdateLocations locations: [CLLocation]) {

let myCoordinate=locationManager.location?.coordinate
        altitude = locationManager.location?.altitude
        latitude = myCoordinate?.latitude
        longitude = myCoordinate?.longitude
        myLatitude.text = String(latitude!)
        myLongitude.text = String(longitude!)
        myAltitude.text = String(altitude!)
    }
```
Code 9.8.

In the fourth line of this code, the combined latitude and longitude info is taken from the location object and stored in **myCoordinate** constant. In the fifth line, altitude of the user is extracted and saved in the **altitude** variable. In the next two lines, combined latitude and longitude info are extracted from the **myCoordinate** constant. The rest is obvious, the text fields in the user interface are populated by the coordinate info.

The complete ViewController.swift is shown in Code 9.9.

```
import UIKit
import MapKit
class ViewController: UIViewController, CLLocationManage
rDelegate {
    var latitude: Double?
    var longitude: Double?
    var altitude: Double?
    let locationManager = CLLocationManager()
    @IBOutlet weak var myMap: MKMapView!
    @IBOutlet weak var myLatitude: UITextField!
    @IBOutlet weak var myLongitude: UITextField!
    @IBOutlet weak var myAltitude: UITextField!

    override func viewDidLoad() {
        super.viewDidLoad()
        locationManager.delegate = self
        locationManager.requestWhenInUseAuthorization()
        locationManager.startUpdatingLocation()
    }
    func locationManager(_ manager: CLLocationManager,
didChangeAuthorization status: CLAuthorizationStatus) {

        if status == .authorizedWhenInUse {
print("GPS allowed.")
            myMap.showsUserLocation = true
        }
        else {
            print("GPS not allowed.")
            return
        }
    }
    func locationManager(_ manager: CLLocationManager,
didUpdateLocations locations: [CLLocation]) {
        let myCoordinate = locationManager.location?.coordinate
        altitude = locationManager.location?.altitude
        latitude = myCoordinate?.latitude
        longitude = myCoordinate?.longitude

        myLatitude.text = String(latitude!)
        myLongitude.text = String(longitude!)
        myAltitude.text = String(altitude!)
    }
    override func didReceiveMemoryWarning() {
```

```
        super.didReceiveMemoryWarning()
        // Dispose of any resources that can be
recreated.
    }
}
```

Code 9.9 (cont'd from the previous page)

9.7. Running the App

When we hit the "Run" button in Xcode and run the app in the simulator, we are presented by the screen shown in Figure 9.19. The simulator cannot of course take GPS signals but a simulated location is shown on the map. The default location is the location of Apple HQ which is seen in Figure 9.19. If you install this app on a real iOS device, it will obviously show your actual location, not a simulated one.

You can change the simulated location from the simulator's "Debug" menu as shown in Figure 9.20. I entered the coordinates of a location at (41.3809° N, 2.1228° E) and the simulator shows it on the map as in Figure 9.21. Can you guess what this famous location is?

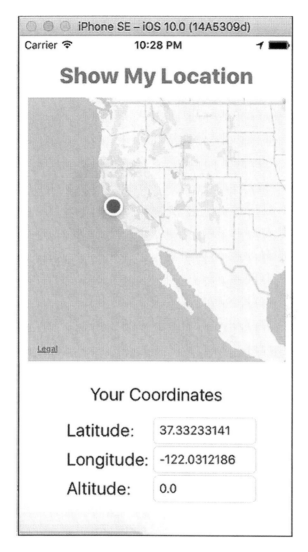

Figure 9.19. Developed "Show My Location" app in the simulator

9.8. Final Notes

Final note 1. I have installed the app on a real iPhone SE and it works as expected.

Final note 2. You cannot change the simulated altitude in the simulator.

Final note 3. If you're planning to go for a safari and use this app there wait until the next chapter where I'll show you sending text messages in Swift. We'll combine SMS sending and location services to develop an app that can be used for sending user's location to a pre-defined phone number easily in case of emergency.

Figure 9.20. Changing the simulated coordinates in the simulator

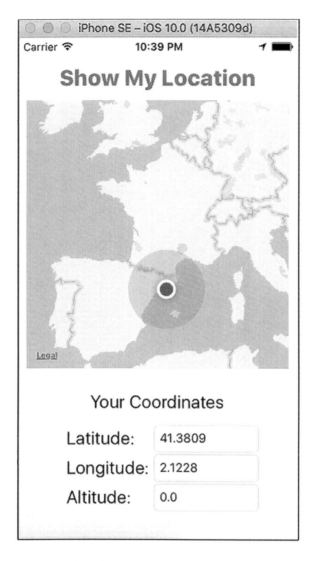

Figure 9.21. Developed app showing a famous point as a simulated location

Chapter 10

iOS APP # 6: S.O.S. MESSAGE SENDER

10.1. Copying a Project

Most of the iOS devices have the capability of GSM connection hence it is important to learn using SMS messaging in iOS. A class called `MFMessageComposeViewController` enables us to design apps that can open the native SMS messaging application of an iOS device with pre-populated recipient and message body fields and send an SMS with a single click. You'll see how this class is used in this chapter.

We'll develop an app which sends the current location using SMS to pre-defined recipients. This app can be useful in case of an emergency in deserts or if you're boozed in a disco when you cannot type text in the message field and need to send your location to a mate to take you home.

We'll extend the app that we developed in the previous chapter, find my location, since we'll send the location of the user and find my location app readily gives us the coordinates of the user. We'll wrap these coordinates and use the `MFMessageComposeViewController` class to send it via SMS. We need to duplicate the "Find My Location" app. For this, find the folder of the project on your Mac and duplicate this folder by right-clicking on it and selecting "Duplicate". A new folder with the name "(project name) copy" will be created. Now, select File → Open in Xcode's top bar and select the new folder you created. We need to rename the project and attach a new bundle identifier to build and run it. For this, select the project from the left pane of Xcode as in Figure 10.1 and rename it something you want from the right pane of Xcode as shown in Figure 10.2.

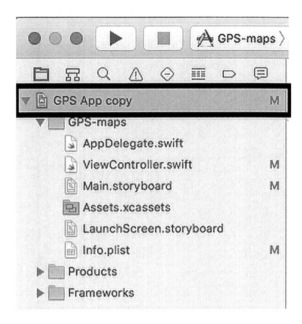

Figure 10.1. Selecting the project in Xcode

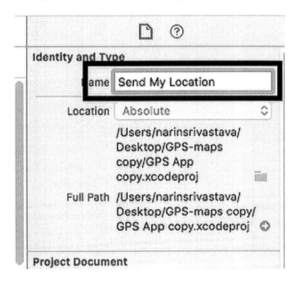

Figure 10.2. Renaming the project in Xcode

After you rename the project, Xcode will ask if you also want to rename files in your project. Select "Rename" in that dialog and then you'll have a copy of your previous project with a new name. After then, in the middle pane, change the bundle identifier to something you prefer as in Figure 10.3.

10.2. Adding New Objects

Let's open the Main.storyboard file and rename the app title and remove the big map object so that we can place a big "S.O.S." button. I renamed the app title as "Send My Location" and laid down a big button as in Figure 10.4. I also deleted the coordinate information labels and text fields since in case of emergency the user won't need to check those numbers. The final layout of the user interface is as in Figure 10.4.

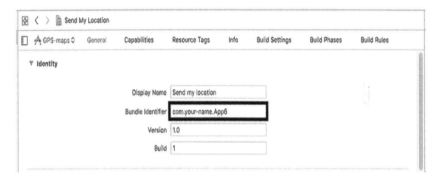

Figure 10.3. Changing bundle identifier

Now, before making any connection, delete all lines related to the previously deleted text fields. After cleaning up, the ViewController.swift file looks like in Code 10.1.

Code 10.1 is the plain version of the code of the app developed in the previous chapter. In its current phase, the **latitude** and **longitude** variables store the coordinate information. Now, we need to connect the big button to the code. Open up the "Assistant Editor" and connect this button as an IBAction. I named the connection as **sendButton**.

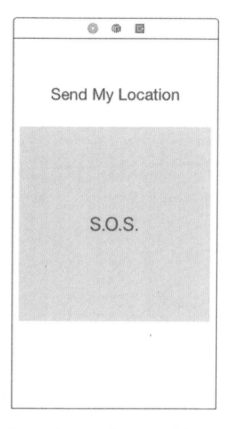

Figure 10.4. User interface of the app

```
import UIKit
import MapKit

class ViewController: UIViewController,
CLLocationManagerDelegate {

    var latitude: Double?
    var longitude: Double?
    let locationManager = CLLocationManager()
    override func viewDidLoad() {
    super.viewDidLoad()
        locationManager.delegate = self
        locationManager.requestWhenInUseAuthorization()
        locationManager.startUpdatingLocation()
    }

    func locationManager(_ manager: CLLocationManager,
```

```
didChangeAuthorization status: CLAuthorizationStatus) {

        if status == .authorizedWhenInUse {
            print("GPS allowed.")
        }
        else {
            print("GPS not allowed.")
            return
        }
    }
    func locationManager(_ manager: CLLocationManager,
didUpdateLocations locations: [CLLocation]) {
        let myCoordinate =
locationManager.location?.coordinate
        latitude = myCoordinate?.latitude
        longitude = myCoordinate?.longitude
    }

    override func didReceiveMemoryWarning() {
        super.didReceiveMemoryWarning()
    }
}
```

Code 10.1 (cont'd from the previous page)

10.3. Adding the SMS Library

We will now add the SMS library. For this, select the MessageUI binary in the Build Phases tab (explained in detail in the previous chapter) of the project properties as shown in Figure 10.5. The "Link binary with Libraries" section looks like in Figure 10.6 after adding this library.

Figure 10.5. Adding the MessagesUI framework

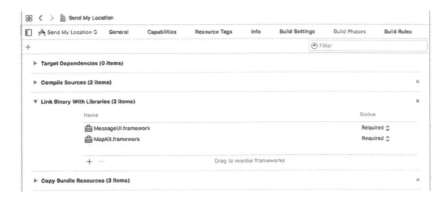

Figure 10.6. The "Build Phases" tab after adding the SMS library

10.4. Adding the Required Delegate Class

In order to use the newly added library, we will add the `import MessageUI` line at the beginning of our code and then inherit from the `MFMessageComposeViewControllerDelegate` class. After these insertions, the beginning of your Swift file should look like below:

```
import UIKit
import MapKit
import MessageUI

class ViewController: UIViewController,
CLLocationManagerDelegate,
MFMessageComposeViewControllerDelegate{
```
Code 10.2

Just after you add the class extensions, Xcode will give an error saying "The ViewController does not conform to protocol MFMessageComposeViewControllerDelegate". Don't worry about this. It means that we didn't include the required methods to conform to the `MFMessageComposeViewControllerDelegate` class. Now we'll add all the required methods.

10.5. Main Code

First of all, let's define a new instance of the messaging class as in Code 10.3 just after the previous variable definitions.

```
let messageCompose = MFMessageComposeViewController()
```
Code 10.3

Now, we'll define a new function as shown in Code 10.4. This function checks if the user's device can send SMS messages. It returns **true** if the user can send SMS and **false** otherwise.

```
func canSendText() -> Bool {
        return
MFMessageComposeViewController.canSendText()
}
```
Code 10.4

We'll use Code 10.5 as the button's function, which will actually prepare for SMS sending.

```
@IBAction func sendButton(_ sender: AnyObject) {

messageCompose.messageComposeDelegate = self
messageCompose.recipients = ["0123456789"]
let SMSText = "Please take me from this location:
Latitude:" + String(latitude!) + " Longitude: " +
String(longitude!)
        messageCompose.body =  SMSText
        present(messageCompose, animated: true,
completion: nil)
    }
```
Code 10.5

The recipients and the message text are defined in this function. You should change the recipient number to the number you want to send your coordinates. You can define more than one number to send the coordinates as an array. The message body will read: ""Please take me from this location: Latitude:" + String(latitude!) + " Longitude: " + String(longitude!)" where your latitude and longitude info will be populated with your actual location.

This code opens the message composing interface for the user to send the coordinates. Note that iOS does not let you to send SMS in the background, it opens up the standard messaging interface and wants the user to be in control by finally clicking the "Send" button there.

In the end, we'll write the method which will tell the message delegate that the message composing is finished (after the user sends the message) as follows:

```swift
func messageComposeViewController(_ controller:
MFMessageComposeViewController, didFinishWith result:
MessageComposeResult) {
        controller.dismiss(animated: true, completion:
nil)
    }
```
Code 10.6

The complete ViewController.swift file is shown below:

```swift
import UIKit
import MapKit
import MessageUI
class ViewController: UIViewController,
CLLocationManagerDelegate,
MFMessageComposeViewControllerDelegate{

    var latitude: Double?
    var longitude: Double?
    let locationManager = CLLocationManager()
    let messageCompose =
MFMessageComposeViewController()
    override func viewDidLoad() {
        super.viewDidLoad()
locationManager.delegate = self
        locationManager.requestWhenInUseAuthorization()
        locationManager.startUpdatingLocation()
    }

    func locationManager(_ manager: CLLocationManager,
didChangeAuthorization status: CLAuthorizationStatus) {

        if status == .authorizedWhenInUse {
            print("GPS allowed.")
        }
        else {
            print("GPS not allowed.")
            return
        }
    }
```

```
    func locationManager(_ manager: CLLocationManager,
didUpdateLocations locations: [CLLocation]) {
        let myCoordinate =
locationManager.location?.coordinate
        latitude = myCoordinate?.latitude
        longitude = myCoordinate?.longitude

    }

    func canSendText() -> Bool {
        return
MFMessageComposeViewController.canSendText()
}
@IBAction func sendButton(_ sender: AnyObject) {

        messageCompose.messageComposeDelegate = self
        messageCompose.recipients = ["xxxxxxxxxxx"]
//Enter a valid phone number here
let SMSText = "Please take me from this location:
Latitude:" + String(latitude!) + " Longitude: " +
String(longitude!)
        messageCompose.body =  SMSText
        present(messageCompose, animated: true,
completion: nil)

    }

    func messageComposeViewController(_ controller:
MFMessageComposeViewController, didFinishWith result:
MessageComposeResult) {
        controller.dismiss(animated: true, completion:
nil)
    }

    override func didReceiveMemoryWarning() {
        super.didReceiveMemoryWarning()
        // Dispose of any resources that can be
recreated.
    }
}
```

Code 10.7 (cont'd from the previous pages)

10.6. Running the App

If you try to run the app in a simulator, it will give a warning saying that it cannot send text messages, which is obvious. You need to try this app in a real device with SMS sending capability. I tried on iPhone SE and iPhone 6S, they both worked fine. When I tap the S.O.S. button, a new SMS composing window opens with the recipient box pre-populated and the message body is a text of my latitude and longitude info. It sends the location info as expected.

Now, let's take a break and get a coffee. In the next chapter, we'll develop another exciting app: a 2D game ☺.

Chapter 11

iOS APP # 7: OUR iOS GAME: BOUNCE THE BALL

11.1. Creating the Game Project and Basic Settings

As we know, games are among the most popular apps. Game developers can earn good money once the gamers get addicted to their games. However, developing a game is not a simple task since a good game should have an exciting story, good graphics, realistic physics rules and efficient code to glue all these together. Fortunately, the game development framework named SpriteKit™ makes our lives easier. SpriteKit has functions and methods for both generating nice graphics and the accurate simulation of game objects according to physics rules. SpriteKit is built-in Xcode 8 hence we can easily start developing iOS games.

In this last chapter, we'll put all our knowledge and SpriteKit in action to develop a simple 2D game: Bounce the Ball. The idea is simple: a ball will move on the scene and the gamer will try to prevent the ball from touching the bottom edge of the screen by bouncing the ball with a paddle that he/she controls with screen touches.

First of all, to create a new Xcode *game project*, select "Game" as the application type as shown in Figure 11.1 and then click "Next". Name your project and then select "SpriteKit" as the game technology in the next window as in Figure 11.2. Save the project on your computer and then you'll see the project file explorer as shown in Figure 11.3 in the left pane of Xcode.

Figure 11.1. Creating a game project

Figure 11.2. Selecting the game technology

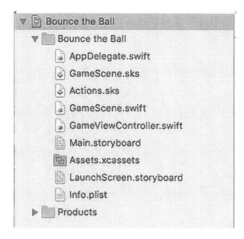

Figure 11.3. Default files of a game project

Comparing these files to the files of the general Xcode project shows that there is a new file type: .sks file. These are SpriteKit Scene files where you can use to visually design the scenes of your game. The code related to game functionality resides in Gamescene.swift and GameViewController.swift files. When you single-click on GameScene.sks file, you'll be presented by the default scene shown in Figure 11.4. In this scene, there's only a default label object that is similar to the label in UIView class. Labels display text in SpriteKit as in other projects. We won't need a label for now in our Bounce the Ball game therefore right-click the label from the scene browser and Delete as shown in Figure 11.5.

For a ball bouncing game, it is obviously better to set the screen in landscape mode. Select the project from the left pane of Xcode and then find the "Deployment Info" section as in Figure 11.6. Here, set the screen orientation as "Landscape Right" and then uncheck the "Portrait" mode.

Open the GameScene.sks again to set the screen size from the Scene Attributes found at the right top pane of Xcode as in Figure 11.7. I selected iPhone SE and Landscape mode but you can select any device you wish.

Figure 11.4. Default scene

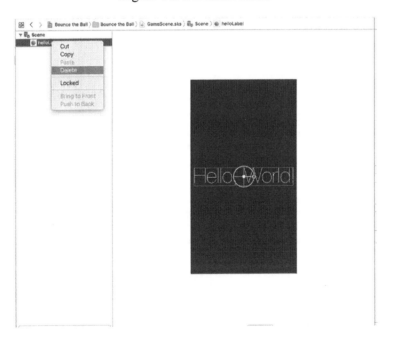

Figure 11.5. Deleting the default Label

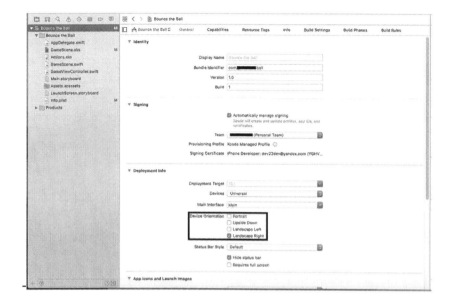

Figure 11.6. Setting the screen orientation in project settings

Figure 11.7. Setting screen size and the orientation in the scene attributes pane

In order to place objects in our game scene, we need to import them as images or data sets in the Assets.xcassets file as we did in previous projects. Open this file by single-clicking on it and then delete the default Spaceship image set. There will be only three objects (hence their images) in our simple game: the background, the ball and the paddle that will bounce the ball. In order to make things funny, I selected a red football shoe as the paddle. The ball is a football ball and the background is a nice spring panorama. You can download these images from the book's website: www.ios-swift.net. Please create new image sets named background, ball and the shoe and place corresponding images to these data sets by drag and drop method. After these operations, your Assets.xcassets file should look like below (creating image sets was explained in detail in previous chapters, e.g. Chapter 7):

Figure 11.8. Assets.xcassets file after creating image sets

Now, open the GameScene.sks again to set the background image. For this, add a "Color Sprite" to the screen (by drag and drop) from the Objects library as shown in Figure 11.9.

We'll set this Sprite as the background image. Select this Sprite and then you can set its properties from the Sprite menu at the right top pane of Xcode. Select its Texture as "background" (name of the image set) and set Sprite's name to "background" (any name can be given) as shown in Figure 11.10.

Figure 11.9. Adding a colour Sprite to the scene

Figure 11.10. Setting the newly added Sprite's properties

The background image is very big compared to our screen size therefore we need to squeeze it to fit. Again in the Sprite menu, set its size to Width: 568 and Height: 320 for iPhone SE as shown below (if you're designing your game for another device, read the next paragraph please):

Figure 11.11. Setting the size of the background Sprite

If you're designing your game for a device other than iPhone SE, then you you'll need to enter *its mapped screen size* which is shown in Table 11.1 (source: http://www.kylejlarson.com/blog/iphone-6-screen-size-web-design-tips/). Since the screen orientation is set as landscape, the width value will be the bigger number and the height value will be the smaller number like W=667 and H=375 for iPhone 6/7.

	iPhone 4	iPhone 5	iPhone 6/7	iPhone 6/7 Plus
Physical Size	3.5 in	4 in	4.7 in	5.5 in
Mapped size	*320 x 480 points*	*320 x 568 points*	*375 x 667 points*	*414 x 736 points*
Rendered Pixels	640 x 960	640 x 1136	750 x 1334	1242x 2208

Table 11.1. Screen sizes of various iOS devices

Note that, the position of the background Sprite has to be (0,0) to fill the screen properly. Now, run the game in the simulator to check if everything is going well as shown below:

Figure 11.12. The scene in the simulator

11.2. Adding the Ball

Let's add the ball to the scene to make our game more exciting ☺. Add a new Sprite from the Object Explorer and select its texture as "ball" (name of the image set), also set the Sprite's name as "ball" as in Figure 11.13. You can drag the ball anywhere you want in the scene (this will be the (x,y) position of the ball and the game will start with the ball in this position).

Since the ball is very big for the screen size, I adjusted the size of the ball as W=30 and H=30 (in fact this is the size of the Sprite that contains the ball).

Important: The z position of Sprites should be set properly otherwise they may randomly disappear during gameplay. The default z position of the background Sprite was 0 so it is OK to set the z position of the ball as 1. These settings are shown below:

Figure 11.13. Adding the ball and setting its basic properties

11.3. Sprite Physics – Moving the Ball

The interactions of Sprites are defined by the physics laws that we set for the game scene and the Sprites themselves. For example, we can set a scene with no gravity or half gravity. Of course, Sprite physics is not only about gravity, it defines the effects of Sprites on each other and many other things. Setting the physics of the scene is in fact a vital part of game development.

Let's see how we define physics of the ball so that when we first run the app, the ball will not stay at its initial place but start moving and bouncing.

Select the ball and then find the section called "Physics Definition" in Xcode's right pane as shown below:

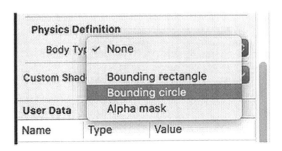

Figure 11.14. Physics definition pane

Select body type as "Bounding circle" as shown in the above figure and then a menu to set "physics properties" related to the ball Sprite will appear as in Figure 11.15 with default values.

The settings shown here can be summarized as follows:

➢ **Dynamic checkbox:** Determines if the Sprite will be affected by collisions etc.
➢ **Allows Rotation:** Determines if the Sprite may rotate dependent on the collision direction.
➢ **Pinned:** Sets if the Sprite will move or not in the scene.
➢ **Affected by Gravity:** Sets if the default gravity of the scene will affect this Sprite or not.
➢ **Friction:** Determines the frictional force the Sprite applies to other bodies – roughness of the Sprite.
➢ **Restitution:** This section sets the ratio of (the energy the Sprite gains after a collision) to (its initial energy). In other words, if this is 1, the collision is perfectly elastic otherwise the Sprite will lose energy when it hits somewhere/something during the gameplay. Also defined as the Sprite's bounciness.

> ➤ **Linear and Angular Dampings:** The "frictional constants" affecting the Sprite's velocity as it moves, the linear and angular parts of this force are set here. If these are nonzero, the Sprite will lose energy as it moves in the scene.

> ➤ **Mass:** A Sprite's resistance to acceleration under an applied force like the mass in real life.

> ➤ **Initial velocity:** The velocity the Sprite will have at the beginning of the game. DX and DY are the components of the velocity in x and y directions. (x is the direction from left to right and y is the direction from top to bottom.)

Figure 11.15. Default Physics Definition for the ball

For now, let's set the Physics Definition of the ball as shown in Figure 11.16.

By these settings, the ball will be affected by gravity, will bounce off without losing its energy and will not have any damping. When you run the game in the simulator, you will see the ball falling off the screen ☺. It is because the scene edges do not have borders by default.

In order to make the ball bounce off the floor, we need to add Code 11.1 inside of the **didMove(to view: SKView)** class in the GameScene.swift file.

```
let borderBody = SKPhysicsBody(edgeLoopFrom: self.frame)
borderBody.friction = 0
self.physicsBody = borderBody
```
Code 11.1

This code creates a border at the edges of the self.frame (which is the whole screen), then sets its friction to 0 (hence the ball will not lose energy during the bounce offs), and finally applies this border node to the scene. After adding this code, our **didMove(to view: SKView)** class will look like Code 11.2 (note that I removed the unused default code):

Figure 11.16. New Physics Definition for the ball

```
override func didMove(to view: SKView) {
       let borderBody = SKPhysicsBody(edgeLoopFrom:
self.frame)
       borderBody.friction = 0
       self.physicsBody = borderBody
    }
```
Code 11.2

Now, let's run our game in the simulator and we will see that the ball will fall and bounce off the floor infinitely (until we stop the simulator ☺). This is because we didn't set any damping on the ball and the Restitution is 1 meaning that the ball bounces off the floor without losing any energy. You can view the short clip of the game at this stage (Video 11.1) on the book's website: www.ios-swift.net.

You can play with the Physical Definition settings of the ball and run in the simulator to see how they affect its movement. For example if you set a linear damping such as 0.2, the ball will lose its velocity continuously as it moves (Video 11.2 on the book's website).

Now, let's remove the effect of gravity from the ball so that we can clearly define the initial force on the ball. For this, select the ball to remove the gravity effect from its Physics Definition pane as in Figure 11.17.

If you run the game in the simulator now, you'll see that the ball stays at its initial place since there's no force acting on it initially. Let's apply an impulse (a sudden force) to the ball so that it starts moving in a direction we want. I applied a force of (dx: 10, dy= 20) by trial and error but you can apply any force you want as long as the ball strikes to all edges of the scene. The code for applying the impulse is given in Code 11.3.

```
let ball = childNode(withName: "ball") as! SKSpriteNode
ball.physicsBody!.applyImpulse(CGVector(dx: 10, dy: 20))
```
Code 11.3

In this code, a **SpriteKitNode** called **ball** is created to access the ball Sprite in the code. Then, the mentioned impulse is applied on the ball in the second line. Please add this code to **didMove(to view: SKView)** and then if you run the game in the simulator, you'll see the ball striking the edges of the screen continuously (Video 11.3 on the book's website.).

Figure 11.17. Removing the effect of the gravity from the ball

11.4. Adding the Shoe

It's now time to add the shoe that will prevent ball hitting the bottom of the scene and bounce the ball. Add a colour sprite close to the bottom edge and select the shoe as the texture as shown in Figure 11.18.

Now, set the size of the shoe as W=100 and L=50 and then the z position to 1. Remember that the z position of the background was 0 by default hence, by setting the z position of the shoe, we guarantee that the shoe will be shown on the background (z axis is from the screen towards the user). These settings are also shown in Figure 11.19 together with the added shoe in the scene.

Figure 11.18. Setting the newly added Sprite's properties

Figure 11.19. Setting the size and the z position of the shoe Sprite

We now need to define physics for the shoe since we want it to bounce the ball when the ball touches it. For this, choose the "Bounding rectangle" in the Physics Definition while the shoe Sprite is selected as shown below:

Figure 11.20. Choosing the "Bounding rectangle" for the shoe Sprite

In this pane, uncheck "Dynamic" and "Allows Rotation" checkboxes since we don't want the shoe to move when the ball hits it as shown in the following figure:

Figure 11.21. Physics Definition of the shoe

11.5. Moving the Shoe

We need to sense the touches on the shoe and move it according to these touches. First of all we need to define a variable to check the state of touching. Since there are only two possibilities: touching and not touching, it is OK to use a boolean variable. Please add this variable declaration before the class definition (just below the **import GameplayKit** line) in your GameScene.swift file:

```
var isGamerTouching = false
```
Code 11.4

The default value is **false** since the user will not be touching at the start of the game. In the default GameScene.swift file, there are readily placed lines regarding the touching. Delete all default code **after the** `touchUp()` function. Then, insert the following code in which functions for sensing the gamer touching and moving the shoe are implemented:

```
override func touchesBegan(_ touches: Set<UITouch>, with
event: UIEvent?) {
        let touch = touches.first
        let touchLocation = touch!.location(in: self)
        if let body = physicsWorld.body(at:
touchLocation) if body.node!.name == "shoe" {
                isGamerTouching = true
            }
        }
    }
override func touchesMoved(_ touches: Set<UITouch>, with
event: UIEvent?) {
 if isGamerTouching{
 let touch = touches.first
 let touchLocation = touch!.location(in: self)
 let previousLocation =
   touch!.previousLocation(in: self)
let shoe= childNode(withName: "shoe") as! SKSpriteNode
let shoeX = shoe.position.x + (touchLocation.x -
   previousLocation.x)
   shoe.position = CGPoint(x: shoeX, y: shoe.position.y)
        }
    }
    override func touchesEnded(_ touches: Set<UITouch>,
with event: UIEvent?) {
        isGamerTouching = false
    }

override func touchesCancelled(_ touches: Set<UITouch>,
with event: UIEvent?) {
        for t in touches { self.touchUp(atPoint:
t.location(in: self)) }
    }
    override func update(_ currentTime: TimeInterval)
{
    }
```

Code 11.5

You can download the source files of the project from this book's website and also copy-paste these codes from there if you want.

In this code, **touchesBegan()** function checks if the shoe Sprite is touched. Then, **touchesMoved()** function moves the shoe by the position method applied on the shoe Sprite using the shoe's updated x coordinate **shoeX**. The **touchesEnded()** function just sets the **isGamerTouching** variable to false when the touching ends. Run the game in the simulator and you can move the shoe to bounce the ball. You can view its clip as Video 11.4 on the book's website. As you can see from this clip, the ball moves dizzyingly fast, you can decrease the initial impulse (see Code 11.3) to have a slower ball if you wish.

The ball bounces infinitely and nothing happens when the gamer misses the ball. The ball bounces off the ground and the game continues. We need a condition to end the game and give points when the user bounces the ball. There can be several ways to set game logic but the simplest is to end the game when the gamer misses the ball (= ball touches ground) and the gamer increases his/her score by 1 when he/she bounces the ball with the shoe. Setting up this logic in the game code requires handling contacts of the Sprites.

11.6. Handling the Contacts and Finalizing Gameplay Settings

In order to handle contacts, we need to extend our main class with the class called **SKPhysicsContactDelegate** in the following way:

```
class GameScene: SKScene, SKPhysicsContactDelegate {
```
Code 11.6

In order to check which Sprites had a contact, we will use "categories". Each Sprite will be added to a different category. We have the ball, the shoe and the ground (bottom of the screen). We'll define the following category variables just below the **isGamerTouching** variable definition in the GameScene.swift file:

```
let BallCategory   : UInt32 = 0x1 << 0
let BottomCategory : UInt32 = 0x1 << 1
let ShoeCategory   : UInt32 = 0x1 << 2
```
Code 11.7

In fact, these are just integers having the values of 1, 2 and 4. However, it is convenient to define the categories in the above manner to track the contacts if there are loads of touching Sprites. The << operator shifts the bits from right to left effectively multiplying the number by 2.

In the first line 0x1 is the byte 00000001, middle one is 00000010 and the last one being 00000100. These are called binary numbers. In binary numbers, each digit has the multiplier of the powers of 2 unlike the decimals which have the multipliers of the powers of 10 per digit. Anyway, don't worry if these don't mean a lot for you. Just keep in mind that 0x1 <<0 is 1, 0x1 <<1 is 2 and 0x1 << 2 is 4.

We'll keep the score of the gamer in an integer which will increment by 1 for each bounce. Thus we can define an integer variable for this aim. Moreover, we'll display this score on the game screen (right top for example) therefore we need a SpriteKit Label to show this info to the gamer. For these, we can add the following code lines just below the category variable definitions:

```
var scoreInt: Int = 0
var scoreLabel = SKLabelNode(fontNamed:"Arial")
```
Code 11.8

Then, add the following code to **didMove()** function in order to access the bottom and the shoe in the game code to check contacts:

```
let bottomRect = CGRect(x: frame.origin.x, y:
frame.origin.y, width: frame.size.width, height: 1)
let bottom = SKNode()
bottom.physicsBody = SKPhysicsBody(edgeLoopFrom:
bottomRect)
addChild(bottom)
let shoe = childNode(withName: "shoe") as! SKSpriteNode
```
Code 11.9

We will now assign bottom, ball and the shoe to the respective categories using the code shown below (please add this code also to the **didMove()** function):

```
bottom.physicsBody!.categoryBitMask = BottomCategory
ball.physicsBody!.categoryBitMask = BallCategory
shoe.physicsBody!.categoryBitMask = ShoeCategory
```
Code 11.10

We want the game engine to check if the ball contacts to the bottom edge or the shoe. If it contacts the bottom edge, the game will be over and if touches the shoe, gamer's score will increment. The following code, which should be placed just after the above code, initializes the contact tests:

```
ball.physicsBody!.contactTestBitMask = BottomCategory |
ShoeCategory
physicsWorld.contactDelegate = self
```
Code 11.11

Finally, please place the following code inside the **didMove()** function to set the position of the score label:

```
scoreLabel.text = "Score: " + String(scoreInt)
scoreLabel.fontSize = 25
scoreLabel.position = CGPoint(x:(self.frame.maxX)*0.8,
y:(self.frame.maxY)*0.8)
scoreLabel.zPosition = 2
self.addChild(scoreLabel)
```
Code 11.12

In the above code, the score label will be positioned at the 0.8 x (screen width) and 0.8 x (screen height) with a font size of 25. You can change this position if you wish.

Finally, let's write the contact handling code. The BallCategory, BottomCategory and ShoeCategory have the values of 1, 2 and 4, respectively (see Code 11.6). Hence if a contact happens and if the contacting Sprites have the categories of 1 and 4, the score will be incremented by one. However, if a contact happens and the categories of contacts are 1 and 2, it means that the ball contacted the bottom edge (the gamer missed the ball). In this case the game will be over. A "Game over." text will appear on the screen. It is also good to remove the ball from the scene. The following contact function is a delegate of the **SKPhysicsContactDelegate** class and this function is added inside the GameScene.swift file (just below all other codes existing in GameScene.swift):

```
func didBegin(_ contact: SKPhysicsContact) {
if contact.bodyA.categoryBitMask == 4 &&
contact.bodyB.categoryBitMask == 1 {

scoreInt = scoreInt + 1
print(scoreInt)
scoreLabel.text = "Score: " + String(scoreInt)
        }

if contact.bodyA.categoryBitMask == 2 &&
contact.bodyB.categoryBitMask == 1 {

let ball = childNode(withName: "ball") as! SKSpriteNode
ball.removeFromParent()
var myLabel:SKLabelNode!
myLabel = SKLabelNode(fontNamed: "Arial")
myLabel.text = "Game over."
myLabel.fontSize = 50
myLabel.fontColor = SKColor.red
myLabel.position = CGPoint(x: self.frame.midX, y:
self.frame.midY)
myLabel.zPosition = 4
self.addChild(myLabel)
        }
    }
```

Code 11.13

When the ball contacts the bottom, the ball is removed using the **removeFromParent()** method:

```
ball.removeFromParent()
```

Code 11.14

After the ball is removed, a big red annoying "Game over." text appears in the middle of the screen. You can download project files including the whole GameScene.swift file on the book's website if you wish. Moreover Video 11.5 on the book's website shows a short gameplay and game over scene of our Bounce the Ball game.

11.7. The Game

Screenshots during the gameplay and the game over scene are also shown in Figures 11.22 and 11.23 (colour figures and clips available at www.ios-swift.net):

Figure 11.22. Bounce the Ball game during gameplay

You can make the game more fun with simple tricks like increasing the initial velocity or controlling the shoe in a nonlinear way.

As you can see from this simple game, developing games is a serious job and requires hard work.

Figure 11.23. The game over scene

EPILOGUE AND FUTURE WORK

I really hope that you enjoyed this book and got some confidence for developing iOS apps. If you would like to share your complaints and suggestions, please feel free to drop me an e-mail at syamacli@gmail.com or alternatively you can share it publicly on the comments section of the book's website www.ios-swift.net.

This book was intended to be a starter's guide. If you have followed this book thoroughly, you should be ready to learn more on iOS app development and the first source for this is, of course, the Internet. I recommend the following websites for advanced subjects:

- http://noeticforce.com/best-swift-tutorials-with-examples
- http://www.ioscreator.com/
- https://www.codeschool.com/learn/ios

I'd like to finish this book with the following quotes which I think have deep meanings:

"If a machine is expected to be infallible, it cannot also be intelligent."

Alan Turing, PhD

"Discipline strengthens the mind so that it becomes impervious to the corroding influence of fear."

Bernard Law Montgomery, FM

Time is everything; five minutes make the difference between victory and defeat.

Horatio Nelson, KB

——————— Keep calm because it's the end ☺ ———————

REFERENCES

1. https://swift.org

2. https://developer.apple.com/

3. http://www.tiobe.com/tiobe-index/,

4. https://developer.apple.com/swift/resources/

5. Neil Smyth, iOS 9 App Development Essentials, eBookFrenzy, 2015.

6. http://www.learnswift.tips/

7. Christian Keur and Aaron Hillegaas, iOS Programming: The Big Nerd Ranch Guide, Big Nerd Ranch Guides, 2015.

8. John Ray, iOS 9 Application Development in 24 Hours, Sams Publishing, 2016.

9. Andrew Johansen, iOS 9: App Development - The Ultimate Beginner's Guide!, CreateSpace Independent Publishing Platform, 2016.

10. Matthew Mathias and John Gallagher, Swift Programming: The Big Nerd Ranch Guide, Big Nerd Ranch Guides, 2015.

11. http://www.kylejlarson.com/blog/iphone-6-screen-size-web-design-tips/

Password for the compressed files downloaded from the book's website www.ios-swift.net: dev2dev

39144837R00121

Made in the USA
Middletown, DE
06 January 2017

Beethoven Harp Quartet { Oistrakh 1ˢᵗ V. / Henri 2ⁿᵈ / Nuk feldberg viola / Piatigorsky cello.

(interchanged violin and viola) Mozart divertimento / Oistrakh - Henri - Segovia

Дорогой друг, я был счастлив побывать в твоем чудном, гостеприимном доме, познакомиться с твоей милой семьей и помузицировать с тобой, что доставило мне особое удовольствие.

От всей души желаю тебе и твоей семье счастья и процветания

Искренне твой
Давид (DAVID OISTRAKH)

David Oistrakh

Very enjoyable every -
Thank you -
(Jascha Heifetz) 1958

Jascha Heifetz

Avec grand plaisir dans votre belle maison merveille...
Cordialement Segovia

Andrés Segovia

Emmy and Henri - Thank you for being lovely hosts, lovely chauffeurs and lovely friends. My parents really appreciate it.
Kate Feiffer
(for Judy and Jules)

Kate Feiffer (for Judy and Jules)

An ecstatic - if perspired -
evening - the joy of music
unconfined (!) -

Isaac Stern

FACING
THE MUSIC

An Inside View of the
Real Concert World

BY

HENRI TEMIANKA
Noted Violinist and Conductor

ALFRED PUBLISHING CO., INC.

To Emmy with Love

Library of Congress Catalog Card Number: 72-92653

*Alfred Publishing Co., Inc.
15335 Morrison Street
Sherman Oaks, CA 91403*

ISBN 0-88284-104-1

Reviewer's Comments . . .

"Delightful . . . amusing . . . informative. Anybody interested in the world of music and concert performers will find this entertaining and fascinating."
—SIR RUDOLF BING

"Whatever Henri Temianka's credentials as a violinist and conductor—and they are impressively full—he has demonstrated his ability to write with genuine artistry. His book is a compelling and delightful reading experience."
—NORMAN COUSINS

"What an enjoyable book. Temianka has the true raconteur's gift."
—RAY BRADBURY

"Frank, witty, and so human . . . I recommend it most heartily."
—YEHUDI MENUHIN

"This charming, funny, and consistently entertaining memoir of a concert violinist and conductor could be the sleeper of the season."
—CHICAGO TRIBUNE

"It is not often that one learns a great deal while laughing, but I did as I read Henri Temianka's 'inside view of the real concert world.' . . . He is one of those rare musicians who sparkles—whether he is making music, conversing or writing—all of it with striking discernment, knowledge, good taste, and wit. His 'Facing the Music' is about as human, warmhearted, and incisive a look of the concert business from the inside out as you will get. It is all applause and adulation and for the young who think that one becomes an artist overnight."
—THE BLADE, Toledo, Ohio

"Anyone who has read Temianka's previous writings . . . knows that he is a master of the fine art of retelling. Over the 264 pages of this volume, Temianka charms with offtimes breezy anecdotes from his own life and sagas of fellow musicians."
—LOS ANGELES HERALD-EXAMINER

"OPUS MAGNIFICENT! Here is one instance where I fail to find words to express my feelings for author Temianka's magnificent literary opus. I could say the book is one of the most entertaining and impressive examples of subjectivity, that is extremely witty, informative, fascinating, et cetera. I could say that 'Facing the Music' has earned a permanent place on my bookshelf—I could say all of these things, and still grope for an even more accurate description of this Scottish maestro's outstanding raconteurism."
—FORT WAYNE NEWS-SENTINEL

". . . as sprightly, as exuberant, as witty and as charming as the author's own performances of Mozart must have been—and no doubt still are. He is one fiddler who hasn't remained on the roof, but who has come down right into the thick of things to explain what's going on to the rest of us."
—HOLLYWOOD REPORTER

"There are genial portraits of the greats of his day—Rubinstein, Menuhin, Oistrakh, Bernstein—much humor and no bitchery, although he does understand and describes the young ambitious musicians who do anything to get to the top and usually fail."
—THE NEW YORK TIMES BOOK REVIEW

Contents

Preface

George Bernard Shaw maintained that as no one could be bothered to read prefaces, these should be strategically placed at the end of the book (although for what reason he imagined the reader readier to apply himself after digesting what the author had to say rather than before, I do not know). As he was referring to his own prefaces for his own works, it may have been a token of his notorious self-esteem that he could not imagine anyone having enjoyed his brilliance and his genius possibly denying himself the guaranteed pleasure of a few more pages of the same literary gems.

Be that as it may, I myself can offer no especial bonus to this entertaining and fascinating account of a violin virtuoso's life, but what I can do is to recommend it most heartily, for albeit the author insists that I myself sprang like a male Minerva, fully armed, from Zeus's head, thereby inferring that I would be thus disqualified from recognizing the agonies and anguishes of that long painful ascent that is a career, nonetheless I can not only recognize the ring of authenticity, but avail myself of the opportunity to assure him that the reading of those early years filled me with a mixture of envy and admiration— envy for the lessons learned and the skills developed along a slower path than mine, as well as the quality of those climactic changes from disappointments to happy surprises; and admiration for the fortitude and resilience he was called upon to show again and again.

Yet I can assure him that I do know some of those rock-strewn paths, hazards that are the easier to overcome the earlier they are met, and that I am by now qualified, not simply by the empathy of one violinist for another, but by having tried to compensate for my early good fortune by deliberately clambering down the mountainside now and again, whatever the risks involved, to teach myself what it is composed of geologically and to get my bearings from all possible angles!

It was foolhardy, but I know now how worthwhile, and I am doubly supported in my convictions on having read Henri's frank, witty, and so human book.

Certainly no broader public career could be brought to the attention of our reading and musical public, in that it concerns a born and cultivated violinist who has followed his chosen instrument into the most varied manifestations of its many incarnations. For he is at the same time the dashing, dazzling virtuoso, the dedicated and selfless chamber music leader and partner, the patient and able teacher, the distinguished and effective orchestra conductor, and finally he is that lively, brilliant, and very human being, that excellent and good colleague, Henri Temianka.

YEHUDI MENUHIN

I

A Virtuoso Is Born

The scene is Carnegie Hall: lights blazing, the auditorium jammed to the rafters, buzzing with expectant chatter. Suddenly a little boy with blond hair appears from the back of the stage. He wears short pants, a velvet jacket. His violin seems abnormally large. There is excited applause, then a hushed silence. The little boy raises the instrument to his chin, lifts his bow, and, lo and behold, heavenly Mozartian sounds emerge. Yehudi Menuhin will never look back. After a sensational debut fame, fortune, and fulfillment are his for life.

Yehudi's career as a celebrated virtuoso is the dream of every young musician as he starts out to conquer the world. Most of the rest of us—and that includes such all-time greats as Johannes Brahms, Fritz Kreisler, Jacques Thibaud, Zino Francescatti, José Iturbi, and Gregor Piatigorsky—started on the bottom rung of the ladder, playing in nightclubs, cafés, and brothels. My own first job, while a student at the Paris Conservatoire in the late twenties, was in a circus. Night after night I trudged up the long narrow staircase to the bandstand perched underneath the roof. Here Maestro Farinelli, the Toscanini of the circus, presided benignly over the musical underworld: a couple of trumpets, trombones, a piano, a double bass, a clarinet, four fiddles, and a cello. I was the last of the fiddles and barely managed to squeeze onto the small platform. Sometimes one leg dangled in empty space. A cloud of garlic hovered permanently over the area, unifying and strengthening us.

When the opening march ended with two earsplitting chords, Maestro Farinelli turned his back to us for the rest of the evening. Peering over the guardrail, the Maestro established ground contact and watched an endless procession of clowns, trapeze acrobats, chimpanzees, dogs, horses, zebras, elephants, tigers, lions, and seals follow one another in the ring. The Maestro's job was to coordinate our music with their acts, making it appear as if the animals were following the music. Did you think horses danced in time? You never played in a circus band. Maestro Farinelli sometimes kept his beat suspended in midair indefinitely, until the horse at last took another prancing step. He would quiver convulsively, arms wildly flapping, to bring up the orchestra if the horse skipped a couple of beats. Maestro Farinelli was a wizard. Not once did horse, elephant, or chimpanzee outwit him.

The moment Maestro Farinelli turned his back on us, the concertmaster promptly placed his violin in his lap and slumped into a trancelike sleep, leaving the three of us to carry on. Five minutes later the second violinist jabbed him sharply in the ribs, and as the concertmaster mechanically resumed playing, the second man went into a coma. After another five minutes came the third man's turn, and finally mine. So it went all evening, except when the Maestro unexpectedly turned around to whisper frantically, "Throw out the lions—man without arms next!"

The sleeping fiddler was hastily called to duty with a vigorous kick in the shin. It all happened so swiftly that the Maestro saw only four dedicated fiddlers playing with tremendous ardor.

I led a Jekyll-and-Hyde existence. At night I mingled with the musical flotsam of Paris; by day with the ambitious young students at the Conservatoire National in the Rue de Madrid. There, my fellow students and I feverishly studied for the fabulous virtuoso careers we all knew would be ours. Day in, day out I switched from Beethoven and Mozart to Maestro Farinelli's polkas and the chimpanzees in the circus. At midnight I took the last métro home to the comfortable apartment of the devoted old French couple who kept me as their star boarder.

The Conservatoire National of Paris, one of the most famous musical institutions in the world, was also one of the shabbiest. Up and down its creaky old staircases had tramped Claude Debussy, Hector Berlioz, Camille Saint-Saëns, Gabriel Fauré, Maurice Ravel, César Franck, Charles Gounod, and all the other musical glories of France. Not that we ever gave them a passing thought. There was one's own future glory to think about. The classroom itself was a bare bleak expanse of walls and floor, crowded with students. My teacher, Jules Boucherit, sat enthroned near the piano. He was an ascetic, sardonic, delicate, extremely handsome, and dark-haired Frenchman, impeccably dressed, the picture of lassitude. He treated the beautiful girl students, who were desperately in love with him, with supreme disdain. A chronic illness often forced him to leave for his mountain retreat for months at a time. Every year the rumor was that this year was Boucherit's last, but he buried all his colleagues over a period of forty years, and at the age of eighty still looked delicate and sardonic. Under the Boucherit system the entire class studied the same composition simultaneously. At the end of an afternoon I frequently had heard Saint-Saëns' "Rondo Capriccioso" twenty-four

times, a devastating experience. All of the students
played at night in cafés, movies, or somewhere, so at the
end of class we rushed off to the métro, racing down the
winding staircase, fiddle cases swinging wildly.

After a few months the circus closed down and Maestro Farinelli left my life. I landed a new job at the Café
Lutétia, which was a great improvement. Instead of
twenty francs an evening, the equivalent of a dollar, my
salary skyrocketed to thirty. Many years later, when I
was reminiscing with the pianist José Iturbi, he exclaimed, "You dirty capitalist! I got only ten francs for
my first café job." I had become what is known in Central Europe as a *Stehgeiger*. Instead of being hidden from
the public, as I had been in the circus, I now was in full
view. Thousands of Parisians and tourists strolled by our
café night after night. I stood on a brilliantly illuminated
platform, flanked by a grand piano and a cello. I was
sharply silhouetted against row upon row of bottles extending above a long zinc bar behind which the *patron*
stood in his shirtsleeves, beaming at the customers. At
the little round tables sat the *midinettes*, the *poules*, the
flâneurs, the *vieux roués*, and the gigolos. Harassed waiters
wearing white aprons, balancing heavy trays above their
heads, wound their way among the crowded tables.
Above the din of the chattering, the clinking of bottles
and glasses, the honking of traffic on the boulevard, and
the shuffling of thousands of feet, our trio poured out the
passionate utterances of Bizet, Saint-Saëns, Puccini, and
Massenet.

Because almost every great French virtuoso had begun
his career this way, I did not feel in the least discouraged.
On the contrary, I was proud to follow in the footsteps
of my illustrious predecessors. The cellist was Polish and
had a mouthful of solid gold teeth, which he exhibited in
a perpetual smile. Both his French and his cello playing
were atrocious. When the three of us played such num-

bers as Emmanuel Chabrier's "España," we badly
missed a percussion section, so two of the waiters helped
us out. Standing by the piano with a tray in each hand,
they would, upon a signal from the pianist, bang them
together over their heads. For just a moment some customers looked up from their drinks, discussions, and
lovemaking. As soon as the piece was over, the waiters
stormed back to the bar to fill their battered trays with
bocks and *apéritifs.*

Summer approached. Since the Café Lutétia and the
Conservatoire were about to close, I began casting about
for another way to earn a living and was tipped off about
the Musicians Exchange, a kind of musical stock market.
The locale, a filthy café in the Faubourg St-Martin, was
swarming with musicians looking for jobs. I had barely
entered when a fat man buttonholed me and said, "You
conduct?"

"*Naturellement.*"

"You know *Madame Butterfly?*"

"*Naturellement,*" I lied.

"*Bon.*" And he told me to be in the suburb of Asnières
that evening at eight o'clock. Théâtre La Salle. Forty
francs. Tuxedo.

I had never conducted, had hardly ever seen an orchestra score, and had forgotten to ask who or what *Madame
Butterfly* was. And the man had disappeared. When I
arrived at the theater, about a dozen players had gath-
ered in the pit—violinists, cellists, a pianist, a clarinetist,
a trumpeter, and a drummer. They paid absolutely no
attention to me. The audience consisted mostly of work-
men wearing their caps aslant, accompanied by wives or
girlfriends. The smell of stale beer, tobacco, and garlic
was all-pervading.

When the time came to start, I looked around, as I had
seen conductors do, tapped the stand with the baton, and

raised my arm authoritatively. Before I could bring it down, the band had begun to play on the accustomed signal from the pianist. They had been playing the show for weeks and knew *Madame Butterfly* backward. After I recovered from the shock, I watched the pianist and tried to follow him. But it was useless—what I heard bore only a slight resemblance to what I saw in the score. My beat got limper and limper; finally I stopped beating altogether and just stood there, watching the musicians mechanically go through their daily routine. Everyone went on smoking; once in a while one of the players would stop in the middle of a phrase to roll a cigarette, lick it to make the paper stick, and light it. The smoke inside the pit became so dense that I could hardly see the players. When my eyes began to smart, I started rubbing them, whereupon one of the girls on the stage pointed at me and exclaimed, *"Pauvre petit."* It was midnight when I terminated my first engagement as a conductor, pocketed my forty francs, and went home.

The next day I went again to the Exchange in the Faubourg St-Martin. Within ten minutes I had another job, as a substitute at the movies for one evening. Thirty francs. Violin. No tuxedo. When I arrived, I went into the pit and found one man there, sitting at the ramshackle old upright.

"Are you the pianist?" I asked.

"Moi, Monsieur, je suis le chef d'orchestre"—Sir, I am the conductor.

He said it with immense dignity. Crushed and silent, I sat in semidarkness for about ten minutes. Then I heard a buzzer and the *chef d'orchestre* said, *"Commençons"* —Let us begin. Whereupon the two of us plunged into the overture to *Faust,* and for the next three hours played on without exchanging another word.

I was glad to escape to Bagnoles-de-L'Orne, a summer resort in Normandy, where the manager of the Grand

Hôtel had been cajoled into giving me a job. Here the rich and gouty came to take the waters. Evening after evening they walked slowly and stiffly into the dining room with its impressively high ceiling and crystal chandeliers. My job was to provide musical entertainment for the guests at dinner, discreetly half hidden behind an elaborate arrangement of potted palms. The hotel manager had not told me much about the job, just the barest essentials: salary, hours of work, and that a tuxedo was *de rigueur*. Also that there would be a second violin, cello, and piano.

As was customary, the second violin remained seated, completely hidden by the potted palms. As the solo violin, I stood while playing and sometimes got my bow tangled in the foliage. The pianist, who was the boss, couldn't see much while banging away at the upright piano, and the cellist was in the worst position of all, being thrice removed from the audience by a barricade of palms, the upright, and his own music stand. But if my colleagues couldn't see, they could at least hear the restrained clatter of the silverware and the china, and the quiet conversational strains of the well-bred. Mine was the strategic vantage point, and I had the job of relating the goings-on in the dining room for the benefit of my colleagues.

I have already implied how important it is for a café violinist to cultivate good relations with the waiters. Allow me to develop this fascinating theme. First of all, customers often ask for a favorite number. One customer may request "La Fille de Madame Angot," another "La Tosca," a third "Come Into the Garden, Maud." In most cases they reward the musician for his labors in one way or another. One customer may send a drink, a second a bottle of champagne, a third a hundred-franc note. Now watch closely: there are three recognized methods of presenting the hundred-franc note.

1. The customer walks up to the podium and discreetly presses the money into the player's free hand while murmuring words of appreciation.

2. He sends the money in advance via the waiter, enclosing it in an envelope with a written request.

3. He hangs on to his cash until after the performance, then sends the waiter over with a banknote, following his progress to the podium, eyes glued on what he hopes is still a hundred-franc note while it disappears into the distance. The waiter appears to be handing something to the violinist while pointing his chin in the direction of the generous customer. The violinist is seen to be fumbling with something that is presumed to be money. The drama ends on a fleeting glance of mutual recognition between violinist and philanthropist, one registering Gratitude, the other Satisfaction and Goodness.

Let us examine these three methods a little more closely. Obviously, the first is the safest. The customer comes in direct contact with the musician, there is no middleman, and no shrinkage can possibly occur while the money is being transferred from the giver's hand to the taker's. The recipient, under the closest supervision of his fellow musicians, returns to his music; later the money is identified and divided. Method Number Two works equally well, particularly if the waiter is honest and has no time to steam the envelope open. The dangers of method Number Three are readily apparent: nothing disintegrates as rapidly as a hundred-franc note handed to a waiter in trust for a third party. The musician has no recourse. He can't very well shout, "Hey, I only got five francs!" It is just barely possible that the customer sent only five francs. In any event, the violinist would promptly lose his job or incur the lasting enmity of all the waiters, the latter alternative being by far the worst.

One evening one of the waiters brought a request from one of the customers: "Valencia." We downed a last gulp of *café filtre*, emerged from behind the upright, and took up our stations. Our rendition of the famous Paso Doble was stirring if a bit ragged. After we had finished the waiter brought us our reward on a silver salver: a five-franc note! For a moment we just looked, too humiliated to say anything. Then the pianist hit out at me: "That's all you deserve for the way you play 'Valencia,' " she said. "Wrong tempo, wrong rhythm, wrong everything! You have no idea of dance music or *le jazz hot*" (the French considered "Valencia" jazz!).

And she was absolutely right. Like most concert artists, I was and am a lousy jazz player. It was the end of my career as a café fiddler. The lady pianist fired me. The next day I left for Holland, the scene of my childhood, where a chance encounter changed the course of my whole life.

I have often thought of that fatal performance of "Valencia" and silently blessed its composer, Señor José Padilla. For it precipitated a train of events that proved to be the turning point of my career. Ever since, I have been convinced that the worst as well as the best performances are divinely inspired. I went directly to the Dutch seaside resort of Scheveningen, my former home. As I passed a café on the boardwalk I stumbled over somebody's clumsily extended foot. The foot belonged to a conductor, Ignaz Neumark, uncharacteristically subjecting himself to a breath of fresh air. He was a friend of my family, whom I had known since I was a child.

"What are you doing here?" he asked abruptly. I explained that I had just been kicked out of my summer job in a café in a French resort, and as a result had time on my hands.

Neumark drew heavily on his ever-present cigarette, peered at me through his thick glasses, and said, "Flesch is in town. I want you to play for him." Carl Flesch was at that time a famous concert violinist, but he was even more celebrated as a teacher. Any young violin student would have been awestruck at the mere mention of his name. I remembered my studies in Berlin two years earlier, when I had been a pupil of Flesch's chief rival, Willy Hess, a representative of the old German school of violin playing; Flesch championed the new "Russian" school. The old German school required that the right arm, the one that holds the bow, be held low enough to clamp a book against the side of one's ribcage, a position that pushes the wrist so high that it sometimes appears as if one were wiping one's nose with every stroke of the bow. The sounds emanating from the violin almost seemed like a kind of byproduct, an unexpected bonus. The new Russian school that Flesch advocated went to the other extreme: the arm was held exceedingly high, emulating the defensive stance familiar to boxing fans. Practically the only thing that Flesch and Hess disciples had in common was that because we were all equally short of cash, we frequently ran into each other in the same cheap hash joints. It would have been unthinkable for the two groups to fraternize. The Flesch students would occupy one long table, while the Hess clan occupied an equally long one across the room. When the food was brought, the Hess students, parodying Flesch's high bow arm, wielded knives and forks in the most grotesque manner, elbows sticking out above their heads. In return, the Flesch students, acting as one, pressed their arms against the sides of their bodies, making the ingestion of food an almost acrobatic feat.

This was about as close as I had ever been to Carl Flesch, aside from hearing him at a concert. The thought of auditioning for him sent me into a panic, particularly as I was out of practice after a summer of commercial fiddling. But Neumark could be tenacious. Of course, I might escape because Flesch was no more eager to hear me than I was to play for him. He was about to leave for

America, where he was head of the violin department at the renowned Curtis Institute of Music in Philadelphia, and he could not see the point of auditioning another young student less than forty-eight hours before he sailed. No matter. Neumark prevailed, I was ushered into the presence, and started playing, miserably I thought. After just one minute Flesch stopped me imperiously. "Put your fiddle away," he commanded. I was crushed. At the opposite end of the room Neumark and Flesch were engaged in a *sotto voce* conversation, while I put my violin back in the case. As I was making a furtive exit, Flesch intercepted me. "Can you come to America with me on Saturday?" he asked. Flesch's enthusiasm was rarely expressed in effervescent terms.

Two days later I boarded the ocean liner that was to take me to America.

Let's face it. Life in Philadelphia is different from life in Paris. Market Street is not the Champs-Élysées, Horn & Hardart not the Café de la Paix. Conversely, the opulent Curtis Institute of Music, formerly a multimillionaire's home, had little in common with the drafty Paris Conservatoire, where it was claimed that all the faculty died of pneumonia. In Paris I had played in the circus, the movies, cafés, and restaurants in a continuous assertion of my early independence. In Philadelphia, Mrs. Edward Curtis Bok (later Mrs. Efrem Zimbalist), the munificent creator of this tiny paradise for geniuses, shortly after my arrival provided me with a monthly stipend, the use of a Stradivarius violin, box tickets to the visiting Metropolitan Opera, and subscription seats for the Philadelphia Orchestra concerts. The change from life in France was violent but painless, and it proved my capacity for rapid adjustment. The Curtis Institute of Music was unlike any other school in the world. Aside from the bounties Mrs. Bok lavished on all the students, there were other fringe benefits. Beautiful girls abounded, especially in Carlos Salzedo's harp class, and they were intrigued by my arrival as a fresh European import and Professor Flesch's new star pupil. Even better, the next summer I received an additional grant to pursue my studies with Flesch at his German mountain retreat in the Black Forest.

In such circumstances who would ever want to be graduated? When it seemed as if graduation as a violinist was inescapable, I took up chamber music. And when I reached the end of that route, the mysterious art of conducting beckoned. It kept me safely at the Curtis Institute for another two years. Can conducting be learned in a school environment? Not really. You can't learn to swim by attending lectures. You can learn to conduct only by conducting, and those opportunities are rare during one's student days. I shall never forget my panic and confusion as I gave my first downbeat in front of the student orchestra: it seemed as if I were engulfed in a raging ocean, with mountainous waves assaulting my ears. I was drowning in a chaos of noise, utterly incapable of distinguishing one group of instruments from another. I tried to assert my authority by reprimanding one violinist who seemed to be distracted by some distant object, invisible to me. "Don't look for conductors over there. The conductor is here," I said sternly, pointing at myself. Then I looked anyway, and so did the whole orchestra. Leopold Stokowski and Artur Rodzinski, my conducting teachers, had tiptoed into the room to observe my first unequal struggle with the orchestra. I was red with embarrassment. Obviously, the Curtis Institute enabled me to expand my musical horizons in many different directions. By the time I emerged from its sumptuous cocoon, I had acquired the basic equipment for functioning as violin virtuoso, string quartet player, and conductor. Among the students it was a common-

place that only geniuses were admitted to the Curtis
Institute, a mere modest two hundred of us. There was
the little violin protégé from Berlin who had been
adopted by Samuel Fels, the naphtha soap king, and who
was promptly dubbed "Little Naphtha." Despite a brilliant early debut, he ultimately abandoned music and
became an executive in the Fels empire. There was Jan
Savitt, who performed feats of Paganinian wizardry and
later unexpectedly became a famous jazz bandleader.
The least gifted violinist in the class, predictably, became a music critic. Those who ultimately floated to the
top were the composers Samuel Barber and Gian Carlo
Menotti. Few of the instrumentalists made it. Amid all
the luxury and the pampering three students attempted
to commit suicide the first year I was there, and one of
them succeeded.

The Curtis Institute, when I was there, was headed by
the fabled and extraordinary Josef Hofmann, who had
made his sensational debut at the age of six. Many pianists considered him the greatest pianist of their time,
possibly of all time. In addition, Hofmann was a me-
chanical genius with more than a hundred patents to his
name, the inventor of shock absorbers, air springs, and
other automobile appliances used by famous manufac-
turers. He was a composer of major attainments, with a
symphony, several piano concertos, and other works to
his credit; I once read a book he had written.

Hofmann was small, with an almost expressionless
face and a dry sense of humor best conveyed by the
following sample of the many letters he wrote me (note
his felicitous use of the dash, one of his trademarks):

> This is my 300th long-hand letter since I came to Cam-
> den for my—vacation. I also am teaching, work in my
> mechanical shop, play the piano occasionally and—
> decompose. Glad to hear that your European engage-

ments look promising. Let's hope for the best. Will write Copley to cable you the date of your first U.S. concert date.

Miss B. may be heard by "us" at anytime during the coming winter season, but I wish to warn her now already that there are no vacancies at the Curtis Institute except for those of—real genius. All is well with us.

Best wishes for a pleasant trip across the big pond. Greetings,

Josef Hofmann

Rumor had it that top faculty at the Curtis Institute received fabulous annual salaries, with the director supposedly getting a cool $100,000. According to one of the most popular stories that circulated among the students, faculty members would repair to the drugstore across the street during the midmorning break, order small Cokes at the soda fountain, and shout in chorus, "Separate checks, please!"

I have been told that Steinway & Sons built special keyboards for Hofmann, on a slightly smaller scale, to accommodate his hands. But despite his small stature, his power was tremendous. At the same time this strange and complex man was capable of a delicacy so exquisite, evanescent, and, yes, feminine that his performance of Chopin's E-minor concerto can never be forgotten by those who heard it. There was a great bond of mutual affection between Hofmann and Serge Rachmaninoff: each would frequently turn up at the other's piano recitals. But this mutual admiration in music was matched by an equally fierce rivalry in automotive matters. On one occasion, years later, I was getting into my new car when Rachmaninoff, spying me from the opposite side of a busy thoroughfare, risked life and limb to inspect its engine at close quarters. He knew that I had been a protégé of Hofmann's and promptly came to the point.

"I always tell Hofmann that he is the world's greatest pianist, and he insists that I am," said Rachmaninoff. "But Hofmann thinks that he is the world's greatest automotive mechanic among pianists, and I *know* that I am." So saying, Rachmaninoff pushed his melancholy Russian face under the hood of my car in an elaborate attempt to convince me of his definitive authority.·

One of the first problems I had had to solve upon arriving at the Curtis Institute was the matter of a lodging. Together with two other students I rented a four-room apartment and we promptly moved all the bedsteads, complete with army blankets, into one room, clearing the other three rooms for lavish entertainment. Next we organized everyone's domestic functions and responsibilities. One roommate was to do the cooking, another the cleaning, and the third would serve as an assistant to both. One Sunday, as economy was the watchword, I volunteered to do the laundry, exhorted everyone to throw his dirty socks, underwear, and shirts into our one and only bathtub, and then proceeded to fill the tub to the rim with soapy water, in order to let the laundry soak, thus rendering the tub unusable for bathing purposes. The next day was an exceedingly busy one at the Curtis Institute, and a poker party that evening interfered with laundry duties. Tuesday was even busier, and there was an orchestra rehearsal that night. I forget what happened Wednesday, Thursday, and Friday, but I remember that on Saturday afternoon the four of us retrieved the sopping laundry from the bathtub and, leaving a trail of soapy water, carried it to the Chinese laundryman at the end of the block.

The experiment in communal living came to an early end and I moved into the home of a lovable old doctor. But in other ways my experiments in pure socialism continued throughout my years at the Curtis Institute.

There was an unwritten law that those of us who lost our monthly stipends in the course of our all-night poker sessions were fed by the winners until the next check came in. When these situations arose, the losers would turn up unannounced for breakfast, lunch, and dinner at the homes of the winners, uninhibitedly wandering from door to door.

After four years I was graduated. The Institute sponsored my New York Town Hall debut as a violinist. They even gave me enough spending money to take a room at the Hotel Majestic, where I tried to take an afternoon nap before the concert, upon strict orders from my teacher. Professor Flesch, an extraordinarily methodical man with a Germanic mind, had explained to me that it was essential to get some sleep before a concert in order to be well rested and refreshed before the great event. But I was not accustomed to sleeping in the daytime. And I was jumpy, nervous, and scared. My mind wandered all over the place. Would I really be able to deliver? What would it be like to walk out onto the stage of that vast auditorium, perhaps filled with more than a thousand people, and with blinding spotlights shining right into my eyes? Would my memory hold out? Flesch had told me a hundred times that the most phenomenal memory was worthless in the absence of self-confidence. "It is not enough," he said, "to know a piece of music from memory. One has to be convinced that one really knows it. Fingers, ears, eyes are all programmed to carry out the instructions of that most miraculous of all computers, the human brain. But when self-confidence gives way to panic, even for a fraction of a second, everything disintegrates."

Flesch was a great teacher, but he would never have made it as a psychologist. The more he explained how fragile memory was, the more scared I got. Only recently I had attended a concert at which the soloist's memory broke down: he started over twice, and each time he stopped in the same place. He finally disappeared backstage, while the whole orchestra sat and waited, and came back with the music. I was convinced that if anything like that happened to me, I would sink through the floor from humiliation. Instead of resting and sleeping, I started going mentally through the program, speeding everything up like a tape-recorder on "fast forward." When I got through the whole program, I started all over again. I mentally drew a musical road map, trying to remember at what point my left hand should go up the D string and when it should stay down on the G string, even though I knew I would have to rely on automated finger memory rather than on brain and ears, especially in the fast passages.

Then I began to have waking nightmares figuring out everything else that could go wrong. A string could break. I had heard about the violinist who was so nervous when attempting a dramatic flourish at the beginning of the Wieniawski Polonaise that his bow had flown wildly up in the air and out into the audience. Another violinist accidentally hit the bridge on which the strings rest; the miserable little object landed beneath somebody's seat, and the performance was interrupted while dozens of people scrabbled underneath their chairs, suddenly creating a landscape of ample bottoms stretching into infinity.

I saw all these catastrophes happening to me. Then my fevered imagination began to wander in a more euphoric direction. I speculated on the reviews that would appear the next morning: "TEMIANKA TRIUMPHS" was the blazing headline in *The New York Times*. "A fantastic sensation was created at Town Hall last night by the first appearance of a young genius with the uncommon name of Henri Temianka." "After eight encores the audience still refused to leave, continuing to scream 'Bravo!'"

Etc., etc. Finally I got out of bed, totally exhausted, and proceeded for the first time in my life to put on tails, the dismal regalia of every concert virtuoso since time immemorial.

I don't suppose history records who invented the diabolical penguin suit. If I ever discover who it was, I shall burn him in effigy. What an insane, absurd contraption! I spent the next two hours getting into it and almost missed my debut recital. The ridiculous tails are the least of it. The real torture begins as one tries to insert the studs in the front of the boiled shirt. Passing one hand through the collar at the top, the other beneath the bottom flap of the shirt, I brought both hands together in a desperate attempt to force the studs through the holes. It was a hundred times more complicated than the feats of wizardry I performed in Paganini's "Witches' Dance" at the concert later that night. By the time I had finally nailed down the studs, my shirtfront looked as if I had been beaten up in a drunken brawl.

My ordeal was not yet over. The white tie came next. Tying a knot in a white bowtie while observing the reverse motions in a mirror is as complicated a maneuver as a moon landing. Perhaps the inventor of that useless piece of attire intended it as a therapeutic ploy. Forty years, four thousand concerts, and four thousand white ties later I have still not learned to cope with the problem. Getting dressed before the concert is more exhausting than the concert itself. It was my first time, but I was so completely absorbed and exasperated that I had no time to be nervous about my impending debut.

Thank God, the concert went well. After it was over, I stayed up all night with my cronies, awaiting the critics' life-or-death verdict. We hovered around Times Square until four A.M. to pick up the early copies of the morning papers. The New York critics were full of praise. Old Charlie Isaacson of the now defunct *Morning*

Telegram waxed positively lyrical. "There is a soul behind the boy," he enthused. "It came through like a
lovely moon peeping through the dense forest." I had to
take a lot of ribbing for that one.

Noel Straus wrote in the *Evening World*:

> His bowing was admirable in flexibility and remark-
> ably light and agile. The final movement of the Concerto,
> the Rondo Capriccioso and the Wieniawski selection
> were startling in their dashing bravura and evenness of
> passage work. Imagination, intelligence and well defined
> style gave his efforts a fascination that elicited more than
> one "bravo" from the numerous audience.

The *Musical Courier* stated:

> . . . one could feel the audience following the per-
> former in spirit.

And the *Musical Leader:*

> The large and distinguished audience was duly ap-
> preciative.

There was a slight difference of opinion among the
other critics. One of them placed special emphasis on my
superior bowing, stating, "He has a mellow, pure, flow-
ing tone and a remarkable right arm. It seems capable of
encompassing any difficulties of bowing with ease." His
chief rival saw great possibilities, but admonished,
"Now the young man needs to work on his bowing
technique." At this early stage in my career I had proclaimed my naïve desire to learn from what the critics
would say. What I learned then and there was to guard
against schizophrenia.

For weeks after my New York debut I walked around
in a state of euphoria. I was flushed and excited over my
success. I had a pocketful of fine reviews. I thought my
career was made. Josef Hofmann sent me to his own

manager, Richard Copley, a delightful old gentleman of
delicacy and an integrity rare in his profession. Mr. Copley printed a handsome brochure with my picture and
my reviews, offering me at a modest price to concert
societies everywhere. I distinctly remember my very
first engagement in Hollidaysburg, Pa. It paid $150, and
some of the fee was left after expenses. Then I had an
engagement in Altoona, a month or so later, and after
that everything came to a grinding halt.

Slowly I began to realize that a young virtuoso has no
prescribed future like people in other professions. A
medical student becomes an intern, then a resident, and
ultimately an established doctor in private practice. He
makes a living from the moment he becomes an intern.
Law graduates are in such demand that they are snapped
up at astoundingly high salaries. No such demand exists
for the soloist, and nobody wants him. The unanimous
response is, "Come back when you are better known."
The soloist is left to wrestle with the question, how is he
to get better known if he cannot make himself heard?

My teacher urged me to go to England. After all, I was
a British subject by birth, and in this materialistic world
one's best chance was supposedly in one's own country.
It struck me as peculiar, considering that both my parents hailed from Poland and I happened to be born in
Scotland during my parents' temporary stay there. Being born in a garage doesn't make one an automobile, I
said to myself, but Flesch prevailed and I went to London. I got a cheap room in a boardinghouse in St. John's
Wood and made the rounds of all the concert managers
in London. Then I waited in my room for that miraculous telephone call. In the meantime I had to eke out a
living, and so I took night jobs in the London theaters.
The orchestras' chief assignment was playing "God Save
the King" at the beginning of the show, partially covered
by a jungle of leaves and branches that extended across

the pit. After that we hung our instruments on wires that had been strung up for the purpose, wound our way to one of the basement rooms, and played poker until we crawled back to play intermission music. On one of these forays through the foliage somebody's head hit my violin, which was a fine eighteenth-century Italian instrument made by Januarius Gagliano. Down it went for the count, split from top to bottom. As fate would have it, the very next day the telephone call for which I had been waiting so long finally came. Harold Holt, one of England's most powerful concert managers, was on the line. Bronislaw Huberman, the celebrated violinist who had interested himself in me since my childhood, had suddenly become ill and had to be replaced immediately. "Mr. Temianka," Mr. Holt tried to say (it took the British several years to become accustomed to my offensively foreign name), "can you take the next train to Leicester? It leaves in one hour." I was so excited that it did not even occur to me to ask what the fee was. Mr. Holt mercifully volunteered: "You will be paid ten guineas," at that time about $50, a nice savings for the concert management since I am sure Huberman's fee was at least twenty times as much. But that was not what was worrying me. The fiddle: Where was I going to find a violin to play that evening? I had no instrument and few friends. Breathlessly I summoned a cab and raced to the repair shop of W. E. Hill and Sons, the famous violinmakers in Bond Street. The redoubtable Mr. Hill, after looking me up and down as if I were some kind of cheap fiddle myself, graciously accepted my broken violin for repair and loaned me the cheapest instrument he had. I barely caught the train. Naturally I traveled third class, but as I walked to my compartment I caught a glimpse of Luisa Tetrazzini, with whom, as it turned out, I was to share the concert that evening. So famous was the fabulous coloratura soprano that all kinds of gourmet dishes have

been named after her, especially chicken. She must have
looked glamorous once, a long time before I met her.
Now she was a heavy-set old lady. She could not really
have been as broad as she was tall, but that is how I
remember her. She was on her third farewell tour of
England. She had earned enormous amounts of money
in the course of her career, but a succession of young
gigolos had helped her dissipate all of it. Her current
gigolo, who doubled as her chauffeur, was the reason she
had to make one farewell tour after another, saying,
"Hello, here I am again," almost immediately after she
had said goodbye for the very last time.

Although I arrived safely, there was no time to rehearse with the pianist, Ivor Newton, an accompanist of
great renown in England. Fortunately, a real accompanist is bountifully endowed with ESP. I had never before
met Newton, and he had never heard me. When I
stepped out on the stage in Leicester, I felt shaky. I need
have entertained no fears. From the very first chord of
Corelli's "La Folia" Ivor seemed to know what I was
going to do before I knew myself. I played on, and I
played well. I relaxed and noticed, when I looked over
my left shoulder, La Tetrazzini standing backstage.
When I finished, I received a tremendous ovation. This
audience, like most audiences, thought it an unbelievable
achievement that an unknown could simply walk out on
the stage at the very last minute and actually play. Un-
consciously they must have been under the impression
that I had never touched a violin before in my life—
maybe a desperate manager had pushed one into my
hand, saying urgently, "For God's sake, please try." Soloists should always make their debuts as a last-minute
replacement for someone else. In fact, I advise the young
debutant soloist with enough money to engage a famous
artist for a concert appearance, on condition that he
agrees to cancel at the last minute. Advertise his appear-

ance widely, announce his indisposition, and then step in and play in his place. A successful career is assured.

When I had taken three or four curtain calls and left the stage for the last time, La Tetrazzini took her dentures out of her handbag, crammed them into her mouth, waddled onto the stage, and curtsied as coquettishly as if she were still twenty years old. The audience applauded vociferously. The English public, although slow to recognize an artist, is fanatically loyal. By the time the artist is no longer able to perform, he has their complete trust. La Tetrazzini was a prime beneficiary of this remarkable English trait. On this particular night the birdlike cascades of silvery coloratura sounds, in the highest register of the female voice, seemed particularly incongruous emanating from the roly-poly body of an elderly lady, but the English public was ecstatic.

With the unaccustomed cheerings of the audience still ringing in my ears, I took the shabby soot-filled night train back to London. The next morning I received a second telephone call from Harold Holt. He sounded quite different. He was delighted with my success, and as Huberman continued ill, Mr. Holt offered me all the remaining concerts the famous artist had been scheduled to play. Mr. Holt was indeed bursting with enthusiasm. No wonder—he was saving a fortune. From his sickbed the great Huberman, my hero since my childhood, wrote me a warmhearted note expressing his happiness that I had been the beneficiary of his illness.

This letter was the first of many. In the early years of my career, when I would voice my frustration and impatience, Huberman would write me other encouraging letters, with occasional admonitions. Once he wrote, "In this profession, one needs a great deal of patience. And you, after all, are very young."

Word of my last-minute substitution for Huberman got around. Gradually I began to gain a reputation as a

reliable substitute for ailing virtuosos. Long-distance
calls and telegrams summoned me to various parts of
Western Europe. Usually I was expected to take over on
a day's notice. In no time at all I found myself speculat-
ing on the state of my more celebrated colleagues' health.
If one of them looked green around the gills, I thought
I had better look over his programs. One day I received
a long-distance call from Holland. A well-known Dutch
violinist, Jan Damen, had been taken ill at the last moment. Could I come and play the Mozart A-major concerto the next day? I promptly agreed, with the reckless-
ness of youth. An engagement was an engagement. The
only problem was, I did not know the Mozart A-major
concerto. I had, it is true, studied it perfunctorily years
ago at the Conservatoire, but I had never reviewed it
since and never played it in public. Normally I would
have wanted a month to prepare for such an event, but
I had settled for twenty-four hours—one thousand, four
hundred and forty minutes. The concerto takes less than
twenty-five minutes. I spent that day and the entire
night memorizing and practicing. When my fingers gave
out, I threw myself on the bed and continued working
mentally, singing aloud or silently. During the rehearsal
the next day, as I negotiated a particularly tricky fast
passage, the conductor said to me, "That passage is impossible. Every time I have had a soloist perform it with
me, he has invariably broken down right there." I was
in a cold sweat as I approached the passage at the concert.
But I managed. The whole performance went well, even
though the conductor gave me some anxious moments.
In one's twenties nothing is impossible.

I developed a routine of calling upon local concert
managers and radio stations wherever I went. One day
I brazenly walked into the leading radio station in Brussels, giving my name to the receptionist. I had never
played in Brussels and was totally unknown. To my

amazement, I was immediately ushered into the office of the president, who welcomed me with great cordiality. Pressing a pen into my hand, he said, "You have come at just the right moment. Your contract is ready. You will play the Brahms concerto on November 12." He shoved the contract in front of me and I signed, in a state of shock. Six weeks later I returned to Brussels to play the Brahms concerto. After my rehearsal with the orchestra on the big stage of the National Broadcasting Corporation, I espied Emil Telmanyi, a prominent Hungarian violinist (and son-in-law of Danish composer Carl Nielsen), rehearsing in front of a microphone. "This is quite a coincidence," I said.

"Well, it's like this," explained my guide from the radio station. "Mr. Telmanyi had been scheduled to play the Brahms concerto. Somehow we got your names confused. We gave you Mr. Telmanyi's contract by mistake. Now you have this major appearance with orchestra, but we had to do something to placate Mr. Telmanyi. So he is playing this little engagement with piano."

Chance plays a part in making a virtuoso career, but the persistence, patience, and ingenuity required of a young and unknown artist to make an initial dent in the consciousness of the musical world are unbelievable. It is a major achievement merely to get people to come and listen for free. One cellist in Berlin, who did not have enough money left for telephone calls, hit upon the brilliant idea of dialing "O" for Operator all day long for several days, inviting all the operators to his debut recital. He depicted the event in such glowing colors that when he appeared on stage, the hall was packed with telephone operators and their friends.

There are other approaches. Some young people arouse the interest of rich patrons who may give or lend them a good instrument and pay for their debut recitals. One colleague of mine, a handsome and gifted young fellow

from some poverty-stricken village in Russia, was told
by his patron to buy himself some clothes. He promptly
did. He bought thirty expensive suits with matching
shirts, ties, socks, and shoes—and lost his sponsor.
Young musicians don't always have the necessary background in human relations. A beautiful and talented
young Mexican pianist, Angelica Morales, teamed up
with her famous octogenarian teacher, Emil von Sauer;
for him it was love at last sight. Carried along initially
by his world renown, they circled the globe giving duo
piano recitals. Some young musicians have been aided by
mature and wealthy ladies whose interest ranged from
the platonic and pentatonic to *molto appassionato* and *con
amore*.

And then, of course, there are the contests. Since
World War II, international contests have mushroomed
all over the globe. Old ones were revived: the Wieniawski Contest in Warsaw, the Tchaikovsky Contest in Moscow, the Ysaye Contest in Brussels (now renamed the
Queen Elizabeth Contest), and the Leventritt Contest in
New York. And there are all the new contests, such as
the Van Cliburn in Texas, the Villa-Lobos in Brazil, the
Enesco in Rumania, and many others in more countries
than you can shake a bow at. These contests create many
opportunities for young performers.

If the contestants come from Soviet Russia, their
chances are excellent because the Soviet government
takes these contests very seriously. Preliminary contests
are held inside the USSR, first locally, then regionally,
merely to determine who is best qualified to represent
the Motherland in the next international contest, wherever it may be. Weeks in advance the Soviet government
sends the selected representatives, the *crème de la crème*, to
the site of the contest, supervised by a chaperon-teacher.
Accommodated in secluded dwellings, the soloists are
trained the way other countries train their champion
athletes for the Olympic Games.

On the other hand, democratic countries are indifferent to musicians; they just don't rank with athletes. The American musician who journeys to an international contest generally has to do so under his own steam. He arrives at the last minute to save on hotel bills, travels by the cheapest means, and takes his chances. If he wins one of the top prizes, he wins a significant sum of money, creates a momentary stir, and with luck commences a real career.

Unfortunately, for every gifted musician who wins a prize at a contest, fifty other gifted musicians have the tag "loser" hung around their necks, which traumatizes them for life and sometimes destroys them. Is there no better way?

Nowadays the inevitable has occurred: professional contestants. Not easily discouraged, they turn up in Geneva, Rome, London, and in any of the thirty or forty world centers that beguile young musicians with the promise of instant recognition. Some of these contestants fall by the wayside in the elimination rounds. Others make it to the semifinals or the finals. Contests become a way of life for them. And it is not always the most gifted player who wins, but the one with the best nerves. For a contest is a very special war of nerves. In an atmosphere of such scrutiny, rivalry, and hostility the most sensitive artist is the one most likely to buckle under extreme tension.

My own career received a substantial assist when I won third prize in the first international Wieniawski Contest in Warsaw in 1935. Henri Wieniawski, a great Polish violinist and brilliant composer of virtuoso music for the violin, lived in the second half of the nineteenth century. My participation in the contest bearing his name was due to a crazy chance meeting. Leopold Muenzer, a formidable Polish pianist who later joined the countless ranks of Nazi victims, wanted to use the piano in my apartment to practice. One day, as he was complaining about a string he had broken, he told me about the first Wieniawski Contest in Warsaw. I had heard about it, but had hesitated to enter, because contests are as unpredictable as roulette. They are all right for those who have nothing to lose, but I was beginning to be known. If I did not win one of the top prizes, my career might be adversely affected. Anyway, the deadline for registration had long since passed; all the contestants had been feverishly preparing for months, while I didn't even know what the requirements were. Muenzer was as obstinate as Neumark. It must be a Polish characteristic. He wired the organizing committee of the contest in Warsaw. They waived the rules, and I was in—with exactly three days to learn some of the Wieniawski caprices, which I had not played before. Then came the long and arduous trip to Warsaw.

The atmosphere there was incredible. A distinguished-looking government representative interviewed all of the candidates, discreetly inquiring into their racial and religious background because granting the first prize to a Jew would have been intolerable to the virulently anti-Semitic Polish government. The international jury, as well as the population of Warsaw, were split into warring factions by nationalistic, chauvinistic, and personal rivalries. Certain teachers who were members of the jury were grimly determined to prevent the pupils of rival teachers from winning the contest, regardless of merit. At the height of one jury dispute one member threw an inkwell at another. The man in the street bet on the contestants as if we were horses. People totally unknown to me would grab me by the arm and say, "I bet a hundred zlotys on you for the first prize. Don't let me down." The concierge in my hotel invested a fortune in me. The President of Poland gave a reception for us in his palace. In this carnival atmosphere a young musician, barely out of the conservatory, was expected to keep his nerve and composure.

The contest took place in the impressive Warsaw Philharmonic Auditorium. The jury was seated at a long table to one side of the stage. Absorbed in listening, they adopted the most extraordinary poses, looking for all the world like Leonardo da Vinci's "Last Supper." The contestant faced them, standing inside a small chalk circle, center stage. First there were the preliminaries, the weeding-out process, in which every contestant had to play a Bach unaccompanied solo sonata, and other compositions with piano, including of course several bravura pieces by Wieniawski. Then came the finals, when the survivors were required to play a Wieniawski concerto with orchestra. The auditorium was always jammed to the rafters, with every last spectator vociferously rooting for his favorite candidate. That's how it must have been (I thought to myself as I stood, trapped, inside the little chalk circle) when the Roman crowds roared at the gladiators trying to kill each other with trident and net. Except that it could not possibly have been quite as noisy and ferocious.

We were all emotionally exhausted by the time the contest was over. Ginette Neveu, the brilliant French violinist who was only fourteen years old at the time, won the first prize. The second prize was won by David Oistrakh. I won the third prize, awarded by Polish Foreign Minister Jozef Beck, later Hitler's infamous crony. Now the doors of Eastern Europe were suddenly wide open to me. David Oistrakh and I had become friends during the contest, and when the president of the jury announced that Oistrakh had won the second prize and I the third, an electrified audience that filled every nook and cranny of the auditorium gave us an ovation, while we embraced each other. When he returned to Moscow, he urged his Ministry of Fine Arts to invite me for a tour of Soviet Russia, and he acted as my official host during my entire stay there. Oistrakh and I were almost inseparable during the full six weeks of my visit. He occupied

a small three-room apartment and even had an inexpen-
sive car. That, to the average Russian, was living like
royalty. My Russian accompanist, Alexei Belenki, was
an average Russian. He lived in a housing development
where he occupied one corner of a room, securing a
modicum of visual privacy by rigging a bedsheet on a
wire across one corner. The occupants of the three other
corners enjoyed similar privacy. How well my accompanist slept depended on the baby in the opposite corner
and the man next to him who worked the graveyard
shift. All that, plus the goings and comings to and from
the communal toilet throughout the night, accounted for
Alexei's chronic fatigue and extreme pallor. He suffered
without a word of complaint, touchingly thoughtful and
devoted to me. He was an excellent chess player, which
created a problem, because Oistrakh and I were also
fanatical devotees of the royal game. What do you do
with a threesome? We solved the problem by inviting the
father of the pianist Vladimir Horowitz to join us. We
played doubles, a game even more complicated than ordinary chess. Oistrakh and I played as partners against
Alexei and Horowitz. Oistrakh opened; Horowitz responded. Now it was my turn. But according to the rules
of the game, I was not allowed to consult with my partner. This meant that I had to analyze and understand not
only my opponent's move and game plan, but also my
partner's! The opening moves were comparatively simple, but by the time we reached middle game, the com-
plexities were monumental.

When I returned to England, everybody asked me
whether Oistrakh and I had made much music together.
I suddenly realized that we had spent every spare minute
hunched over the chessboard, oblivious to the world
around us.

My treasured friendship with David Oistrakh continued to his death, despite the myth to the effect that all

musicians are envious of each other, that no real friendships are possible among them. One day I ran into Jussi Bjoerling in a restaurant in New York. He said to me, "I thought that man sitting in a corner was Fritz Kreisler, but then I realized it couldn't be, because the two of you were having such an animated conversation. Surely no two violinists can be that friendly." I felt flattered to be mentioned in one breath with Fritz Kreisler, and assured Jussi that it was indeed the famed violinist and composer.

What makes a violinist into a virtuoso remains a mystery to me. Looking back, three chance happenings guided my career in ways that I could have neither planned nor foreseen. Because I was a lousy jazz player, I ended up in America studying with Carl Flesch. Because I happened to be near the telephone when Bronislaw Huberman took ill, I got my first career break; had I been at the corner grocery store at that moment, someone else would have had that chance. And because I happened to meet Leopold Muenzer in London, I won a prize in the Wieniawski Contest and started my international career.

2

The Soloist

Why does anyone want to become a soloist? It is one of the toughest professions in the whole world. It requires nerves of steel, the constitution of a bull, the stomach of an ostrich, the hide of an elephant. Violent changes of time zones, climates, dietary customs, people, and languages assault body, emotional balance, and digestive tract. Extraordinary physical coordination and prodigious feats of memory are required. On tour day after day I am propelled through seemingly endless turbulent skies, from Paris to Tokyo, from Sydney to London, from Moscow to Bombay. Sometimes I feel like a human rocket.

The career of a soloist calls for total involvement, nothing less. Take the case I know best: a concert violinist. With his ears he listens, with his eyes he observes his fingers, the bow, the violin, the conductor, the music, the audience, the box office. Both arms are in use, from fingertips to shoulderblades. With chin and neck he holds the violin in an iron vise, to prevent the precious and delicate instrument from slipping, falling, and breaking into a thousand fragments. He has to control every muscle in his face to preserve a presentable appearance. Invisibly beating time with his big toe inside his patent-leather shoe, standing on a stage under hothouse conditions for hours on end, precariously swaying, soaked to the skin, in a state of near-panic that his memory may fail him and bring the entire performance to a grinding halt in the presence of several thousand people, the soloist braves the dangers and torments that always lurk in his path.

The slightest injury, a mere scratch on the tip of the little finger of the left hand, which an average person might scarcely notice, amounts to total incapacity. Otto-kar Ševčík, the famous violin pedagogue whose innumerable books of exercises have spread terror among young violin students around the globe, was blinded in one eye when his E string broke explosively. Two of France's finest violinists, Jacques Thibaud and Ginette Neveu, perished in air crashes. So did William Kapell, the young American pianist, and Guido Cantelli, the thirty-six-year-old Italian conductor whom many considered Toscanini's heir apparent. Massive concert grands have collapsed on the knees of piano soloists; performers and conductors have fallen off platforms (in the case of Otto Klemperer, such a fall later led to brain surgery). At least one conductor lost his life in the line of duty: in the seventeenth century, when some conductors beat time by stamping a cane on the floor, Jean-Baptiste Lully speared his foot and died of blood poisoning. Many a soloist's luggage has been lost at airports or stranded in railroad stations on every continent, depriving him of a change of clothes and the most elementary necessities just before a concert. The life of a soloist is filled with grime and punishment.

It is also a lonely profession, especially for pianists. In between such glamorous capitals as Paris and Tokyo lie Dubuque, Iowa, Whitefish, Montana, and provincial towns in Holland, England, and Japan you haven't even heard of. When the pianist arrives, frequently at an impossible hour of the day or night (plane schedules being what they are), it can be a frustrating experience, particularly if he can't speak the language. English may be the nearest thing to a universal tongue, but few people in Fukuoka, Japan, Mendoza, Argentina, or even Helsinki know it. It may be raining or snowing. After the pianist checks into his hotel he sits, sometimes sentenced to one or more days of solitary confinement. The piano available for his concert performance may or may not be first-rate. (I would be happy to have a thousand-dollar bill for every lemon I have encountered.) If nobody in the local town takes an interest in him prior to his concert, the soloist can be the picture of loneliness. If they smother him with companionship, he goes out of his mind because of the lack of privacy and the assault on his personal life. Local newspaper interviewers may come and drag out of him the same life history that he has just been badgered into giving to other interviewers in Winnipeg or Guadalajara. The best hotel in a small town may be first class, but it is often third-rate. Sometimes huge trucks roll by all night.

Eventually, the soloist transacts the business for which he originally came. He dons his white tie and tails, walks out onto the usually overheated stage, enchants the audience while perspiring through his outermost garments, prays that the audience will not applaud between movements and that no infants will cry during them, autographs several hundred programs backstage afterward, politely hides his annoyance when strangers crowd in on him and feels lonesome if they don't. Finally he becomes the guest of honor at a reception where he is the only one who doesn't get a chance to eat or drink because he has to smile and shake hands with all of the guests. Then he goes back to that marvelous hotel, packs his bags, and goes on to the next provincial town to repeat the experience. If he stays until the next day, he can read the local critic's discourse on what was wrong with his performance.

Violinists, cellists, and singers are slightly better off than pianists. They have to take someone along to accompany them at the piano. This accompanist is an important personage, although mostly ignored by the public. The relationship between soloist and accompanist frequently deepens in time. Solitude does cement relationships. Singers in particular become utterly dependent on the inspired support and coaching of their pianists. One thinks of such partnerships as Franz Rupp and Marian Anderson, of such accompanists as Ivor Newton and Gerald Moore in England—the latter achieved star rank. Sometimes the accompanist gradually assumes the role of factotum, unofficial personal manager, travel agent, secretary, redcap, bellhop, lover, or husband.

Pianists are vexed by never knowing what kind of piano they will be playing at the next concert. But they are blessed in comparison with cellists. For years the airlines have waged all-out war on cellists, giving them the choice of placing their cherished treasures in the cold, unfeeling hands of some airline official, who will dump the instrument into the plane's yawning baggage hold, or paying half a fare for a seat next to the owner, where the cello rides in splendor. When I traveled with the Paganini Quartet, our cellist engaged in endless debates with bureaucrats at the airports, pointing out that his cello did not eat, did not use the lavatory, and could be held between his knees on the plane. It did not really need another seat. When the employee was just about to send the cello to the baggage hold, my friend would threaten the airline with a $200,000 suit if anything happened to his valuable instrument. He had long practiced this peroration and delivered it with a dramatic inflection that struck fear in the hearts of his antagonists.

Then he would walk off with his cello and board the plane, leaving the bureaucrats cowed and beaten.

Sometimes we used another stratagem. While one of us was presenting the airline tickets at the desk, the three others would proceed to the gate, camouflaging the cello as best they could. We would wait at the gate until everybody else was aboard, then at the very last minute present ourselves. The gatekeeper's usual reaction was, "What have you got there?" We would reply, "It's a bass balalaika." Since the plane was just about to take off, he would feverishly consult his instruction book. Nothing about bass balalaikas; only half-price tickets for cellos. With the employee in total confusion, we would push on through the gate, carrying the cello before us like a battering ram.

Forty years ago Fritz Kreisler used to say that all he knew of every city in the world was the railway station, the leading hotel, and the concert auditorium. It was briefly thought that the air age, with its dramatic reduction in travel time, would enable a performer to have more leisure between concerts. What a delusion! Concert managers saw a golden opportunity to cram more performances into the soloist's schedule. In the good old days a tour of Japan or South America meant two or three weeks of delightful relaxation on a luxury ocean liner. Famous artists like Nicolò Paganini remained in one city for months on end, making many appearances before moving on to the next town. Ignace Paderewski traveled in his own private railway car, complete with grand piano and such elementary conveniences as cooks, butlers, and valets. Modern technology has changed all that.

In the jet age you find a soloist playing in New York one night, in Paris the next day, and in London or Amsterdam one day later. Almost every self-respecting conductor of international reputation holds at least two major orchestra directorships. The unwritten laws of that mysterious thing called prestige make it imperative that these two orchestras be in cities as far from each other as possible. For instance, Andre Previn was simultaneously director of the Houston Symphony Orchestra and the London Symphony Orchestra. William Steinberg had Pittsburgh and Frankfurt at the same time. Zubin Mehta was director of the Los Angeles Philharmonic and the Israel Philharmonic; Antal Dorati led the National Symphony in Washington and the Stockholm Philharmonic. Pierre Boulez jetted between the New York Philharmonic and London's BBC Symphony, Georg Solti between the Chicago Symphony and the Orchestre de Paris, Lorin Maazel between London's New Philharmonia and the Berlin Radio Orchestra, to which he was about to add the Cleveland Orchestra. Eduard Van Beinum, who was simultaneously at the head of the Los Angeles Philharmonic, the Amsterdam Concertgebouw, and the London Philharmonic, died of a heart attack at fifty-seven, thereby reducing the statistical average of a conductor's life expectancy, normally no less than eighty-five. When the North and South Poles develop population centers and symphony orchestras, it is a safe bet that the two positions will be occupied by the same conductor.

To add to the discomfiture of the soloist, he must, absolutely must, practice on his instrument no matter where he is. Andrès Segovia told me that he practices five or six hours a day, every day of his life. Practicing would be no great problem if there were such a thing as a soundproof hotel room. But as everyone knows, hotel room walls consist of two layers of wallpaper. Heifetz was once practicing in his New York hotel toward midnight, anxiously preparing for a Carnegie Hall recital. His phone rang. An angry female voice demanded that he cease making noise. He replied with dignity, "But I am Jascha Heifetz." She retorted, "I don't care if you're Lawrence Welk. I want to get some sleep."

Huberman, who suffered from chronic insomnia aggravated by an abnormal sensitivity to noise, always carried a little book in which he had entered the numbers of the quietest rooms in all the hotels in which he had stayed. As he had been a perpetual wanderer since his early prodigy days, the book contained a monumental amount of information. Whenever he stayed in a new hotel, he would stalk the corridors in his pajamas through the sleepless night, making notes about the locations of noisy elevators, streets, public rooms, bars, and restaurants.

One of the most prestigious engagements for a soloist is an appearance with a leading orchestra. Anyone who can boast of playing with the New York Philharmonic, the Boston Symphony, the Philadelphia Orchestra, or another leading orchestra is on his way to the top. But to some conductors the soloist is only a necessary evil, tolerated for box-office purposes. There have been serious conflicts between soloists and conductors, with one or the other walking off the stage in a huff. On one occasion Klemperer was accompanying a violin soloist in a modern work that he hated. In the middle of the performance somebody in the audience got up and walked out; whereupon Klemperer turned around and exclaimed, "Thank God, somebody understands it."

Most famous violin soloists have started out as prodigies—what the Germans call *"Wunderkinder"* (literally, "miracle children"). By the time they reach puberty, or even before, the violin has virtually become an extension of themselves, an extra limb. Menuhin made his debut when he was eight or nine, Heifetz and Kreisler at thirteen, Mischa Elman at fourteen, Henrik Szeryng at a laggardly sixteen. Pianists rarely emerge so soon; cellists never: the size of the instrument stands in their way. Josef Hofmann made extensive tours as a piano prodigy at the age of nine, but the Society for the Prevention of Cruelty to Children stopped him in the middle of his United States tour.

Some soloists come up through the ranks. Alfred Wallenstein was first cellist in the New York Philharmonic under Bruno Walter, gradually becoming fed up with the job and making no effort to hide his boredom. Nothing is more frustrating to a conductor than to see a player, especially the leader of a section, remain unresponsive to his desperate cajolings and urgent exhortations. When Wallenstein finally left the orchestra to become a conductor, Walter congratulated him and added, "I hope you will be lucky enough never to have Wallenstein as your first cellist."

Gregor Piatigorsky was discovered by Wilhelm Furtwängler while he played in a café opposite the opera house in Berlin. Piatigorsky had only recently escaped from his native Russia, with nothing except his cello and the clothes on his back. He considered himself lucky to have found a job, any job. Night after night he played such popular potpourris as *The Merry Widow* in the smoke-filled atmosphere of the café. One evening toward midnight a tall man with a scrawny neck and bald head walked in. It was Furtwängler, who sat down at one of the little marble-topped tables to relax with a glass of Pilsener. Suddenly he pricked up his ears at the sound of a cello rising above the little piano trio. That was no ordinary cello player. Piatigorsky's fabulous tone instantly captivated Furtwängler, as it was to captivate millions of others in years to come. At the end of the piece Furtwängler walked up to him, introduced himself, and hired him on the spot as solo cellist of the Berlin Philharmonic. Piatigorsky's appearances with that famous orchestra eventually propelled him into his glamorous solo career.

No layman can imagine the many different fears that beset soloists. Fear of space, for instance. One has probably been practicing for years in a little room with a low ceiling, virtually touching the four walls. The sensation of walking onto the stage of a vast auditorium filled with thousands of people, then into blinding lights, is overwhelming. If any artist tells you that he always feels supremely confident as he strides into that yawning abyss, call him a liar. What helps me is to breathe deeply, a dozen or more times, before going on the stage. Sometimes I take a mild tranquilizer an hour before the concert; it relaxes me, just enough. Paderewski used to hold a metal ball filled with warm water for twenty minutes, not merely to warm his hands, but to enable him to achieve complete mental concentration before walking out onto the stage. Once, ready to begin to play, he walked toward the stage when he was stopped by the electrician with a question about the lighting. "Now I have to start all over," muttered Paderewski, who turned around and went back to his metal ball for another twenty minutes. Many great artists have had to give up their solo careers because the nervous torment became unbearable. Vladimir Horowitz would stand in the wings in a state of uncontrollable fright prior to a concert and had to be pushed onto the stage. He ultimately suffered a total breakdown and for many years ceased to give public performances. Glenn Gould has also stopped playing in public.

But it is not only a matter of nerves. The excitement of the stage affects the performer's chemistry, propelling the adrenalin on a dizzy course through his system. How well that body chemistry is controlled may well determine whether or not the hopped-up performer reaches undreamed-of heights of inspiration, or whether arms, fingers, ears, and brain become so overstimulated that the perception of speed, dynamics, and artistic concept is distorted. I have never understood why certain jazz players resort to the use of stimulating drugs during performances. Nature provides the needed stimulants in abundant measure.

Then there is the soloist's ever recurring fear of a fatal memory lapse. I once had a remarkable experience with the French pianist Robert Casadesus. During a chance meeting on a lengthy train trip, we discussed the subject of memory in detail. Casadesus, having arrived at his destination, left the train. I later learned that this normally unflappable artist, so completely reliable and confident, had suffered a memory lapse at his concert that night. The reason was, of course, quite clear to me.

The searching light beam of intellectual analysis can become a death ray. Piano soloists will tell you that violinists, cellists, and singers have it made. For every single note they play, the pianist has to memorize and play six, eight, even ten notes. In addition, the piano repertoire is infinitely larger.

Victor Borge, who started out as a serious concert pianist, told me that he was so petrified with fear for his memory before his debut that he pasted some paper slips with music cues inside the piano, where only he could see them. He tried the system out and it functioned beautifully—at the rehearsal. When he came out on the stage that night, a blinding spotlight shone on the piano, making it impossible to read anything. Borge's desperate contortions, as he jumped up in genuine panic and peered inside the piano, brought down the house. In that moment Victor Borge the pianist-comedian was born.

My own closest brush with memory failure came when I played the Beethoven concerto with the Residentie Orchestra in Rotterdam. In the middle of the first movement there is a break between two phrases that is supposed to last a fraction of a second. Suddenly I could not remember where to move my hand to start the new phrase. For two or three seconds the whole universe seemed to be in suspended animation. An unbelievable silence hung over the entire auditorium, neither orchestra nor audience breathing or moving. It was like a film that suddenly stops, frozen on a single frame. Then, as inexplicably as all motion had ceased, it resumed. My hand moved to the right position, my bow resumed its up and down strokes, and everybody started to breathe again. The rest of the performance, all remaining thirty-five minutes, went beautifully. At the end I received a thunderous ovation, as if I had performed some heroic feat. Audiences love the human element.

Aside from the specters of space and memory, the soloist must also know how to deal with acoustics. What he has been accustomed to hearing at home bears no resemblance to what he hears on the stage. To the inexperienced soloist, the acoustical distortions, so different from one auditorium to another, can be shattering. A violinist may feel as if soap had been spread on the hair of his bow. Suddenly practically no sound emerges from the violin. Is his glorious tone reaching out to his audience, keeping every last listener enthralled? Or is it all being absorbed and destroyed by the heavy draperies framing the stage? How does the soloist know? He doesn't, until he receives reassuring noises from the audience at the end of his performance.

Is the life of a soloist really as tough as I have depicted it? It all depends on who he is. Many artists adore it. After all, they receive more ego gratification and recognition in a week than most people do in a lifetime. They bask in the glory of it all. Vladimir de Pachmann, an eccentric Polish piano virtuoso, was so completely at ease that he would interrupt his performance to crawl underneath the grand piano to fix a loose pedal in full view of his large audience. After several minutes of uninhibited shenanigans, he would dust off his tails, return to his bench and continue the performance. If he was dissatisfied with the way he played a phrase or fast run, he would slap the offending hand with the other, innocent one, exclaiming, "Shame on you!" Then he would repeat the phrase to his satisfaction, and, beaming ear to ear, shout enthusiastically, "Bravo! Bravo, de Pachmann!" When he was invited to play for Queen Victoria at an afternoon musicale in Buckingham Palace, he insisted on washing his own teacup. In the middle of one performance he recognized a friend in the audience. He stopped cold, walked up to the footlights, and in tones of utter surprise exclaimed, "For God's sake—if it isn't Gottfried Schmulovitz! Since when are you in town?" He insistently motioned him to come and shake hands and for the next five minutes engaged him in animated conversation, snatches of which were overheard by the audience. De Pachmann inquired about the man's wife, his children, his business, and took out his engagement book and made a lunch date on the spot. Then, thoroughly satisfied, he went back to his piano and continued where he had left off. I have always secretly envied him.

Sir Thomas Beecham, also totally at ease on the concert stage, was so disgusted with his noisy audience while conducting the overture to an opera at Covent Garden that he turned around and shouted, in the presence of the Royal Family, "Shut up!" It made the front page in all the London papers. Adila Fachiri, a Hungarian concert violinist, combined panic with aplomb in an incident unique in the annals of music. When her memory failed her, she fainted, falling dramatically to the floor—but not until she had carefully handed her valuable violin to the concertmaster. Once Josef Hofmann came out on the stage, sat down at the piano, got up again, leaned over toward a lady in the front row, and asked, "May I please see your program, madame? I forgot to look." If this last sounds farfetched, bear in mind that soloists play several programs in the course of a tour, giving local concert societies a choice. After playing four or five one-night recitals a week for a month or longer, my accompanist and I became so nonchalant that we walked out on the stage one night without looking at the program. It happened in Arendal, a little fishing town on the southern coast of Norway. Playing from memory, I started with Corelli's "La Folia" and continued with Lalo's Symphonie Espagnole. There seemed to be a certain amount of restlessness in the audience. I was puzzled. During the intermission a lady came backstage. "I thought that Brahms sonata sounded strange at the beginning," she said, "but when you played the second piece, I *knew* it couldn't be the Mozart A-major concerto. What's going on?" Shamefacedly I returned to the stage and confessed my error to the audience. They accepted it with charming good grace. Then I explained that I could not start over again because I was delaying the ship that was to take me to the next concert. The captain, a passionate music lover, then dismissed the printed schedule in order to enable me to finish my concert. My all too human error, the unusual circumstances, and my explanation in the most ungrammatical Norwegian ever heard in Arendal created an extraordinary bond between the audience and myself. When the concert was over, the entire audience walked with me to the nearby ship in the moonlit night, and waited to wave goodbye as the ship sailed away.

The soloist's life has certainly not been tough on Artur Rubinstein. In his mid-eighties he continued to give concerts for adoring audiences around the world, at astronomical fees. He has a lovely wife, gifted children, beautiful homes in Paris and New York, and the energy, vitality, and *joie de vivre* of a man half his age. Cellist Pablo Casals, in his mid-nineties, continued to play the cello, compose, conduct, and teach. Jascha Heifetz, past seventy, and still without an ounce of superfluous fat, played as beautifully as ever and shared his knowledge with a new generation of gifted students. If we extend the select circle of soloists to include conductors, we stumble upon a whole club of fabulous octogenarians. It is difficult to resist the conclusion that the life of a concertizing musician, for all its frustrations, is animated by some extraordinary, mysterious, revitalizing force. Compare it with the life of the most famous actors of our time: Humphrey Bogart, Gary Cooper, John Garfield, Tyrone Power, Clark Gable, and a host of others died in their forties and fifties. Conductors and soloists not only remain healthy, some of them make fabulous fortunes. Toscanini owned an island in Italy, Heifetz a yacht in Southern California, Herbert Von Karajan a private plane, and Zlatko Balokovicz, a Yogoslav violinist, a gaggle of Strads. Menuhin has homes in England, Switzerland, and California, Huberman lived in the former Austrian Imperial Palace in Schoenbrunn. Musicians from Handel to Rubinstein have owned superb art collections. The grand old men and the younger superstars command fees of up to $20,000 for a single evening's entertainment. There is another group of $5000 or thereabouts stars. There is a whole galaxy of rising stars, young stars, and not-so-young stars earning fees that may vary roughly from $1000 to $2500 per evening. Some of them do well one season and worse the next, others are steadily marching toward the top. You can tell by the way their managers treat them. A manager goes all the way out to the airport to welcome a $10,000 artist. He goes to the hotel to pay his respects to a $5000 artist. He takes the $2000 artist out to lunch. The minimum-fee

artists, those under $1000, are "squeezed in" at the office
between incessant telephone interruptions. In the early
1970s more than two hundred piano virtuosos were under national management in the United States alone!
Probably half of them are household names to the informed music lover. Svyatoslav Richter, Gary Graffman,
**Leonard Pennario, David Bar-Illan, Emil Gilels, Jeffrey
Siegel, Rudolf Serkin, Vladimir Ashkenazy, Daniel
Barenboim,** and at least fifty others are equally well
known. How much do they earn annually? The top ones
at least several hundred thousand dollars, while those at
the bottom may be barely able to pay their rent.

But it's not the more than two hundred I'm worried
about; they, in a sense, have already made it. It is the
thousands of other pianists who are in trouble because
the supply is infinitely greater than the demand. The
same is true of violinists, singers, cellists, guitarists—in
fact all musicians. Conservatories and music schools
across the country turn them out in unlimited numbers,
heedless of the lifetime of frustrations that lies ahead.
Those who are successful will be on the road most of the
time, leaving behind a well-fed fatherless family. Those
who are not successful have togetherness, but little else.
Nonetheless thousands stick to their profession with incredible tenacity, ignoring vicissitudes, catastrophes,
and failures. There can be only one conclusion: there
must be more to music than meets the ear.

3

Heir for the G String

Most musicians are born poor. I can think of only two notable exceptions: Felix Mendelssohn, whose father, Abraham, was the founder of the famous Mendelssohn banking house; and Ernest Chausson, the French composer. In both cases wealth did not bestow longevity: Mendelssohn died at thirty-eight and Chausson at forty-four, when he lost control of his bicycle and crashed into a wall. I was luckier than most. My father, who had a beautiful voice and started out as a cantor in a synagogue, was a reasonably prosperous diamond merchant in Rotterdam by the time I was introduced to the fiddle. It seems that my affinity for music was discovered when I was two years old. A monstrously active child with an infinite capacity for mischief, I suddenly turned into a little angel when taken to my first concert, an organ recital. Pure hearsay, but from that day on, my fate was sealed. There was no doubt in my parents' minds that they had produced a new Mozart, or at least another Paganini. Just four years passed before my father placed the first tiny fiddle in my hands, gave me my first violin lesson, and accompanied me at the piano. For my seventh birthday I was given lessons with a real violin teacher. I went to his house in awe, having no idea of what a real violin teacher was like. Was he tall? Small? Did he have a beard? Would he try to hit me with the fiddle, or stand me in a corner? I was thoroughly scared.

It turned out Mr. Carel Blitz was small. That comforted me a little. He wore a pince-nez, and had a little black mustache and neatly combed brown hair. He had a friendly round face, and his little steps, as he walked across the room, were full of bouncing energy. Immaculately dressed, he wore pearl-gray spats over shoes that shone like mirrors. Mr. Blitz greeted me warmly, took my fiddle, and stood it upside down on his forehead. With both arms spread wide he did a precarious balancing act crossing the room. Turning triumphantly, he took my bow and balanced it on the tip of his nose. Immediately I felt a growing confidence in my new teacher. Then Mr. Blitz sat down at the piano, carefully pulled up his trousers to preserve the creases, and played a few sweeping arpeggios, filling the room with harmonies. "Come on, my lad," he said, "let's play." He tuned my tiny fiddle for me (I still have it—hanging on the wall in my den) and played a tune. I, of course, had never heard anyone play so beautifully, and instantly vowed that some day I would play like Mr. Blitz. When he handed the violin back, it felt quite different. It felt warm and comfortable. All of a sudden all the notes turned up in the right places. While I played, Mr. Blitz accompanied me at the piano, improvising as he went along. A cigar stub dangled from his lips. Once in a while Mr. Blitz would shout an encouraging "Come on, Paganini!" above the din. On other occasions he would transfer the cigar stub from mouth to hand and sing along in a childlike falsetto in order to convey the true phrasing and character of a tune. During his singing spells the piano accompaniment continued uninterrupted; the cigar stub held between two fingers traveled across the keyboard, leaving a trail of ashes. Soon Mr. Blitz became the fixed star by which I judged all other values. Our association lasted for many years and developed into a deep friendship.

Unlike Mr. Blitz, all too many teachers make their students' lives miserable. Forced to repeat one passage over and over again, playing the same exercises day in and day out, the poor sufferers understandably begin to look upon music as the Devil's own invention. My teacher never made this mistake. He adapted his methods to my age and mentality. When frequent repetition of a difficult passage was really indispensable, he would say, "I bet you a guilder you can't do it, *schlemiel!*" making one of his comic faces and putting a coin on the piano. Naturally I snapped at the bait. My pride was involved, and so was money, an unbeatable combination. Finally Mr. Blitz had to implore me to stop repeating the passage. Could anything be more detestable than scales? My teacher found a way of making them palatable. He accompanied them at the piano, giving free rein to his imagination. Fragments from the Beethoven concerto popped up from nowhere, quite possibly followed by "The Last Rose of Summer." There was just no telling where his ceaseless quest for inspiration might lead. On one occasion, as I was mangling a difficult four-octave scale in B major, a running counterpoint on "Yes, We Have No Bananas" erupted in the bass. Mr. Blitz and I burst out laughing. In short, this first teacher of mine, without benefit of Dale Carnegie or Sigmund Freud, had done what any real teacher does instinctively: he had found the key to my heart. Once he had my trust and affection, he knew I was ready to absorb all he could give me.

I disappointed Mr. Blitz only once, and I shall never forget the occasion. On that particular Wednesday, as I walked into the room, I imagined a slight restraint in my

teacher's usual welcome. Instead of asking for my latest
story, he immediately said, "Have you practiced well
this past week?" I emphatically affirmed that I had spent
more than three hours each day in consecrated communion with my violin.

"That's fine," he said, without conviction. "Let's begin."

I placed my fiddle case on the grand piano and opened
it. My jaw fell. The case was empty! With dark forebod-
ings I backed toward the door, awkwardly muttering
something about returning in a minute. As I ran home,
my little legs hit the pavement with the speed of drum-
sticks. All to no avail! My fiddle was not in the house.
Red with humiliation, I went back to Mr. Blitz. He
walked to the cupboard, opened the door, and solemnly
brought forth my violin—which had been there since the
previous Wednesday.

Mr. Blitz composed—anything from a foxtrot to a
symphony. His most astounding specialty was a simultaneous improvisation on the piano and violin. Seated at
the keyboard, with the violin tucked under his chin, he
would open with a thunderous blast on the piano; a
flamboyant cadenza on the violin followed. Then, drawing the bow across the open strings with his right hand,
he would create a perfect illusion of two persons playing
at the same time. During the whole performance he
never took his cigar stub out of his mouth. This particular show was usually reserved for newcomers, whom he
impressed by announcing that he was about to perform
an unknown concerto by Tchaikovsky. After he had
finished and been lavishly complimented, he would re-
veal that he had just been improvising.

There seemed to be no end to the wonders and surprises Mr. Blitz had in store for me. Jauntily swinging
his cane, wearing his hat at a rakish angle, he was forever
exploring his native city. He was known in every café in

Rotterdam, where he initiated me into the mysteries of the green cloth. All I know today about the noble pastime of billiards I owe to his farsighted mentorship. He had discovered long before that there was a considerable similarity between the techniques of using a violin bow and a billiard cue, hence many an exciting billiard game was really a violin lesson in clever disguise. Mr. Blitz was not a severe teacher—he almost never scolded me. I think it was his complete confidence in me that made me feel I could not possibly fail him. At one point I found it exceedingly hard to cut short a soccer game in order to practice in the solitude of my room. Frequently it became a contest between the Devil and Mr. Blitz. Mr. Blitz usually won, for I just could not disappoint him. For these early beginnings in self-discipline and perseverance I thank my teacher to this day.

I met my next teacher when, upon the advice of Bronislaw Huberman, I moved to Berlin at the age of fifteen. It was only then that I began to realize what I had lost. The new teacher knew all about technique and nothing about humanity. Once he screamed at a student that her Berlin debut, scheduled for the next day, would be a total fiasco. It was—no young artist could make a successful first appearance after such a destructive prediction. There was a sadistic streak in Professor Willy Hess. He was a magnificent specimen of a man, with an aquiline nose, white hair combed straight back, and a Kaiser Wilhelm mustache. His violin students and the chamber music class prepared a wonderful surprise for his sixty-fifth birthday. For weeks we rehearsed the Bach Double Concerto in D Minor for Two Violins and String Orchestra. The soloists were two private students, Georg Kulenkampf and Tossy Spivakovsky, both of whom later had brilliant careers. We all contributed from our meager funds to buy a magnificent rug. A huge framed photograph of the orchestra was ready in time for a

surprise presentation on the morning of his birthday.
Then, the night before, all the students deposited their
instruments on the floor of my room, which was situated
across the street from the professor's penthouse apartment. As the only light switch was near the door, I had
to memorize the location of all the instruments before
making my way to bed in the dark.

The professor was an early riser, so we all congregated
in my room at six-thirty the next morning. Then we
crossed the street with fiddles, violas, cellos, basses, music stands, and music, and stealthily climbed up six
flights of stairs. The tiny elevator had not been built for
string orchestras. Besides, we were afraid of spoiling the
surprise if we made too much noise. The maid let us into
the music room, and when we were finally unpacked,
seated, and ready to play, she went to call the unsuspect-
ing Herr Professor. As he opened the door to his studio,
the downbeat of the mighty concerto reverberated. Our
professor did not lose his composure. Would anyone, if
he suddenly came upon an orchestra playing in his apartment at seven A.M.? There he stood, arms akimbo, looking magnificent in his dark-blue velvet jacket, even at
seven A.M., while we fiddled away for the next twenty
minutes. Finally the concerto was over, and in the ensuing silence his senior student delivered a carefully prepared address, concluding with the presentation of the
rug and the photograph. Herr Professor's reply was
brief: he thanked us and then admonished us never again
to use the same edition of the Bach concerto, as it was full
of inaccuracies and replete with bowings and fingerings
of which he disapproved.

Professor Hess was in many ways a remarkable man.
He played from memory every étude that had ever been
written. "Kreutzer Number 13 next time," he would
scream to his students, and perform the piece flawlessly.
We learned a lot from him about the technique of violin

playing. But a real teacher is infinitely more than a man who sells trade secrets. He is a creative artist, a sensitive sculptor who, instead of clay, molds the youthful mind and heart—a man of mellow wisdom who hands down to a new generation his priceless artistic heritage, to be cherished until it is handed down again a generation later. Of all the teachers I have known, Piatigorsky was perhaps the only one whose intuitive gifts matched those of Mr. Blitz. He once told me about a talented young student who was not progressing. Piatigorsky was baffled and concerned. At every lesson he would play for the student, showing him how it really ought to sound. Each week Piatigorsky tried more and more desperately, playing his heart out, hoping his own mastery would be transferred by osmosis. Instead, the student got worse and worse. One day, as he was again worrying about his pupil, a sudden revelation hit Piatigorsky. "I'm playing too well," he realized. "I'm discouraging the student." At the next lesson Piatigorsky deliberately played more casually. The student seemed to do a little better. Was it imagination? Piatigorsky was so encouraged that the next time he made a few mistakes, a wrong note here, a bad slide there. The student visibly pricked up his ears. When his turn came, there could be no possible doubt: the boy was improving. Piatigorsky was overjoyed to see his stratagem working. The worse he played, the better the student performed. Piatigorsky threw himself into the situation with enormous gusto. He took pride in playing worse than he had ever played in his whole career. A couple of weeks later the student made a brilliant success at graduation. As Piatigorsky went up to congratulate him, he found his student surrounded by well-wishers, one of whom asked, "What do you think of Piatigorsky?" "As a teacher—great," said the boy. "As a cellist—lousy."

The first famous artist to interest himself in my career

was Bronislaw Huberman.* As a fourteen-year-old boy I had played for him repeatedly, and traveled with him throughout Holland to carry his violin case and turn pages for his accompanist at his concerts. There was good reason for my hero-worship of this extraordinary man. Although little known in North America, Huberman had been a revered artist on the European concert stage for almost two generations. Like Paganini before him, he had only to announce, "Huberman will make his violin sing," and concert halls were sold out in a matter of hours. The devotion of European audiences to this extraordinary artist was unique. Women were known to carry his photograph with them wherever they went. Princes and princesses, dukes and duchesses, statesmen and captains of industry could be found in their idol's anterooms.

Huberman was born in 1882, near Warsaw, the son of a Jewish lawyer. At the age of twelve he played the Brahms concerto in Vienna, in the presence of Johannes Brahms himself, and was embraced by the master after the performance. From that moment on Huberman went from triumph to triumph; his career as a prodigy was comparable to Yehudi Menuhin's some thirty years later. When I heard Huberman for the first time, I was a mere boy, a budding violin prodigy myself. My excitement while waiting for the great man to appear on the stage was uncontrollable. Finally an invisible hand opened the door and Huberman stepped out on the stage. He did not walk; his flat feet shuffled along the floor. As he came closer I saw a small, balding man with a bony head, a grotesquely protruding lower lip, and a big, impressively curved nose. He was hollow-chested and had sloping shoulders. But his outstanding characteristic was his eyes: he was walleyed, and when he ap-

*The same virtuoso whose illness several years later started me on my career in England.

peared to be looking at one person, he actually was looking at someone else, as I was to discover later when I met him.

Huberman hardly smiled as he acknowledged the audience's initial applause. He was intensely nervous and went through a number of agonizing motions before he could bring himself to play. First he produced a piece of rosin from his hind pocket and proceeded to draw the hair of the bow across it several times with unnecessary vehemence, a job he could have done just as well backstage before the concert. Then he began to tune his violin, turning each peg. After he had tuned his violin thoroughly and loudly, he went back to putting on some more rosin, evidently oblivious to the fact that he had already done so. Then he repeated the tuning formula, producing sounds no member of the feline family could have improved upon.

Finally he drew his violin to his chin and struck out with his bowing arm. In that selfsame instant an incredible transformation took place: he had closed his eyes and was no longer walleyed, he had raised his violin heavenward, and his whole body seemed to participate in this upsurge. Huberman was no longer a hollow-chested little man with sloping shoulders. He had become all spirit, a divine messenger of the world's greatest music. A wave of exaltation engulfed him and his listeners alike.

At the end of the concert Huberman received a delirious ovation. He was a symbol of spiritual strength. His was the triumph of a truly great personality. He achieved the incredible paradox of being grotesquely homely in repose and superbly beautiful in action.

Recently, when I listened to some recordings that Huberman made at the height of his career, I received a cruel shock. Judged by objective standards, Huberman's playing was so full of flaws that these recordings should never have been allowed to reach the public. No violinist of our day revealing such imperfections could hope to run the critics' cruel gauntlet. Yet Huberman's success had not been created by the ignorant. From Brahms onward, all the greatest musicians of the age had acclaimed him as a great artist. What accounted for it?

Much of the conviction that Huberman's performances carried, I concluded years later, resided not in his playing but in his powerful personality. The conviction of his playing was simply an extension of his uncompromising convictions as a person. In his forties, at the height of his career, he had become intensely interested in the Pan-European ideas of Count Coudenhove-Kalerghi because he foresaw the threat of another world war and fascism. He promptly stopped playing the violin and enrolled in social and political science courses at the Sorbonne, and for two years he did not play a single concert. Such an act of renunciation at the height of a great career would have been a sacrifice for any person, but in his case it was a double sacrifice, for he had an excessive regard for money. How many of us would willingly part with a fabulous income rolling in at a steady pace, year in, year out? To Huberman every dollar was like a hundred. Yet he had the strength to give up the money and the adulation of his public in order to devote himself singlemindedly to a new ideal.

After finishing his studies at the Sorbonne, Huberman traveled across Europe, making speeches in favor of a Pan-European movement that would unite the unhappy and torn continent into one great unit. Had men like Huberman succeeded, the Second World War might never have happened. But Europe was not ready for it.

Huberman was not a natural orator because he had a pronounced lisp, and this, in addition to his appearance, would have discouraged a lesser man. But Huberman seemed oblivious to his own handicaps; and he spoke with such tremendous conviction that he made his listeners oblivious too.

While he was on a tour of Indonesia in 1936, Huberman's plane crashed into a tree. He was among the survivors, but many of his fingers were broken, as was his left wrist, and a rib had punctured one lung. Huberman's career as a concert violinist seemed ended forever when he was only fifty-four. With the mad obstinacy of a man incapable of realizing that he is defeated, Huberman underwent treatments of every imaginable kind. He had daily massages. He devised exercises for his fingers and his hands which he carried out painfully for hours on end, day in, day out. He suffered grievously, physically and mentally.

Two years later I heard him again, when he resumed his career in Holland. He played more beautifully than ever. During the two years of enforced idleness he had gone through a purifying process, technically and emotionally. The concerts he gave thereafter were among the most memorable of his entire career.

One of the most remarkable aspects of Huberman's mysterious hold on people was the fact that it could be sharply divided along geographical and racial lines. His success in Germanic countries, such as Germany, Austria, and Holland, was fabulous. So was his reception in Slavic countries, such as Russia, Poland, and Czechoslovakia. On the other hand, he was consistently unsuccessful in almost every Latin and Anglo-Saxon country he ever visited. I could never explain this phenomenon to my own satisfaction. Huberman did have a mystical quality that was perhaps in harmony with the Slavic spirit. His mysticism and solemn dedication to his art perhaps had a profound appeal for Germans. What mattered to the Slavic and Germanic psyche was Huberman's unforgettable moments of exaltation and ecstasy. Huberman took them into a different world, and if there were imperfections in his playing, they were oblivious to them. But to the Anglo-Saxon mind, ecstasy was immoderation, exaltation a lack of understatement.

When Hitler came to power in 1933, Huberman immediately canceled all his engagements in Germany and declined to make further appearances there. Very few men indeed, in those early days of Hitlerism, had either the integrity or clarity of vision to make so clearcut a decision. Artists who cherished their careers wanted to believe that Hitler's bark might be worse than his bite and that business would continue as usual. Huberman stood to lose more than anyone, for Russia and Germany had been the scenes of his great triumphs ever since childhood. Russia he had lost with the advent of Bolshevism; Germany he now voluntarily renounced. Huberman reigned so supreme in the world of art that it was to him that Furtwängler, conductor of the Berlin Philharmonic Orchestra, turned with an impassioned plea that Huberman be the first "to break down the wall that keeps us apart," and to return to Germany to play for the German people. Huberman's reply in the form of an open letter to Furtwängler was published on the front pages of the world's leading newspapers. He resolutely refused to accept for himself alone privileges that for racial, religious, or political reasons were now denied to his fellow artists of lesser prominence.

He defined the interpretation of great music as "the artistic projection of that which is highest in man," and exclaimed:

> Can you expect this process of sublimation, which demands complete abandon to one's art, from the musician whose human dignity is trodden upon and who is officially degraded to the rank of a pariah? Can you expect it of the musician to whom the guardians of German culture deny, because of his race, the ability to understand "pure German music"? . . . In reality it is not a question of violin concertos nor even of the Jews; the issue is the retention of those things that our fathers achieved by blood and sacrifice, of the foundation of our

European culture, the freedom of the individual and his unconditional dignity unhampered by fetters of caste or race.

So saying, Huberman in the fateful year of 1933 renounced the Germany of Hitler and with it the largest part of his career. He continued to live near Vienna in Schoenbrunn, the Austrian Versailles, where before him Austria's princes and emperors had held sway. Now these princes of the blood traveled to Schoenbrunn to pay homage to Huberman. With the invasion of Austria in 1938 all this came to an end. The great artistic empire over which Huberman had once reigned supreme lay in ruins around him. Huberman became a wanderer for the remainder of his days.

Although Huberman's career as a concert artist was almost finished, his greatest task still lay before him. For many of the persecuted Jews fleeing before Hitler's hordes the only haven left was Palestine. Huberman conceived the then fantastic idea of creating a national Jewish orchestra in Palestine. He traveled back and forth between Europe, Palestine, and the United States, collecting money for the orchestra wherever he went, speaking at gatherings, and giving benefit concerts. He auditioned thousands of orchestra players. The task of raising a complete symphony orchestra from among thousands of destitute refugees scattered all across the globe, many of them without passports, then transporting them to a small and turbulent territory in the Middle East, establishing permanent homes for all of them, and organizing a concert schedule that would keep the new orchestra going through the year—all this would seem a mad project for a single human being to attempt. Huberman carried it out. There was no rest for him. He established one of the world's topnotch symphony orchestras in a part of the world that had never before known what it was like to have any symphony orchestra at all. The violin section of the orchestra was so extraordinarily talented that choosing a concertmaster became a baffling problem: every man in the section was a former concertmaster. In a final spirit of compromise five concertmasters were appointed, each to serve alternately.

As a crowning achievement Huberman brought Toscanini to Palestine to conduct the miraculous new orchestra. For months the whole Jewish population of what is now the State of Israel lived in a delirium of excitement. One woman who gave birth to twin girls during Toscanini's visit named them Tosca and Nini. In 1938 Huberman himself appeared as soloist with the orchestra, before an audience of thirty thousand.

During the years of the Second World War Huberman lived quietly in a suburb of New York City, playing only a very occasional concert, an almost forgotten man in the mad hustle and excitement of the industrial New World. But while he was himself condemned to inactivity, he still found time to encourage others as he always had. Every since my childhood, I had occasionally played for him and benefited from his advice and wisdom. He was a constant source of inspiration to young violinists on the threshold of their careers. On the occasion of one of my New York appearances Huberman specially came to the city to be present, and at the end of the concert, with his customary generosity to a younger colleague, he stood up and shouted "Bravo!"

It was because of Huberman that I went to Berlin in the 1920s and discovered the real world of violin playing. In Rotterdam I had been at the top of the heap; here I was low man on the totem pole. Prodigies from around the world converged on Berlin, in fierce competition with each other. Whether they came directly from Russia and other parts of Eastern Europe, or from the

United States, South America, or Germany itself, the majority had one thing in common: they were East European Jews or their descendants. The history of violin playing abounds with such glorious names as Elman, Heifetz, Oistrakh, Menuhin, Stern, Milstein, Szeryng, and Perlman and Zukerman among the younger generation. The statistics leave no room for doubt: an unbroken tradition of great violin playing has emerged from the ghettos. Even Kreisler, Joachim, and Szigeti, though they were Austrian or Hungarian, were only a generation or two removed from the ghetto.

Why did the ghetto inhabitants play the violin? The most popular explanation is that a Jew who could escape with his life during a pogrom could also escape with his violin. But why, then, not a piccolo or clarinet? Because the throbbing, sobbing warmth of the violin expresses Jewish sorrow, yearning, and even joy as no wind instrument could. The inexpressibly sad, madly exuberant tunes of the Jewish ghetto have become familiar to millions because of *Fiddler on the Roof.* After the violin the clarinet was indeed next in popularity among the Eastern Jews. Then came the bass, also known as the bull fiddle, double bass, or contrabass. No Jewish wedding was complete without a trio consisting of fiddle, clarinet, and bass playing "Mitzve Tanzels," the traditional Jewish dances. The quality of these little bands was seldom superlative. At one wedding a mischievous child supposedly turned one of the pegs on the scroll of the bass while the bass player was resting, lowering the pitch of one string beyond recognition. The bass player frantically ran after the fleeing child. Finally he cried out, "Please, I won't hurt you. Just tell me which peg you turned!"

There is another reason why Jews, particularly under the domination of the czars, took up music: they were either barred from the liberal professions or admitted to them only in the insignificant numbers the ignominious quota system allowed. The few avenues not closed to them included literature and music—hence the Sholem Aleichems and the Heifetzes. There was also a practical side to it: superior knowledge and exceptional talent alone made possible an escape from the ghetto; they were the magical keys that could open the doors to a better life. America ought to hold the czars in grateful memory, for such fine symphonies as the Philadelphia Orchestra and the New York Philharmonic were built in large measure by gifted Jews who escaped from Russian oppression.

One can imagine what pressures frustrated parents exerted on a gifted child. The desperate hopes of entire families were focused on him, and his parents were ready to gamble everything on that one lottery ticket. In the worst cases the child was seen as a future meal ticket, while in many others fathers and teachers had visions of vicarious glory denied themselves. Jascha Heifetz's father, for example, was an obscure violinist. Heifetz, Menuhin, and scores of others never knew normal childhood: while other children frolicked, they practiced endlessly, and the long hours of ruthless early training left indelible emotional scars. Some parents were unbelievably competitive. When Mischa Elman failed to make an appearance in Vienna, though he had played in every other European capital, his father was asked why. "Against whom should he play?" he countered.

The trouble with the musical profession is that every student starts out with one singleminded fierce ambition: he is going to be the next Heifetz if he is a violinist, the next Rubinstein if he is a pianist. And if he does not have that ambition at the start, his parents will not rest until he has. It is a situation that might almost be called the Heifetz Syndrome. One woman, accompanied by her little boy, went to the Carnegie Hall box office to buy two tickets for Heifetz's forthcoming recital. "Please give me two tickets at two-fifty," said the woman. "Sorry," said the ticket man, "no tickets left at two-fifty." The woman gave another glance at the posted list of ticket prices. "So give me two tickets at three-fifty." "Sorry," said the man again. "Well, what *have* you got?" said the exasperated woman. "All that's left are a few tickets at six-fifty." Whereupon the woman turned to the little boy, sharply slapped his face, and exclaimed, "Now, Ikey, will you practice?" How many Heifetzes and Rubinsteins are there in any one generation? Imagine the frustrations in the legal profession if every law student were determined to be Chief Justice of the Supreme Court, in the sciences if a physicist or biochemist felt he was a failure unless he won the Nobel Prize, or if a writer's sole goal were to make the best-seller list. There is no other profession as unrealistic as mine. Orchestras throughout the world are littered with the broken dreams of the Heifetzes who haven't made it. Believe me, no string player starts out with the intention of joining an orchestra.

The strange and mysterious thing about those who haven't made it is that they are often as good, or almost as good, as those who have. The differences can be so slight. Personality, persistence, health, the human environment, luck, and that unpredictable something called the human potential all play a part. I once had a pupil who at the age of fifteen seemed destined for a great career. She was strikingly beautiful, charming, and unspoiled, with the physique and endurance of an Olympic champion. She would go horseback-riding all day and then play for me as if she had spent the time practicing the violin. She won major awards, gave a New York recital, and at sixteen made her nationwide debut on the air playing the Brahms concerto (one of the most difficult of all) with Leopold Stokowski and the NBC Symphony.

It was a spectacular performance. She seemed to have it made. She went to New York to continue her studies. Her mother went along, leaving the rest of the family in California. Then her mother died, and the distraught girl disappeared from sight. Later, after two unhappy marriages and five children, she took to drink. Then she came back to me for lessons, trying to take up where she had left off. It was hopeless. The marvelous spirit that had animated her as a child had vanished. She played notes, not music. She had become grossly overweight and flabby. The last time I saw her name was in a small newspaper item which reported that the authorities had removed her children from her custody because of her neglect.

Talent remains a mystery. How does one recognize it? Even that is a mystery. One is reminded of Leonard Bernstein's father's reply when he was asked why he did not give his son more early encouragement: "How was I to know he would grow up to be Leonard Bernstein?" In the field of music some talents are immediately recognizable, while others develop slowly beneath the surface, imperceptible to the outside world. Mozart was an example of the first, writing masterpieces in his teens. On the other hand, the trite music Beethoven wrote at twenty gave no inkling of the stupendous genius that developed. Mendelssohn wrote his first symphony when he was twelve, Brahms waited until he was forty-three. Benjamin Britten, at the age of nine, wrote melodies which he later incorporated into his popular "Simple Symphony." Dmitri Shostakovich wrote his first symphony, an enduring masterpiece, when he was nineteen. Charles Ives developed much later in life, meanwhile prospering as an insurance agent. Ralph Vaughan Williams went to Paris to study with Ravel when he was thirty-five, the age at which Mozart died.

No effective musicmaking is possible without profound emotional involvement. In most professions emotion is considered a handicap. Some of the most hackneyed phrases in English are "Don't get emotional," "Keep cool," and "Let's be objective." In every field except the arts, from surgery to politics, emotions are supposed to be bottled up. The musician who bottles them up is a dead duck. From early childhood on he is trained to express his emotions with the utmost freedom, to liberate them from all restraint. The music of the great masters repeatedly exhorts the interpreter to play with passion. *Allegro molto appassionato* is the indication at the beginning of the Mendelssohn violin concerto, and one of Beethoven's most famous piano sonatas is known as the "Appassionata." The music of such great romantic composers as Chopin, Schumann, Tschaikovsky is filled with fiery passion. The violin virtuoso's most potent weapon in projecting that passion is his vibrato. "Vibrato" is that peculiar oscillation of the tone produced by the rhythmical shaking of the left hand and arm. If you are not a violinist, try extending your left arm forward, palm up. You will recognize the correct position as that of an Indian beggar asking for a bakshish. Now start shaking the entire arm. After one minute you will feel as if it were ready to drop off. We violinists sometimes keep it up for six to eight hours at a stretch. That's vibrato. Next time you go to a violin recital or orchestra concert you will have a new appreciation of what it means to be a violin virtuoso.

I remember how shocked I was when I heard a nine-year-old girl play the Wieniawski concerto at the Wieniawski Competition in Warsaw with an almost shameless display of voluptuous emotion: she was doing musical bumps and grinds. Can this passion, once released at an early age, be brought under control? In such a supercharged emotional atmosphere the role of the teacher becomes particularly sensitive. The impres-

sionable adolescent student tends to become a hero-wor-
shiper, particularly if the teacher is a famous artist.
Which is why in this profession so many old men have
married young girls, all students. When he was past
eighty, Pablo Casals married a pupil in her twenties. The
Hungarian composer Zoltán Kodály, the pianist Josef
Hofmann, the Belgian violinist Eugène Ysaye, and a
well-known Swiss violin teacher, Oscar Studer, are all
examples of music patriarchs wedded to adoring young
women.

Because teaching music is a tough way to make a living, some teachers develop flexible ethics with the passage of time. One of my favorite stories is about the
teacher who was asked how much he charged for his
lessons. "Well," he said, "I have lessons for twenty-five
dollars, but nobody takes those. I also have lessons for
ten dollars. Finally, I give lessons for five dollars, but, to
be honest, I can't recommend those." In Holland one
cello teacher was a genius at boosting his income. He
taught in both The Hague and Amsterdam, forty minutes apart by train. One day he eyed the cello of a pupil
in The Hague with distaste. "My dear boy," he said
paternally, "you cannot continue to play this appallingly
bad instrument. It so happens I have just seen a marvelous instrument in Amsterdam. I'm going to try to get it
for you in trade for your cello, provided you can afford
to add five hundred guilders." The grateful student, or
his parents, scraped together the five hundred guilders.
Whereupon the teacher went to Amsterdam and re-
played the scenario with another pupil there, but this
time the marvelous instrument he had seen was in The
Hague. The teacher pocketed another five hundred guilders and exchanged the cellos.

In Berlin some music teachers shamelessly hang out a

shingle claiming, "Six weeks from the beginning to concert maturity." Vladimir de Pachmann, that irrepressible practical joker and eccentric, noticed one of those signs when he first arrived in Berlin, still an unknown, to make his debut there. He rang the doorbell and asked, "Can you really make a concert pianist out of me in six weeks?" "Absolutely," affirmed Herr Professor. "All right," said de Pachmann, "let's start. Where do I put my hands?" De Pachmann proved himself an eager, uncommonly gifted pupil. Before the first lesson was over he could already play a scale, slowly. The next week he played all the scales, faster. To his teacher's speechless amazement he was playing Czerny études the third week, Chopin études the fourth, and in the fifth a Beethoven sonata with a few wrong notes deliberately sprinkled here and there. The sixth and last week he rattled off the Brahms B-flat-major concerto. At the end of the lesson he produced two tickets from his pocket, saying, "Herr Professor, you were absolutely right. I am ready for the concert stage. Please come to my debut recital tomorrow night!"

A new phenomenon in teaching has emerged in recent years. His name is Shinichi Suzuki, and he has taken the violinistic world by storm. His concept of teaching is predicated on the revolutionary proposition that playing the fiddle can be "fun." He teaches literally thousands of little Japanese children by rote, leading them in snake dances through rooms and across fields while they play pieces like "Pop! Goes the Weasel" in unison. Since three- and four-year-olds can hardly be trusted to practice by themselves, Suzuki insists that their mothers also learn to play the fiddle. Rumor has it that Suzuki will next enroll pregnant housewives, so that not a minute need be wasted when a baby is born.

The virtuoso's proficiency must reach such a degree of automated perfection that it will stand up under the grimmest onslaught of nervousness and panic on the stages of London, Paris, New York, and Tokyo. Even this is not enough. The foolhardy aspirant to a solo career must have a fully memorized repertoire to meet the demands of today's concert world. David Oistrakh has told me that he had thirty-five violin concertos ready for performance in any one season. Since a violin concerto averages a half-hour in length, this repertoire covers seventeen and a half hours of memorized music that the performer must be able to toss off with the confident mien of a sleepwalker. Of course, Oistrakh did not play only concertos: he was also expected to perform from memory dozens of sonatas and smaller pieces. In his last years he had taken up conducting. I asked him how he liked it. "Great," he said. "I mostly use the score so I don't have to remember all the notes. And if I lose my place, the orchestra goes on playing anyway."

There have been notable exceptions. The French violinist Jacques Thibaud made a brilliant career with an exceedingly small repertoire, largely because the public never tired of hearing him play the same favorite French chestnuts. Anyway, Thibaud was a charming *bon vivant* who would rather spend his time with beautiful women, gourmet food, and vintage wines than practicing with his violin. One evening in the greenroom after a concert an admirer asked Thibaud to write a few lines in his autograph book. "What shall I write?" asked Thibaud of pianist Moriz Rosenthal, who was standing next to him. "Write your repertoire," answered Rosenthal helpfully.

Thibaud lived in grand style; Oistrakh, by contrast, was perhaps the world's most underpaid musician. The fees his managers collected in 1970 for a single appearance were somewhere around $8000; most of this went to the Russian government, a good portion went to management, and only a few hundred dollars of expense money went to the man who commanded and richly deserved these fees. When Oistrakh visited us in Los Angeles he was amazed at the comparative luxury in which we live (humble enough compared to the Shangri-las of the movie stars). He kept looking around, repeating with an air of incredulity, "No musician in Russia lives like this." I assured him that there were dozens of musicians in Los Angeles living as well, and some much more luxuriously. Then Oistrakh, the most celebrated of all Soviet violinists, told me of the jealousy and unpleasantness to which he had been subjected in Moscow for owning two automobiles. "Did you do anything about it?" I asked. "Yes," he answered, "I sold one car."

Classical musicians in general are the most underpaid people in the world. For every Rubinstein and Menuhin there are a hundred others who emerge from leading conservatories with impressive diplomas, only to end up as virtually anonymous orchestra players or modest accompanists, at a scale of remuneration that would make a plumber indignant. What, then, motivates thousands of young people to take up classical music? I think it is primarily a passion that is not to be stilled. It is the overwhelming need for self-fulfillment felt by those who are gifted or who think they are. I remember when I was only nine I prayed before going to sleep, "Dear God, please let me be another Huberman." Then, as an afterthought, I offered God a compromise: "And if you can't let me be Huberman, can I please be another Flesch?" It's lucky Flesch never found out about this.

I am constantly asked to audition and advise young people planning to embrace serious music as a career. One young violinist appeared to me to be totally ungifted. While I was still struggling with my thoughts, wishing to be honest without destroying him, he asked me point blank, "Do you think I could have a career like

Fritz Kreisler?" I gave him a candid answer, advising him to take up another profession. A year later he came back. His playing had not perceptibly improved. "Now you surely agree that I can make a career like Kreisler?" he queried eagerly when he finished playing. I said I did not. I never heard from him again, and his name has not yet made the headlines.

The expectations of that boy were, in varying degrees, the expectations of almost every one of my fellow students in the conservatories of Paris and Berlin and at the Curtis Institute. They were the cream of the crop, the gifted ones selected from among hundreds of other aspirants after the most exacting entrance examinations and auditions. Not one of them has ever been heard from! Even so, the species is in no danger of extinction. The violin as we know it is four hundred years old. But the Old Testament already refers to the "kinoor," which is generally translated as "violin." And Nero is said to have fiddled while Rome burned. So there is a slight hiatus of several thousand years between the kinoor and Nero, and Nero's first known prominent successor in the trade, the seventeenth-century Italian violinist Arcangelo Corelli. The species flourished on Italian soil, reaching its peak in the first half of the nineteenth century with Nicolò Paganini. Then the Eastern Jews took over, to be replaced in turn by a tidal wave of emerging Oriental talent. All dire predictions to the contrary, the species survives abundantly—unscathed, unbloodied, and unbowed.

4

Life on the Circuit

To many a music lover the life of a soloist must seem to be pure glamour: audiences shouting "Bravo," beautiful ladies swooning at his feet, champagne suppers, interviews in the newspapers, and, in between, communion with Beethoven, Bach, Mozart. How spiritual and elevated an existence! There is that. And there is the other. For instance, I ran into my old colleague Szymon Goldberg, just back from a provincial tour of Poland. He immediately wants to know whether he can stay with me (so much nicer than a hotel—cheaper too). I say okay because Szymon always has unusual experiences.

During a recent concert, Szymon relates, no sooner had he started playing Beethoven's Kreutzer Sonata when it became apparent that something had gone wrong with the toilet, which unfortunately was located directly behind the stage. Despite serious misgivings and an inability to concentrate on the glorious music, Szymon struggled manfully through the entire first movement, accompanied not only by the piano, but by the ceaseless repetition of the toilet filling up and flushing, filling up and flushing, sometimes producing a most violent *crescendo* where Beethoven had indicated a *dimi-*

nuendo. At the end of the first movement it became obvious that the show could not go on. As no stagehand seemed to be available in that dismal little Polish town, my friend had no choice. He placed his violin and bow on the piano, disappeared backstage, removed his tails, and climbed up on the old-fashioned toilet with its tank rigged up high against the ceiling. He worked at it for five or ten minutes and was covered with falling plaster and dust, commodities abundantly available in Poland. The operation was successful, so Szymon dusted himself off as best he could, washed his hands, slipped back into his tails, and returned to the stage to give an inspired performance of the remaining movements of the Kreutzer Sonata. Ah! The glamour of it all!

A concert tour is a kaleidoscopic experience: deadly boredom alternates with unexpected incidents and exciting encounters. While standing and waiting at a northern Michigan airstrip in the early 1950s, I thought up a new game to pass the time. "Events most unlikely to occur," I called it, talking to myself and chuckling with smug self-approval as such images flashed through my mind as Kosygin making the decision for Christ at a Billy Graham revival meeting; Casals wearing a toupée; the Queen of England abandoning the throne to marry Elvis Presley; a U.S. Ambassador abroad attending a cultural event. Suddenly I was shaken out of my reverie by someone exclaiming, "I'm Harry Truman." I started violently. The most unlikely event of all had occurred: former President of the United States Harry S Truman stood in front of me with outstretched hand, waiting for me to grasp it. No mistaking that sharp face, the broad-brimmed hat, the steel-rimmed glasses. He had stepped off a hedge-hopping DC-3 for a breath of air, noticed a man with a violin case, and in his characteristically direct manner had walked straight up to me. I introduced myself in turn and explained that I was in the middle of a concert tour. Mr. Truman said, "You know, people always think that the 'Missouri Waltz' is my favorite piece of music, but that's not true! It drives me nuts when they start playing it every time they see me. My real love is chamber music. I have at home the recordings of all nine Beethoven symphonies." *(Sic!)* It turned out we were to be on the same plane. Mr. Truman quickly jumped aboard and I followed. He introduced me to his traveling companion, Paul Butler (the late Democratic National Chairman), and we sat down together. The plane was almost empty. Mr. Truman wanted to know all about my violin. I told him it was one of the most famous violins ever made, a masterpiece by Antonius Stradivarius, dated 1727, when the great violinmaker was eighty-three. It had belonged for many years to the legendary Nicolò Paganini, who had played it in hundreds of concerts and cherished it to his dying day. Mr. Truman got very excited, and, nudging Paul Butler, who was across the aisle, passed the information on. Then Mr. Truman asked to see the historic instrument. I carefully took it out of the velvet-lined leather case and showed it to him, a miraculous creation of fragile wood, in some places only two-tenths of an inch thick, which had withstood the wear, tear, and vicissitudes of almost two and a half centuries. Stradivarius' magic hands and then Paganini's had again and again touched those exquisitely chiseled and varnished pieces of maple and spruce, so incredibly delicate, now glittering in the bright morning sun. We were enjoying a gentle, smooth ride on that perfect September day high above the Midwestern plains, so when Mr. Truman asked me to play something, I planted my feet firmly apart, lifted my bow and fiddle, and played a Bach solo sonata for violin, the droning of the engines providing an unaccustomed accompaniment.

I stopped after the first movement, but Mr. Truman

applauded so enthusiastically that I continued to play the remaining seven movements of the sonata. When I finished, there was more applause, in which the stewardess and a couple of passengers in the back of the plane joined. "I have never seen or heard a Stradivari violin at such close range," said Mr. Truman, obviously very impressed.

The seatbelt signs came on as we circled over Kansas City. Mr. Truman cordially invited me to visit him on my next trip. As soon as I arrived home I sent him one of my recordings as a memento of our meeting. His acknowledgment was not long in coming. It began:

> Dear Mr. Temianka,
> Your record arrived in broken condition. It must have had some very rough handling from the post office. I was never more disappointed in all my life!

Considering Mr. Truman's experiences in the course of his long career, I felt flattered. I immediately sent him a replacement, this time the Schumann piano quintet, which I had just recorded with Artur Rubinstein. The record evidently arrived in one piece, for Mr. Truman wrote, "I shall think of you whenever I play it," and renewed his invitation for me to visit him. Some months passed before I returned to Kansas City. I went directly to the Truman Library in Independence, where Mr. Truman was expecting me. He received me with great cordiality and gave me a handsome autographed picture of himself. Not exactly a summit meeting, but surely a day to be remembered.

When I get really bored, I write limericks. When I concertize in the state of Washington—playing nightly in towns strung across hundreds of miles of mountains, the Columbia River, and apple orchards—places like Ellensburg and Moses Lake leave me frustrated. Other places like Pasco produce imperishable masterpieces:

A little old lady from Pasco
Made a fortune by selling Tabasco.
An astonishing switch
From her previous pitch,
As a call girl she was a fiasco.

And if the famous American composer Walter Piston will forgive me, when I concluded a concert with his sonata for violin and piano, I wrote:

If you don't like my playing, okay.
That's your right which I'll always insist on.
But I think it's a cause for dismay
That the last thing we play should be Piston.

What an interesting life I lead! Following Pasco and Wenatchee—the mysterious Orient. After twenty-six and a half hours and twelve thousand miles on the same plane, traveling with the sun and subjected to its blinding rays from start to finish, I arrive at the Djakarta airport. The customs shed, like its counterparts in Tahiti, Fiji, and New Caledonia, is not air-conditioned in the tropical heat. Alas! No travel agency representative shows up at the airport. I hail a cab in the universally familiar deaf-mute language, and head for the Hotel Indonesia, where the desk clerk stoutly maintains that I have no reservation. All my arguments are to no avail, so I despairingly pick up my bags and fiddle, explore beautiful downtown Djakarta at night, and ultimately, through a maze of pedicabs and sweating humanity, glimpse what looks like a golden Balinese temple. It turns out to be Djakarta's newest hotel, which, when it is finished, could well be an enchanting place to rest one's weary bones. For the present, swarms of construction workers are brushing past me in the dark, hauling cement mixers, lumber, bricks, toilets, and all the things construction workers haul when they construct. Meanwhile, I am communicating in sign language, until I realize that the older generation still remembers Dutch, my childhood language. The old man at the desk relents when I tell him my sad story, and I am allowed to remain overnight, the distinguished first guest in this future palace. Throughout the night construction workers are noisily marching past my uncurtained ground-floor window. The next day on to Singapore, where I have my first concert on this whirlwind tour of the Orient.

At the violin recital in Singapore at the Old Victoria Theatre my accompanist is a little fat Chinese lady, incredibly intense and incredibly unmusical. If she were a little less unattractive, I could suspect her of having been engaged by the local impresario for extramusical reasons. Every time she realizes she has made a mistake, she wildly throws up her arms, looking like a bird that has just been shot. Meanwhile dozens of real birds, unbelievably, are flying around backstage before, during, and after the concert—this is apparently as routine in Singapore as the performance of the national anthem, at the beginning of the concert, via two ancient loudspeakers suspended somewhere near the stage. The sound is ghastly. No one sings along. I stand motionless, respectful, sweat already pouring down my neck. Lizards are climbing up the walls.

Nevertheless, the concert is successful, and the Singapore audience is grateful. After the concert things start to look up. A young Chinese doctor takes me in tow for a visit to the Singapore underworld. At midnight we end up in garishly lit Bugis Street, one short block so crowded with little sidewalk tables that we can hardly wind our way between them. Painted transvestites, prostitutes, gigolos, and pimps, rakishly dressed in all the colors of the rainbow, are jostling one another and us while we search for an uncrowded table. Still wearing my white tie and tails, I am surprisingly inconspicuous. My doctor friend lays me ten-to-one that I cannot tell who, in this crowd, are the men and who are the women. I decline. To bed at four A.M., after packing bags for the hop to Hong Kong in the morning.

After a concert in Hong Kong, I went on to Macao. The *China Mail* described my visit as follows:

THINGS ARE REALLY SWINGING IN MACAO
Tourism is booming, hotel rooms are booked out, woman wrestlers are going to wrestle—and on the cultural front world-famous violinist Henri Temianka will give a recital at the Don Pedro Theatre tomorrow night at 9:00 P.M.

Macao must be the only place in the world where the performing artist walks straight from his bedroom onto the stage. The Portuguese government sponsors the concert series, which takes place in an auditorium on the top floor of the Municipal Library. As part of the contract the artist enjoys the government's hospitality in the form of a large and comfortable bedroom overlooking Red China across the river. When it came time for the concert, I turned my back on China, took violin in hand, opened the bedroom door, and bowed to the audience. Later I signed the guest book that contained such names as Benjamin Britten and Helen Traubel.

After Macao, I returned to the mysterious West. On the long flight home I succumbed to another incorrigible hobby. After a couple of martinis, Tom Swifties came tumbling off the assembly line as I observed the faces, figures, and eating habits of the passengers, and began to fantasize:

Give me another pork chop, he said swinishly.
I lost my toupée, he stated baldly.
He pinched her bottom, asininely.
I sat on my Strad, he said brokenly.
We're going to operate, he said incisively.

You've got a coronary, the doctor said heartily.
We're all out of flowers, she said lackadaisically.

Life on the circuit in the States is not too different.
It's a hot and humid summer day, and I am about to
solo with the Philadelphia Orchestra at the open-air
Robin Hood Dell. I am to play Lalo's popular Symphonie Espagnole with Dimitri Mitropoulos. The rehearsal
goes well enough, but we have no sooner begun the
concert than the first ominous drops of rain begin to
splash on his bald pate and my precious violin. Both of
us pretend to ignore it. The orchestra players move a
little farther back into the shell; they are not as exposed
as we. It begins to rain harder, and still harder. In the
audience people put up their umbrellas or cover their
heads with programs and newspapers. My fingers slide
and slither across the strings. The water streams freely
down the conductor's cranium and neck. Neither of us
is going to be the first to yield. Then a hand on my
shoulder: the manager, less prideful and fanatical than
the performers, has come to stop the show.

One time I arrived in a small Midwest farming community to give a recital. The president of the concert
organization took fierce pride in the fact that in twenty-
five years he had never missed a concert, but this time he
was confined to bed with a serious illness. Since the
imminent threat to his unblemished record was a grave
blow to his morale, we went to him, loading a small
upright piano on an open cart. My accompanist played
outside the front door, while I fiddled through the recital at the foot of the president's bed. His record was
saved, and we moved back to the auditorium to repeat
the entire program.

It brings back memories of World War II when I often
played for battle-shocked soldiers in the hospitals. Mira-
cles happened. Patients who, I was told, had been totally

withdrawn for months broke out of their isolation for the first time and began to communicate memories that antedated their war experience. I have also played in hospitals for tubercular patients and for friends who were dying of cancer. Their response was so powerful that I sometimes had difficulty maintaining my composure. In Montreal four associates and I played the marvelous Schubert quintet for Otto Klemperer, the German conductor I idolized, who had broken a hip. The room was crowded with doctors and nurses who came to listen. One of my most touching experiences was a surprise serenade for Dr. Max Osborn, a German art historian, who, after fleeing from Germany, lived, destitute, in a sordid little basement room in New York. Tipped off that it was his seventy-fifth birthday, I and my three associates in the Paganini Quartet somehow managed to squeeze into the little basement and play a Beethoven quartet. I doubt whether the most lavish gift of money could have meant more to the sick old man at that moment.

Sometimes a tour can be physically dangerous. After a concert in some remote community, I had gone to bed with a high fever and a serious flu. When I phoned ahead to cancel the concert we were to give the next evening, the committee chairman in charge reacted as if we were about to drop the H-bomb on her. I heard myself softheartedly promising that we would be there, the entire Paganini Quartet with its four celebrated Strads. More dead than alive I got into the rented car the next morning and sat next to the violist (who did the driving) in a state of abject misery, every once in a while dozing off. The road was a solid sheet of ice that January 23. Half a dozen times we miraculously escaped colliding with oncoming trucks slithering from side to side. I really didn't care. I just dozed off. A little later I opened my eyes—and saw a car coming straight at us, no more than twenty feet away. I blacked out at the moment of impact. When I came to, I was wedged in our wrecked car. My very first thought was, "Thank God, now I don't have to play the concert." My second thought was, "What happened to the violin?" Ultimately ambulances and tow trucks arrived, and I ended up in the hospital in Hillsdale, Michigan. All I could talk about was my violin. Where was it? Had it been damaged? At one in the morning two state troopers brought it to my hospital bed. I gingerly opened the case. Every movement I made caused the most agonizing pain, but the famous Strad was without a scratch. The reason? Precious violins are protected as no human being is. Wrapped in heavy silks, bedded in a form-fitting velvet-lined leather case, my precious Stradivarius was far better equipped than I to stand the impact of that head-on collision. I had always been especially worried about my priceless historical violin, and the many terrible things that could happen to it. The accident changed all that. I suddenly realized that my violin could take care of itself; the one to worry about was me.

At times in the hospital I started thinking about a special concert program that would be medically oriented. It would include such works as Beethoven's string quartet, Opus 132, the slow movement of which bears the inscription "Holy Song of Thanksgiving by one recovering from an Illness," Grieg's "Heart Wounds," and Marin Marais' "Gallbladder Operation." Marais, a seventeenth-century Frenchman, was one of the first composers to engage in writing program music. His "Gallbladder Operation" for viola da gamba and harpsichord bears such annotations by the composer as "The patient is bound with silken cords," "He screameth," etc., etc. At that thought I lost interest in the program.

Three weeks after the accident I told my orthopedist that I wanted to resume what was left of my concert tour. He replied that I was out of my mind and that he would not assume the responsibility for the decision. I went anyway. It was a novel experience. Wheelchairs at every airport upon departure and again upon arrival. Wheelchairs to get me backstage, where a bed or couch had been readied for me. Painkillers before and after every concert, and plentiful supplies of brandy. I wore a brace so tight that I could barely breathe, and I moved my bow with the greatest difficulty. Never mind, I was active again, making music. Perhaps no one who is not a musician can understand how powerful a force this musicmaking is. I am deeply convinced that my recovery was greatly speeded up by my premature activity, not endangered as the doctor had anticipated. During the first week I barely made it from the wheelchair concealed behind the curtain to the center of the stage. I put on a good act, and the public never knew.

There is an extraordinarily close relationship between the practitioners of music and medicine. On Tuesday evenings when in Los Angeles, I conducted the Los Angeles Doctors Symphony Orchestra, which consists of about seventy general practitioners, internists, gynecologists, ophthalmologists, pediatricians, radiologists, psychoanalysts, dentists, even veterinarians, some of whom drive fifty miles to attend rehearsals. The orchestra is long on violins, short on brass. Two of the bass players and one bassoonist are women. When there are gaps in the ranks for which no doctors are available, the members relent sufficiently to permit the inclusion of a doctor's wife or a nurse. In desperate situations—say the absence of a first trombone player, which is as conspicuous as a missing front tooth—no questions are asked: it is assumed that anyone who can play the trombone has been a patient at some time or other, or at least has watched *Dr. Kildare*. Naturally, the quality of the players varies. Dr. Bernard Korn, a past president of the orchestra, played the Kabalevsky violin concerto as a soloist with orchestra—from memory. The performance was as smooth as a tonsillectomy.

Sometimes I was asked why I bothered with amateurs when I have a first-rate professional orchestra of my own. The answer is the doctors' enthusiasm and love for music inspired and refreshed me. After all the tragedy they witness in the course of their daily work, great music has a profound meaning in their lives. And when I worked with them, they ended up playing better than they can. It is really quite a phenomenon. Many warm friendships have developed.

Almost every year the Doctors Orchestra goes on a goodwill mission abroad, giving concerts for medical benefits, with every doctor paying his own way. We have raised money for a hospital in Peru, the Red Cross in Greece, and the Cancer Institute in Israel. Between concerts the doctors present learned papers at the universities, go sightseeing and souvenir-hunting, and do all the things other tourists do. When I didn't feel well, I kept it a deep dark secret, for fear of finding seventy doctors at my bedside, each with a different box of pills.

Prominent soloists are engaged to appear with the Doctors Orchestra. Which reminds me that Vienna too had a Doctors Orchestra. When they invited the tenor Leo Slezak to appear with them, he declined, stating, "I would rather have my appendix removed by the Vienna Philharmonic."

The medical profession is filled with men who had originally chosen music as their profession; conversely, a number of medical students have ended up in symphony orchestras. Boyd Neel, founder and conductor of a widely known English chamber orchestra, and later Dean of the Royal Conservatory in Toronto, for a while tried to pursue both professions simultaneously. At the conclusion of his debut concert in London he had to be rushed to the hospital under police escort to deliver a baby. The next day the obstetrics profession lost a practitioner. Dr. Jerome Gross, an eminent surgeon in Cleveland, continued to give concerts as a violinist, including solo appearances with the prestigious Cleveland Orchestra. Jean-Pierre Rampal, the world's most celebrated flautist, was a third-year medical student when he switched to the musical profession. The vicissitudes of World War II forced Andries Roodenburg, a Dutch concert violinist, to earn his livelihood as a specialist in internal medicine, which was his original training. At night he exchanged scalpel and stethoscope for violin and bow, and continued to make major appearances with such orchestras as the Buffalo Symphony under William Steinberg. When I last saw Roodenburg, he expressed his frustration at having to spend so much of his time away from his music. Dr. Leo Eloesser, at one time a chest surgeon of great prominence in San Francisco, would have been lost to the world of medicine had he not been turned down after auditioning for a job as second fiddle in the Heidelberg Symphony Orchestra. He celebrated his ninetieth birthday with a flying trip around the world, interspersed with attendance at medical congresses from Buenos Aires to Tokyo and string quartet sessions with fellow fanatics everywhere. Music must be a lifegiving force.

5

The Virtuoso in Shirtsleeves

Would you believe that Yehudi Menuhin stands on his head every day as part of his Yoga exercises, and that he once hired a taxi in Dallas and drove nonstop to Los Angeles in thirty-five hours, taking turns at the wheel with the cabbie? That Isaac Stern likes to keep two different TV programs going in his hotel suite, simultaneously making outgoing calls on one telephone and answering incoming calls on another? That David Oistrakh traveled to his concerts with a tape recorder slung over his shoulder on which he listened to the gurgles of his grandchild? That Gregor Piatigorsky for years made only right-hand turns when he drove because he couldn't make left-hand turns? That many musicians are great cooks, bartenders, and ping-pong players? That one musician friend wired his collection of musical instruments and equipped them with lightbulbs and lampshades, so that his whole house was illuminated by trombones, bull fiddles, and bassoons?

Who are these colleagues of mine, these strange men in penguin suits whom the public applauds and admires from afar? They are egomaniacs, Christlike altruists, hermits, extroverts, introverts, wits, halfwits, and eccen-

trics. They range from Albert Schweitzer to Oscar Levant; they are as divergent as Yehudi Menuhin and Duke
Ellington. Sometimes we sit up until the small hours of
the morning, playing music or exchanging the latest
anecdotes from Buenos Aires and Vladivostok or copying the latest recipes from Paris and Rome. For most of
the great virtuosos love to eat, cook, and tell stories, as
well as play music.

A recipe of mine that was in a cookbook devoted to
recipes by concert artists won a prize in a contest. That
prize means more to me than the one I won fiddling in
the Wieniawski Contest. If you missed it, you can't
afford this yawning vacuum in your life. Here it is:

WIENER SCHNITZEL AS I COOK IT

1 pound veal cutlets	*½ cup butter, margarine,*
2 eggs	*or other frying fat*
1 cup bread crumbs	*1 lemon*
salt to taste	*pepper to taste*
1 to 2 cloves garlic	

FIRST   Buy, borrow, or steal choice filets of veal and
have them pounded. Dip them on both sides into beaten
eggs, then into bread crumbs, and repeat this process *da
capo* and *ad libitum*. Salt as desired.

SECOND   Rub garlic into frying pan. Melt generous
amount of butter, margarine, or other fat for frying until
very hot.

THIRD   Place filets in frying pan and thoroughly brown
on both sides until dark brown. Turn heat down, cover,
and allow filets to simmer for half an hour.

FOURTH   Shortly before removing filets, squeeze fresh
lemon juice over them and sprinkle with fresh ground
pepper.

Serves 4.

At the end of the recipe the editor of the cookbook added:

> NOTE   Mr. Temianka prefers a mixture of butter and margarine for frying and also suggests that garlic lovers may squeeze garlic juice over filets instead of rubbing pan, but *molto moderato.* Furthermore, he directs you to garnish with boiled new potatoes or whipped potatoes; serve with a fresh green salad, a stein of dark German beer, and imported German (Düsseldorf) mustard, and you have a dinner fit for a conductor!

There must be a relationship between sensitive ears and sensitive palates, for the love of good eating and drinking seems to me to be more prevalent among musicians than among members of any profession. I think I first became aware of the love affair between Music and Gastronomy when, as a young student, I met the violinist Jacques Thibaud, who was ideally suited for the career of a virtuoso. While many of the prominent artists live in a perpetual state of anxiety and fear, Thibaud carried himself with the careless air of a grand seigneur. On a number of afternoons I dined with this Prince Charming prior to concerts scheduled for the evening. Many artists at such a time are unable to get anything down except a poached egg or milk toast and weak tea. Not Thibaud. We had a round of double-sized *apéritfs,* and then Thibaud turned to the menu and the wine list and gave them the benefit of his most solemn attention, as befits a French gourmet of the highest order. He planned the dinner with as much care as a concert program and the results were equally felicitous. He treated guests and waiters alike with the exquisite courtesy of the true gentleman. We spent most of the afternoon around the table, winding up the proceedings with the finest cognac and a great many stories. What particularly stands out in my memory is that even on these very

earliest occasions, Thibaud never patronized me though
I was then only a youthful student.

Thibaud's passions in life were women, food, wine,
and music, in any order. He once went on an amorous
escapade, covering his tracks with a flurry of telegrams
to his wife at home:

CONCERT IN BERLIN FANTASTIC SUCCESS. SEVEN ENCORES.
LOVE. JACQUES.

ROME RECITAL SOLD OUT. IMMEDIATELY REENGAGED. JE
T'EMBRASSE. JACQUES.

WARSAW CONCERT UNBELIEVABLE TRIUMPH. MILLE BAIS-
ERS. JACQUES. Finally he returned home. During dinner
the servant brought a telegram for Madame Thibaud on
a silver salver:

BRUSSELS APPEARANCE SENSATIONAL. RAVE REVIEWS. I MISS
YOU. JACQUES.

I don't know whether Jacques tried to utter the time-
honored "I can explain everything," but if he did, the
words were lost in the fracas.

In the course of one of our periodic meetings Thibaud
reported on the culinary ecstasies he had experienced.
He had just returned from a concert in Lyon in the
South of France. As a matter of course, he made his
traditional pilgrimage to the nearby Restaurant de la
Pyramide, one of the world's most celebrated restaurants. There he could choose from the most fantastic
gastronomical productions, a feast for the eye as well as
the palate: whole saddles of hare, ducks, woodcocks, par-
tridges, quails, all presented on huge silver platters.
There had been a *Barquette de moules sur un lit d'épinards*
—mussels cooked in white wine, wrapped in a buttery
boat-shaped pastry, served on a bed of spinach, and covered with a delicate rose-colored sauce.

During the leisurely conversation that punctuated the
three-hour feast, Thibaud asked Monsieur Point, the legendary owner of the Pyramide, what he considered the

most difficult dish in the world to prepare. Monsieur Point thought long and hard. Finally he answered, slowly, *"oeufs sur le plat"*—fried eggs. Thibaud almost fell off his chair. They spent the rest of the afternoon in a discussion of the utmost profundity dealing exclusively with the subject of fried eggs.

Stories abound attesting to musicians'—especially composers'—love of good food and drink. Gioacchino Rossini, who wrote such operas as *William Tell*, spent the second half of his life planning new gastronomic recipes instead of operas. One famous dish, *Tournedos Rossini*, is an enduring monument to his culinary talents. Rossini, it is said, composed with such facility and became so obese that he preferred to rewrite a page of music when it fell to the floor, rather than pick it up. Max Reger, a German composer of immoderate productivity, was equally immoderate in his eating and drinking habits. Watching him down a whole row of bottles of beer, the English conductor Sir Henry Wood declared, "I knew he had a tremendous output—but his input is even greater." After Reger played Schubert's "Trout" Quintet at a friend's house one evening, an admirer sent him a magnificent trout in token of appreciation. Acknowledging the gift, Reger offered to play Haydn's "Ox" Minuet the next time around.

George Szell was so addicted to good food that he couldn't bear the thought of entrusting the choice and preparation of the menu to a mere railway chef. We often traveled by train from Glasgow to Edinburgh for an evening concert, and Szell arrived at the railway station almost collapsing under the weight of bottles of the finest wines, caviar, lobster, French sourdough bread, Viennese apple strudel, and all the things that make the life of a virtuoso bearable. Behind him staggered the orchestra's factotum, carrying buckets of ice, dishes, glasses, etc. Of course, we did not consume these trea-

sures prior to the concert. They were carefully deposited
in the dressing room backstage to await the return train
trip. Throughout the concert we worried about the gradually melting ice supply, rearranging the bottles and tins
between the overture and the symphony and again during the intermission. The last piece on the program always seemed endless. But it was worth all the trouble.
No banquet at the Ritz ever compared with our supper
on the midnight train home. We enjoyed many more in
years to come.

Szell, whose glorious conducting career ended with
his death in 1970, was often portrayed as a high priest of
humorless solemnity, dedicated to his music to the exclu-
sion of everything else. Those who have this image of
him would be amazed if they could read the letters he
wrote to me from all over the world. Here is one he sent
from Australia:

Dear Friend,
   Just now I bought a new bottle of Shaeffer's fountain
pen ink (the kind that you tip before opening so as to let
some ink flow into a small compartment—which makes
it easier to fill the pen). There's a label on the bottle with
the following admonition:
   SCREW TIGHTLY BEFORE TIPPING
   What would you think of making it obligatory to hang
this sign around the necks of all hotel chambermaids?
                              Yours very cordially,
                              Szell

Clearly, Szell valued my opinion in such matters.
   At social gatherings Szell and I made a hit with an act
we had practised assiduously: the Mendelssohn concerto, performed as it had possibly never been performed before. Standing behind me, Szell would hold
my bow, coordinating his up and down strokes with the
movements of my left hand on the strings. To make this

spectacular stunt more plausible, I once had a doctor friend put my right arm in a plaster case and explained to our audience that, unwilling to disappoint them despite a recent accident, I had called upon George Szell to save the evening. Grinning from ear to ear, George thereupon plowed into the Mendelssohn concerto with diabolical zest.

Musicians generally avoid eating heavily, if at all, before concerts, but they make up for it afterward. I once took David Oistrakh, his wife, Tamara, and their son, Igor, to the Farmer's Market in Los Angeles, the outdoor supermarket to end all supermarkets. It has dozens of stalls serving cooked food of a hundred different nationalities. I asked the Oistrakhs to remain seated while I purchased vittles for the whole party. Knowing their appetites—they were full-bellied heavyset Russians—I bought enough to feed a regiment. When I returned to our table, they had all disappeared. They came back, one by one, staggering under mountains of food they had purchased: Russian borscht and piroshki, Mexican tamales, Jewish cheesecake, Italian ravioli, Spanish paella, Japanese sushi, Chinese won ton soup, Austrian apple strudel, and plain American hamburgers. I was appalled. Half an hour later the table had been picked clean as if by a swarm of locusts.

Early on I had discovered Oistrakh's idea of a "light" supper when we went to Frascati's immediately following our concert at the Shrine Auditorium. When he asked what I had ordered and I said "steak," he shuddered. "How can you eat such heavy food so late at night?" he inquired solicitously. "And what did *you* order?" I asked. Well, Oistrakh had ordered a huge platter of chopped liver, followed by blintzes with sour cream, all washed down with a pitcher of beer. After that, I knew what to prepare when he came to our home.

Oistrakh's comments on life in this country and in

Russia were priceless. When I mentioned John Kennedy's razor-thin 1960 victory over Richard Nixon, he said, "That would have been impossible in my country; one of the two candidates would have had ninety-nine percent." One day he asked me to show him the "Jewish Quarter." I drove him to nearby Bel-Air and showed him the palaces of some of the movie magnates and captains of industry. Oistrakh's jaw dropped in amazement. The Moscow ghetto was never like this.

The happiest times have always been when we have chamber music at our house—veritable orgies of informal musicmaking, gastronomy, and story-swapping, with everybody in shirtsleeves. The warmth of musical and human empathy is unique. As we play, unrehearsed, a quartet of Beethoven or Mozart, there are extraordinary flashes of insight, thrilling moments of truth when we share the same concept of an exquisite phrase, sculpt the same melodic line, linger and savor the same *ritardando* or *diminuendo*. In those moments we spontaneously look up from our music, exchanging ecstatic smiles and glances. It is a level of spiritual communication granted few human beings.

Among all these heartwarming experiences one chamber music session stands out as perhaps the most extraordinary of all. On a quiet Sunday afternoon the phone rang. It was Isaac Stern, who had just landed at Los Angeles International Airport having unexpectedly caught an earlier plane. He wanted to know if it would be possible to scare up a couple of quartet partners for the evening. Such improvised sessions were not unusual, but when Isaac called from the airport, he had given me a two-hour ultimatum.

Fortunately, I was in luck, and as soon as the quartet had been completed, I phoned to invite a few friends, in accordance with the best traditions of such evenings. One of them was the president of a society that annually presents a series of quartet concerts in Los Angeles. The Paganini Quartet, of which I was the leader, had appeared there frequently, until the society adopted a new policy under which "local" musicians were no longer to be invited. Los Angeles had come of age and was going international. I had never commented on this decision, but when the society president asked me who was playing quartets at my house that evening, I said airily, "Oh, just a bunch of local musicians." The four of us were playing a Beethoven quartet when he arrived, a little late, and found Jascha Heifetz playing first violin, Isaac Stern second, myself handling a big viola, and Gregor Piatigorsky playing the cello. Piatigorsky, Heifetz, and I all lived in Los Angeles, and Stern is a native Californian. I relished the stunned expression on the society president's face—and I never heard any further remarks about "local musicians."

The name Heifetz has entered the language as a synonym for perfection. I have heard people groping for a superlative that would adequately describe perfection, in one field or another, then blurt out, "He is the Heifetz of martini mixers!" Because Heifetz never questioned his reputation, I believed the stories that he played only the first violin part at string quartet sessions. Usually he invited a third violinist to sit on the sidelines, to play second violin in case the original second violinist developed an uncontrollable urge to play first violin. So this particular night I had a problem. Isaac Stern could hardly be expected to play second fiddle all evening. The chamber music sessions at our house were always totally democratic and relaxed. It was not only a matter of camaraderie and modesty; everyone felt that playing second violin genuinely enriched his experience. Playing second violin is like being inside the music: the first violin may get most of the tunes, but the second gets a closeup view of the marvelous changes of harmony, the rich texture, and the interplay among the four instruments.

My problem was solved when, after finishing the first quartet, we all stood up and I turned to Isaac, saying, "Would you like to choose the next piece?" "Ah," responded Stern, "you want me to play first violin?" And, taking no chances, he immediately moved into a strategic position, blocking the first chair. Heifetz graciously acquiesced, and we were in business. But Jascha did more than acquiesce: he strove to adapt himself to the leadership of the first violin, willingly subordinating himself, revealing again the drive for perfection that is the essence of the authentic Heifetz legend. It was an unforgettable evening.

Freddie Schang, my concert manager, wrote in the guest book: "Tonight was the night that I learned the way to love quartets—you must cuddle up and be close."

Schang was right. You must sit so close, preferably on the floor, that the fiddlers have just enough room left to draw their bows. That's communication.

Piatigorsky's evening never finished with the last quartet. Enormously tall, distinctly resembling the late boxer Primo Carnera, he sank into an overstuffed armchair, chainsmoked cigarettes, and, sustained by generous helpings of Scotch, held forth by the hour in a Russian accent of immeasurable thickness.

One never knew what to expect next. On one occasion he seemed to be intoxicated by a new subject he had been investigating. "I have been studying the love life of the pigs," Piatigorsky announced with deadly seriousness. "It is absolutely fascinating," he added, proceeding to treat us to a two-hour monologue that was as explicitly clinical as anything by Kinsey or Masters and Johnson.

Strangely enough, the cello has little box-office appeal. Size has nothing to do with it, for the violin, which is smaller, and the piano, which is larger, do much better.

Perhaps, in the puritanical era that lies just behind us, the explicit wrapping of legs around the instrument, combined with its deep, sensuous sound, provoked intolerable guilt feelings on the part of the audience. If the theory has any validity, the cello should now be in for a grand renaissance, emerging as a new kind of sex symbol. Which reminds me that some years ago the manager of a chic department store in London angrily confronted a charming young lady who was trying on a dress. "Madame," he said, "the salesgirls complain that you are making obscene motions while trying on our dresses. This is a respectable store," "But," answered the charming young lady, "I am Raya Garbousova, the concert cellist. I am only trying to make sure that my cello will fit."

Like all good Russians, Piatigorsky was happy only when he was miserable. One day he told me he had dislocated his shoulder and could not play the cello. "Unfortunately," he added, "it is not permanent!"

There are basically two kinds of musicians: those who loathe practicing and those who must compulsively keep their hands on their instruments, six, seven, eight hours a day. I belong to the first category and have never been able to understand the second. I believe there really is such a thing as practicing too much: by overpracticing, one can become a robot, a human computer, spewing out notes with incredible, deadly perfection. Fritz Kreisler hated to practice. I have seen him learn a piece on the stage in front of three thousand people, looking over his accompanist's shoulder and trying to memorize the piece he was practically sightreading. The glowing gypsylike warmth of his playing more than compensated for all the minute imperfections. Yehudi Menuhin, who was the most famous prodigy of our time, has some of that same nonchalance. One leisurely day we drove together to Stockton, where we had a concert that evening. We

spent a relaxed afternoon at the hotel; almost all performers take a good nap before a concert. Around five
o'clock Yehudi jumped out of bed, threw a couple of
scores on my bed, and asked me to follow them while he
whistled the music. The two pieces, one by Arthur Benjamin, the other by Camargo Guarnieri, two contemporary composers, appeared on that evening's printed program. Yehudi had planned to learn them, but there
hadn't been time. He disappeared into the bathroom and
began to shave and whistle. Soon he reappeared with his
face covered with soap, the music emerging from behind
a mass of white blobs.

I had to stop him after four bars because he had
skipped a couple of notes. I made the correction, and he
continued. A little later I had to stop him again. Thus we
continued to the end. Then Yehudi started again at the
beginning. He did not repeat the old mistakes but made
a smaller batch of new ones. On the fourth try the piece
was note-perfect. Then we rehearsed the other piece.
That evening Yehudi played both compositions from
memory without a flaw.

Practicing is a sublimated form of slavery: the virtuoso
is in its bondage for life. Whether one practices much or
little is a matter not merely of his mental and emotional
makeup, but of his physiology as well. One virtuoso may
be battling incipient arthritis while another just bounces
along. Some are blessed and others are cursed.

A lot of musicians are gadgeteers. Emil Telmanyi, the
Hungarian violinist who married the daughter of Danish composer Carl Nielsen, had his guest bathroom at the
top of a flight of stairs. To save his friends the embarrassment of finding the room occupied at the end of an
arduous climb, he installed a red-and-green-traffic-light
system, visible from the ground level, that was operated
by the bolt that secured the bathroom door. When I was
in Vienna recently, I found that my friend Rudi Buch-

binder, a young Austrian pianist, had removed the in-
nards of his old upright piano and singlehandedly installed an opulent liquor bar. The outward appearance
of the piano was unchanged. It was only after Rudi
touched a secret sliding panel that I discovered how
greatly the piano had been improved. Heifetz too loves
gadgets, and the phone is one of them. There was a
period when Heifetz appeared to set considerable store
by my judgment. He would phone to ask my advice, and
although he never followed it, he would always phone
again when the next problem arose. Perhaps I should not
have said that he consulted me. He would make a statement, and then, after a strategic silence, I would walk
into the trap and give my opinion. At one point, after a
lifetime of concertizing, he had remembered the injunc-
tion of his master, Leopold Auer, that every artist has an
obligation to pass his heritage on to the next generation.
Heifetz was about to give his first master class and he was
concerned. On this occasion Heifetz informed me that
he was planning to audition not only players, but even
those who merely wanted to audit the class. I pointed out
that this was contrary to all custom and that there were
perfectly respectable teachers who had long since given
up playing and who would be needlessly humiliated if
they were compelled to audition. But Heifetz didn't see
it that way. "If they don't audition, they can't attend,"
he said with finality.

Not long thereafter he called me again. He had seen
an announcement of my own forthcoming master class
and wanted to come and listen. "Not unless you audition
first," I answered drily. I have rarely heard Heifetz laugh
with such delight.

In San Francisco one day I came upon an enchanting
cartoon of Heifetz, inspired by an interview that contained the absurd statement, "Heifetz's playing is perfect, regardless of whether he holds the violin above or

below his chin." The cartoon showed Heifetz playing while holding the violin in his mouth, and it showed two little old ladies in the audience, one saying to the other, "He says he can *feel* the music better this way."

The cartoon never made the printed page, but I was allowed to make several copies of it, one of which I presented to Heifetz when we had our next quartet session. Heifetz, an inveterate practical joker, is convinced to this day that I cooked up the whole thing myself, a fact that really impressed him. At any rate, he asked me to autograph the drawing, and in return I asked him to autograph my copy. He did, with undisguised skepticism, for he wrote on the drawing, *"Si non e vero, e ben trovato,"* which, loosely translated from the Italian, means, "True or not, it's damned clever!"

While some musicians go through life totally humorlessly, others will lay their careers on the line for a practical joke. The Concertgebouw Orchestra briefly had an eccentric French concertmaster who one night stood in a darkened doorway waiting for a cop to pass on his beat. When he finally heard approaching footsteps, he violently kicked the door and started running with his fiddle case. Naturally the cop ran after him and locked him up for the night. The next morning, when his identity was revealed, the Frenchman indignantly protested that Holland was a police state where a man couldn't have a little exercise without being harassed and persecuted.

I used to specialize in irreverent parodies of all my colleagues, playing "God Save the Queen" in the style of each famous violinist, and imitating his manner of speaking as well as the way he walked on stage. I was too successful: several times my imitations caused a major diplomatic crisis. Prior to one of Mischa Elman's periodic London visits I had parodied his high-pitched voice and inflections. I would phone various friends of his and announce in a grotesque falsetto, "This is Mischa." It cracked them up.

Shortly afterward Elman arrived in town and began phoning his friends. To his amazement one and all collapsed with laughter. The more he insisted "This is Mischa," his voice rising higher with excitement, the more hysterical the laughter became. Only after he angrily slammed down the receiver did the truth begin to dawn.

On another occasion I had imitated Huberman's playing shortly before his arrival. Even though I worshiped him, I felt no compunction in emulating his shuffling gait, his grotesquely protruding lower lip, his peculiar mannerisms. As the great man came out on the stage at his next concert, there was such embarrassing hilarity that my friends had to get up and leave. The strangest twist, and it was what made them laugh the most, was that it suddenly seemed as if *Huberman* was parodying *me*.

Yehudi Menuhin's wife had heard of my parodies and asked me to do them at a party, in Yehudi's presence. Afterward Yehudi drew me aside and asked anxiously, "Do I really play like that?" I succeeded in allaying his fears.

When musicians are at their best, they are among the world's most lovable, generous, and unpretentious beings. When it comes to supporting good causes, whether in music, politics, medicine, or education, they donate their services, and sometimes their money, lavishly and with limitless affection. Yehudi Menuhin, Isaac Stern, Victor Borge, Gian Carlo Menotti, and Gregor Piatigorsky all came to raise funds for my deficit-ridden California Chamber Symphony as if it were the most natural thing in the world to do, sometimes traveling thousands of miles for the purpose. Musicians of every faith, from Pablo Casals to Jascha Heifetz, journeyed to Israel to demonstrate their devotion to that valiant music-loving country, generously giving moral and artistic support. Zubin Mehta, a Parsi Indian, flew to Israel to conduct the Israel Philharmonic during the Six-Day War, in magnificent disregard for his own safety. Dame Myra Hess, that noble English pianist, remained in London during the blitz, maintaining public morale with daily concerts in the heart of the burning city. Casals, Toscanini, Huberman, and Adolf Busch set examples of integrity and courage during the Mussolini and Hitler days. It may also come as a surprise to some that so many great musicians remain modest, free of petty vanities. At our many memorable chamber music sessions at home friendly fights developed because violinists like David Oistrakh and Yehudi Menuhin insisted that they wanted to play second violin. I remember the time when a friend, a great European pianist, was in financial distress following his wife's catastrophic illness. Knowing that Artur Rubinstein was an admirer and friend of his, I phoned Rubinstein long-distance. Although Rubinstein, already past seventy, was due home very late that night after a concert and a strenuous flight, he invited me to an early breakfast the next morning. He wrote out a four-figure check in our friend's name, and handed it to me, saying, "If the situation were reversed, I know he would do the same for me."

Musicians can also be so petty and ungenerous that I sometimes wonder whether there is any other profession in which envy and jealousy are so shamelessly displayed. I have been present at dinner parties at which the whole evening's conversation was devoted to running down a distinguished but absent colleague. On such occasions it is impossible to overlook the fact that music is one of the most competitive professions. Even those who have reached the top seem to feel insecure, and their intolerance toward each other can be frightening. One day I went to a piano recital by Artur Schnabel. Afterward at a dinner party I saw Moriz Rosenthal, the famous last disciple of Franz Liszt who had given a piano recital that same afternoon. When he asked me whether I had heard his concert, I truthfully told him why I hadn't. He laughed hollowly, walked over to the piano and sat down. "What did Schnabel play?" asked the sprightly octogenarian sarcastically. "Beethoven's Sonata Opus 57," I answered. "Ha!" muttered Rosenthal, and played the first few phrases abominably, full of the most appalling clinkers. "That's how Schnabel plays it," he said. "Now, let me show you how *I* play it," and he played the entire sonata from start to finish, in a desperate effort to prove to me, a young whippersnapper, how superior he was to Schnabel and how wrong I had been to go to Schnabel's concert instead of to his. All through dinner Rosenthal told caustic stories about his rival. After the dessert nothing could have prevented him from returning to the piano to play the remaining pieces of Schabel's entire program—first the way Schnabel had supposedly played them, then the way Rosenthal played them. I was allowed to name only one piece at a time, in order to give him more opportunities to snort, "Ha!" before he went on to the next parody. Some time later I had dinner with Schnabel. Schnabel knew that I was fond of cigars, so after dinner he offered me a splendid Havana, with the comment, "You will observe that my cigars are not equipped with gold bands bearing my name. I leave that to my colleague Artur Rubinstein." Rubinstein, at that time, was more successful in America than Schnabel. That he could even afford his own personalized cigars was more than the flesh could bear.

But all this is child's play compared to the scenes that occur night after night in the greenroom backstage, following a concert. (Why that strange name? Could it be because so many musicians are green with envy while hypocritically congratulating a colleague after his performance?) The greenrooms of famous concert halls are vibrant with history. All four walls are covered with autographed pictures of the immortals who have performed there. Tschaikovsky, Paderewski, Caruso, Rachmaninoff, and all the other glories of the past gaze down impassively at the busy crowds milling and elbowing their way through its narrow confines. For most greenrooms are hopelessly inadequate in size. After a concert at Carnegie Hall it is not unusual for a hundred or more "friends" to call on the triumphant soloist. Suffocating while interminably trapped on a narrow stairway, they finally manage to squeeze into the tiny greenroom, a few at a time. There they go through the ritual of shaking hands with the soloist, barely managing to stand their ground while being pushed from behind.

In Osaka I experienced a refreshing change from the usual routine. As I entered the greenroom at intermission several women were waiting for me. One promptly ripped the sweat-soaked shirt and undershirt off my back, proceeding to iron it on a board that had magically appeared. Another Japanese lovely threw me onto a couch and started massaging my back, while a third brought a bottle of beer. I was sorry when the bell rang announcing the end of the intermission.

Some artists go to extraordinary lengths to avoid actually congratulating their colleagues. One well-known cellist came to see me backstage after a concert. I strained to hear the expected compliment above the din of the crowd surrounding us. "I had a sold-out house in Minneapolis last night," he said, pumping my hand, and turned away. Lines more commonly used to escape the torment of complimenting a colleague are, "That Beethoven Concerto is certainly a marvelous piece," or "What a beautiful violin. What is it?" implying that such merit as the performance may have had was due entirely to the instrument. One possible gambit is to point out that the instrument doesn't play by itself. But there is a disadvantage in letting the adversary know that he has drawn blood. Far better to reply, "Yes, isn't it great? I paid only ten thousand bucks for it and was recently offered sixty-five thousand," which leaves the performer in possession of the battlefield.

A virtuoso is so used to being pampered, fêted, and flattered that some of us end up taking an awful lot for granted. Frederic Lamond, a Scottish-born pianist who achieved fame as a Beethoven specialist, partly because he looked astonishingly like Beethoven, once asked me to get him a guest room in my apartment house in London. After he left I received a letter from him. I assumed it was a thank you note and opened it casually. It began:

> Dear Mr. Temianka!
> I didn't like the apartment. My bedroom was much too cold, a lady in the room to my left took a bath at 1 A.M. every night, and the man on my right kept throwing his boots around the room so that I could never sleep.

Luckily he didn't hold it against me. The letter ended with cordial regards and expressed the hope that he would see me again on his next visit to London.

Almost every famous virtuoso is surrounded by a coterie of admirers, in some of whom friendship with the great man gradually assumes obsessive proportions; their humdrum lives are raised to a different plane. They may get to see the great man perhaps only once in the course of a year, either because he plays another concert in their city, or because they cheerfully travel halfway around the world for the sole purpose of basking in his presence, maybe for a few hours, maybe a few minutes. No matter. When they return home, they can report to all their friends, "As Artur said to me only yesterday . . ." or "I told Isaac. . . ." Only the first name is used— *bien entendu.* You never say Rubinstein or Stern—that's for the peasants. Indeed, how else is one to convey one's status, one's exquisite intimacy with the famous virtuoso? Sometimes I am perverse enough to pretend I don't know whom they are talking about. "Jascha who?" I will ask innocently, as if there were a choice between the one and only Jascha and maybe Jascha Picasso, Jascha Nixon, or Jascha Bernstein. It spoils their whole game. Some of them cling to their heros like barnacles, even bulldozing their way into exclusive supper parties following the concert. Bulldozing barnacles—now there's an image! The virtuoso is helpless. He is stuck with his hero-worshipers. His devoted friends have traveled hundreds of miles to visit him. They always come backstage when the virtuoso is most in need of privacy, demonstrating their special status by clasping him in an embrace of unilateral fervor.

After the concert they insist on being admitted to the virtuoso's dressing room immediately following his sweat-soaked return from the stage, even though the attendant assures them the virtuoso has pleaded for privacy until he has had a chance to change his clothes. "But," they say as they cut a swath through the crowd of autograph-seekers, "he is expecting me," suggesting that the virtuoso's heart will be broken if there is an instant's delay. So they barge in and find him changing his underpants.

Interestingly enough, most of these people settle for one virtuoso. He becomes their idol, the center of the universe. I knew one elderly woman who started virtually every sentence with "Artur. . . ." It seemed to have become a grammatical necessity. Some performers are astonishingly adept in dealing with their hero-worshipers. It was worth the price of admission just to watch, for instance, David Oistrakh beat a strategic retreat after a concert to the waiting cab, while smiling and nodding serenely at his fans.

Would the virtuoso be happier without his fans and admirers? Forbid it, Almighty God. He basks in the glory, the adulation, the affection, the hospitality, the offerings. A virtuoso cannot live by fees alone. When the concert is over, he sheds his penguin suit and is reborn in shirtsleeves. I have seen the then seventy-five-year-old Artur Rubinstein do an imitation of Pavlova as the Dying Swan, skittering across the room at four A.M. with arms aflutter, while someone else played the piano for him. I have heard Piatigorsky at dawn improvise a cello solo purporting to be a conversation in a Moscow street between Prokofiev and Shostakovich, the one represented by the bass register, the other by the strident notes of the upper string. None of us remembers which was which, so blissful was the effect of the all-pervading champagne bubbles. Virtuosos really are human.

6

Chamber Music:
the Highest Form of Art,
the Lowest Form of Entertainment

I became interested in chamber music at a very early age, and to me Mozart's string quartets and quintets have always seemed the purest form of musical ecstasy. Not, however, in the manner in which I heard them performed during my student days in Paris. Benevolent Parisian amateurs would invite me to participate in their slaughter of the sublime masterpieces of Mozart, Beethoven, and Debussy. My only incentive as a hungry student was the reward of a gastronomical orgy at the end of the evening. I soon learned to arrive at these parties later and later, until I had perfected the fine art of timing my arrival to coincide with the last cacophonic chords. On one of those occasions the first violinist's A string broke, and as it fell to the floor the cat began to play with it. *"Tiens, tiens,"* said the Frenchman, "look at the little kitty playing with his grandfather's intestines!"

It was only much later that string quartet playing began to have a different kind of meaning for me. But I

have never been able to understand the unconcern of
some amateur quartet players with such considerations
as beauty of sound, intonation, ensemble, or phrasing. It
would almost seem as if they were trying to prove that
great music survives, no matter what. One can only sur-
mise that what these amateurs hear inwardly while they
play bears no relationship to what comes out. Amateurs
seem to take their involvement in chamber music as an
article of faith, the way Hindus cleanse themselves in the
waters of the Ganges. Imagine dropping Clorox in the
Ganges before engaging in the ritual of purification! Let
me add immediately that some of my best friends are
amateurs whose devotion to chamber music sometimes
transcends humanity. At one of our sessions in San Francisco, one quartet player, a famous chest surgeon, was
interrupted by the telephone in the middle of a Haydn
quartet. He came back to his chair, planted the viola
firmly under his chin, and without saying a word
resumed where he had left off. It struck me that he
played faster than usual. Only when we had come to the
end of the composition did he excuse himself, explaining, "I must rush to the hospital. There's an emergency."

Some amateurs actually achieve high standards of excellence. Martin Kamen, the codiscoverer of Carbon 14,
gives a good account of himself in such complex works
as the Bartók quartets; he also plays the Bach solo sonatas
from memory on his viola. Simon Ramo, the triple
genius of science, industry, and business, methodically
investigates every violin bowing and fingering as if it
were an integral part of his TRW empire.

My professional involvement with chamber music
started quite early in my career. One day during my San
Francisco residence shortly after World War II began, I
received a long-distance call from Mrs. Elizabeth
Sprague Coolidge in Washington. I had known the legendary name for many years. What musician didn't?

Mrs. Coolidge had long been the *grande dame* of modern music. She had commissioned works by virtually every living composer of consequence, from Bartók to Stravinsky, and many of them had dedicated their compositions to her. The concert hall at the Library of Congress in Washington bears her name. Universities and colleges from one end of the country to the other had been able to organize chamber music concert courses thanks to her generosity. She was an undisputed patron saint of chamber music. Unfortunately, like the two other patron saints of chamber music of that period, Mrs. William Andrews Clark and Mrs. Gertrude Whittal, Mrs. Coolidge was almost totally deaf. It is extraordinary that this trinity of angels all shared the tragic defect of the greatest chamber music composer, Beethoven.

Nonetheless, Mrs. Coolidge could hear music and she lived with and for it all day long. She used a huge brass ear trumpet, and when she went to a concert, where she always had front-row seats, her chauffeur carried in an amplifying box large enough to have hidden a body. She continued to play the piano, with the aid of an amplification device built into the instrument, the end of which she plugged into her ear. She and I used to have marathon sonata-playing sessions that would end when I was totally exhausted, while she was barely hitting her stride, rosy-cheeked and animated. She was strong and imperious, a big, rawboned woman of frightening energy and impatience—and a whim of iron. On one occasion—she was well into her eighties—I phoned to say that I was in Boston. She asked me to come right over and I told her it would take me about an hour to get ready. Ten minutes later my phone rang. "This is Mrs. Coolidge's chauffeur, sir. I am downstairs. Mrs. Coolidge is waiting for you in the car outside." Mrs. Coolidge wanted what she wanted when she wanted it. She never inquired: she commanded and she expected to be obeyed.

When she was refused, she was visibly shocked, as if someone had rudely knocked her hat off.

Her first phone call to me from Washington was typical. She gave me the briefest explanation about a Beethoven Sonata and Trio Cycle that was due to begin at the University of Southern California in Los Angeles *the next evening.* There were to be five concerts on five consecutive evenings, all with different programs.

This is the kind of project that requires weeks or even months of dedicated preparation, and Antonio Brosa, the Spanish violinist who was to have played a key role in the concerts, had been suddenly taken ill. But Mrs. Coolidge, with a magnificent disregard of all logic, ordered me (there is no other word) to take the next train to Los Angeles. It would have been impossible to argue with her, and in any event, if I had turned her down, she probably would never have forgiven me. And I needed all the help I could get in starting my American career.

The next morning I found myself in the Frank Lloyd Wright house of the English cellist Warwick Evans, a magnificent specimen of a man. With him was Gunnar Johansen, an equally handsome Danish pianist and a ladykiller. An open box of cigars was within arm's reach at all times. It seemed ridiculous to contemplate any kind of serious rehearsal, since we had barely met and would have to play the first program the same evening. There seemed to be only one sensible thing to do: smoke the excellent cigars that were so hospitably tendered, drink the best martinis in Southern California, and listen to the marvelous stories and impersonations in which Warwick excelled. Nonetheless, and I would have no one think otherwise, we did play through the program from start to finish, and being experienced musicians with a background in chamber music, we stuck together through thick and thin.

The concerts went reasonably well, but the real fun

began afterward, when the three of us, joined by Otto Klemperer, arrived at the house of Alec Templeton, the blind pianist-comedian, with whom I was staying. Alec promptly sat down at the piano, Warwick stood up in front, and together they improvised the most ribald London music hall acts, parodying in a spirit of uninhibited exuberance and desecration the marvelous Beethoven tunes we had just played at the concert. All of us were helpless with laughter, except Klemperer, who watched us with an expression of total amazement. I think it was beyond his comprehension that anyone could find Beethoven's glorious music a subject for levity.

The argument as to precisely what constitutes chamber music has never been completely resolved. The official definition is music in which each player plays a *different* part, in contrast to an orchestra, in which a number of players (violinists for instance) all play the *same* part. For all practical purposes this means that there is generally not more than a handful of players, and a conductor is not normally required. The nature of the music is intimate. And since the most widely practiced form of chamber music is the string quartet, with only two violins, one viola, and one cello, the texture is extraordinarily transparent, requiring the highest degree of craftsmanship. It is a form of music that has long eluded those who relish the crashing of cymbals.

The small band of the initiated who attend quartet concerts constitute a sort of secret society that jealously guards its fancied supremacy. To those who shy away from it, it is known as the highest form of art, but the lowest form of entertainment. All of that is slowly changing, perhaps as a result of the stereo revolution. For now, in the narrow confines of the average living room, turning up all the dials makes it possible to have a string quartet sound like Judgment Day.

In any event, a professional string quartet is a union

of four musicians dedicated to the strangest proposition ever made: all men are born equal. In a string quartet someone is always slower than someone else, and the others inevitably have to adapt to the slowest rate. In its worst moments a string quartet appears like the hopeless entanglement of four umbilical cords. It is the artificial marriage of four grown men. Furthermore, since most quartet players are in fact married, a professional string quartet actually consists of eight human beings. Can you really expect the wife of the second violin to admit that the first violin is superior to her husband? Ten to one she says to him in the privacy of their bedroom, "Darling, you play much better than Temianka. Don't let that s.o.b. lord it over you." You begin to get an idea of the friction and hostilities that can be generated in a string quartet. It is a situation that makes for some terrible frustrations, as can be seen from the high incidence of suicide among string quartet players. Interestingly enough, it is always the second violin or the viola who breaks down. With few exceptions, the second violin is a frustrated man to begin with, otherwise he would play first violin.

Violists are forever trying to prove that the viola is a completely different instrument from the violin, and that violinists don't know how to play it. Actually the viola is only a bit bigger and lower in pitch, and playing it is like getting adjusted to a smaller or bigger bicycle. Whenever we had a jam session at home, distinguished colleagues like Oistrakh and Menuhin often played the viola, acquitting themselves with honor.

Why have cellists been immune to similar depression? I think the sheer size of the instrument bolsters the player's ego. He feels important, he looks important, and his instrument produces a bigger sound than the viola. At one party following a quartet concert, when my cellist thought I was out of earshot, I heard him boast to some admirers that the cello was really the heart and soul of the quartet. "It gives the rhythm, the heartbeat; it is the foundation on which everything rests," I heard him say. He had a point. In any event, just hearing him make the claim reassured me that he was unlikely to do away with himself. Musicians are entitled to all the ego satisfaction they can get.

Strangely, if first violinists and cellists are less inclined to suicide, they show a high incidence of premature death through heart attacks. Jack Gordon, leader of the Gordon Quartet, died of a heart attack at forty-nine; as did Alfred Dubois, leader of the Artis Quartet, at fifty-one; and Robert Maas, cellist of the Pro Arte and subsequently of the Paganini, at forty-seven.

String quartet aficionados frequently argue about the merits of the individual members of a famous string quartet, lauding one to the detriment of another. Note, however, that the argument almost invariably concerns the first violin or the cellist, particularly the latter. The virtuosity of the first violin is more or less assumed, since everyone knows he is the leader. But if you want to be recognized as a connoisseur, you must rave about the cellist. Never mind how he plays—just be sure to get your bid in first. Your expert opinion is repeated from listener to listener, spreading through the auditorium like wildfire. Your reputation is made. Don't waste your time on the second violin or viola. Nobody notices them. I know what I am talking about. For twenty years I was the leader of the Paganini Quartet. The story of how it got started matches anything in *Scheherazade.*

Toward the end of 1945 I made one of my periodic visits to Washington, this time to play the Beethoven Sonata Cycle at the Library of Congress, at the invitation of Mrs. Coolidge. One evening she suddenly asked, "Why don't you form a string quartet? I will engage you

to play the Beethoven Quartet Cycle at the Library of
Congress next month."

The Beethoven Cycle consists of seventeen major
works, each a monument and a milestone in the world
of chamber music. Mrs. Coolidge might just as well have
asked a theatrical producer, in the process of forming his
own repertory company, for a festival of all of Shake-
speare's plays, beginning this Friday. She was quite unable to understand my qualms, but after listening to me
for two minutes with a stiff face, while peering at me
through her gold-rimmed pince-nez, she mentally put
her hat back on her head and said, "All right, we'll do it
next October." This was starting at the top, and the
temptation was great. But then I thought of the enormous difficulties involved in getting the right partners.
I had long wanted to form a quartet, but never could find
the ideal players. I promised that I would inquire and
report back to her. Then I went on to New York to give
a Carnegie Hall recital.

I never went to a party more reluctantly or more ir-
resolutely than the one in New York on New Year's Eve,
1945. I almost didn't go. But I went, and another chance
encounter changed my life. At this particular rendez-
vous with destiny I had no sooner entered the front door
than I found myself looking into the eyes of Robert
Maas, who was then only forty-five, though he looked
far, far older: the tragic experience of World War II had
left an indelible mark. Until the war he had been the
cellist of the world-famous Pro Arte String Quartet, but
in the summer of 1939 he had returned to his native
Belgium for a vacation, leaving his associates in the
United States. The war separated them, and he eked out
a living by playing in a café in Brussels—under the constant threat of deportation because he refused to play for
the occupying German troops.

It was unmistakably he. There was no other face like

Robert Maas's. He had a huge bald dome, grizzled eye-brows as thick as mustaches, a big nose that jutted out, and a large mouth that curled up at the corners when he smiled, a little like the funny painted smile of a clown. At the back of his bald head was a little fringe of dyed hair that he meticulously combed at frequent intervals while fondly eyeing what could be seen of it by a side-ways mirror. He looked emaciated. He told me he had arrived only a few days earlier and had been introduced to a mysterious old lady who seemed much interested in music. She invited him to her home the following day. Robert went with his cello and played a Bach solo sonata for her.

As Robert arrived at this point in his story, I suddenly thought of Mrs. Coolidge's quartet. He had been a mar-velous cellist before the war, but how did he play now? How had the long years of illness, deprivation, and deg-radation affected his art? The next day he played a Bach sonata for me. The six solo sonatas of the great Johann Sebastian Bach, those for violin and those for cello, con-stitute the acid test by which the fraternity of string instrument players judges its individual members. In playing a Bach solo sonata, you stand naked before your judges. There is no piano or orchestra to shield you; every note must be there. The ultimate is demanded in control of the bow; the most intricate motions of left and right hand must be coordinated with the jeweled preci-sion of the finest Swiss watch. Some laymen may be bored by a Bach solo sonata, but a professional will im-mediately be ensnared, watching like a hawk from begin-ning to end, carefully weighing every note, solemnly deciding which way to cast his vote.

All the doubts I had entertained about Maas were magically dispelled after his first note. I knew instantly that I was in the presence of a master, a great cellist, and a great artist. His style of playing was monumental.

There was a throbbing, indestructible rhythm that drove the music on to its inevitable destiny, neither hurrying nor halting, and there was an extraordinary feeling of unity between him and his cello as he bent forward, controlling his instrument, driving his bow deep into the strings to produce a tone of unique vibrancy and breadth. His range of dynamics extended from the palest pastel blue to the most dramatic and violent reds, and in the bass register a fathomless black. Yet, for all his dramatic power and fervor, his playing was characterized by classic reserve and impeccable taste.

When Robert finished playing, he told me what had happened at the home of the mysterious old lady who had befriended him. She had asked him what he now proposed to do, what the future held for him. Maas had said he wanted to be, once again, a partner in a great string quartet. The old Pro Arte Quartet was no more, so he hoped to create a new quartet. The lady (Robert refused to divulge her name) had wanted to know what this would cost, and Maas had named what he thought was an astronomical sum. To Maas's amazement, the lady gave the plan her immediate endorsement and sent him on his way to find three partners. Robert's and my paths had clearly crossed.

Two days later I was introduced to Robert's mysterious patron saint. She was Mrs. William Andrews Clark, the widow of the copper king and United States Senator, one of the most incredible figures in American history. When Senator Clark died in 1925, at the age of eighty-six, he was the uncrowned king of Montana. According to Senator Robert LaFollette, he was "one of the hundred men who owned America." Senator Clark's fifteen-million-dollar Fifth Avenue mansion had a hundred and twenty-one rooms, thirty-one baths, four picture galleries, fifteenth- and sixteenth-century tapestries, statuary, French porcelain, and imported ceilings. It is some measure of Senator Clark's ego that, well past eighty and unable to understand why his wife did not provide him with a male heir, he sent her to a gynecologist. The senator had had two sons by a previous marriage, one of whom, William Andrews Jr., was the founder and long-time patron of the Los Angeles Philharmonic Orchestra.

Compared to the opulence with which the senator had surrounded himself, Mrs. Clark now lived modestly. Instead of a private railroad train, she merely had a gleaming limousine and a uniformed chauffeur; instead of the regal mansion, only a lavish apartment on upper Fifth Avenue overlooking Central Park, with a Peter Arno doorman, a maid, a cook, a secretary, and a withered old lady companion dancing attendance. As I was to discover later, she also had a rarely used, spectacular château in Santa Barbara and a rustic farm with five bathrooms and swimming pool not far from there.

As a young girl Mrs. Clark had lived in Montana, the daughter of a French-Canadian doctor. She was a gifted musician who studied the harp. When she was eighteen, Senator Clark became interested in her, and as his protégée she went to Paris to study music. A few years later he married her. She became deaf in her twenties, but she could still hear music with a hearing aid and, like Mrs. Coolidge, she lived for music.

Music was the only thing that could induce her to leave her apartment. Sitting in the front row at Carnegie Hall or Town Hall, equipped with the most advanced hearing aid, she drank in every note. When her health was particularly good, she thought nothing of attending two, even three concerts a day. On one occasion she attended a three P.M. matinée at Town Hall, stayed in her seat awaiting the five-thirty twilight concert, and returned for the evening recital at eight-thirty.

Every once in a while I meet people who derive a weird satisfaction from repeating ad nauseam that "money isn't everything." They would have loved meeting Mrs. Clark—a woman who could have everything that money could buy, yet who had been deprived of almost everything worth having. She had lost the sight of one eye early in life, and the strain in the one remaining eye severely limited her ability to read. One daughter died of meningitis early in her teens, and her surviving daughter was strangely withdrawn and had the curious habit of maneuvering backward while engaged in conversation, executing a series of mincing steps that ultimately landed her and her partner in conversation at the opposite end of the room. At one point the daughter bought a stupendous château on the Hudson for a reported half million dollars, and then spent a similar sum to remodel it. As the work approached completion she suddenly concluded that she would be frightened living in such a remote spot, and she never moved in.

Almost everything Mrs. Clark touched turned to tragedy, yet she perked up at news of a catastrophe. It was not that she rejoiced, but in a life of overwhelming boredom and isolation catastrophe meant unaccustomed drama, action, and to the extent that life was not snuffed out totally, the chance to do something constructive. On such occasions the air was filled with electric vibrations.

And so, thanks to Mrs. Clark, on June 6, 1946, the four members of what was to become known as the Paganini Quartet met for the first time in San Francisco. The Quartet created a sensation from the very beginning. After we had been rehearsing for only two weeks, RCA Victor offered us an exclusive recording contract. The following year we won the recording industry's award for the best recording of the year with our three Beethoven Opus 59 quartets, the "Rasoumovsky." Public curiosity was so great that our world debut at the University of California at Berkeley was sold out long in advance. We were in *Time* magazine. Chamber music, for so long the stepchild of the concert world, had come a long way. Our four concerts at the University of California were followed by a New York debut, two concerts sponsored by the New Friends of Music. Mrs. Coolidge's project, the Beethoven Quartet Cycle in six concerts at the Library of Congress, was followed by concerts across the United States and Canada, a series of recordings for RCA Victor, and a trip to Europe to play the Beethoven Cycle in Brussels and concerts in Paris, London, and elsewhere.

It would be impossible for a layman to understand the blood, sweat, and tears required to create and maintain a great string quartet. With only four people involved, every musical decision has to be arrived at by consensus or compromise, for if the leader imposes his will, sullen acquiescence will inevitably leave its mark on the quality of the performance. But arriving at an agreement can be unbelievably time-consuming. The dead sheet of music in front of the performer is only a set of primitive hieroglyphics, little dots etched on telegraph poles, little shorthand messages like "*p*" or "*f*" to indicate soft and loud. But how soft is soft, how loud is loud? The potential for a long-drawn-out argument over this kind of issue in a string quartet is beyond belief.

Sometimes in the course of these endless discussions I found myself thinking of the millions of children starving in Asia, or cancer research, or the H-bomb. In such moments I would wonder whether it all made sense, though the curious thing was that most of the time I was totally involved. The correct interpretation of a *crescendo* in bar eighty-four of the first movement of a Beethoven quartet was vastly more important to me than anything going on in the outside world, because this mad passion for relevant detail is at the core of all superior musicmaking. Contrary to the popular concept, great performers do not put their trust in "inspiration." Each piece of music demands thousands of tactical decisions and value judgments. If the decisions and judgments are correct, and if the performer has the technical ability to implement them, all the ingredients are there to inspire. Without these ingredients, inspiration is hot air.

7

Wood, Glue, and Genius

Shortly after my reunion with Robert Maas and my meeting Mrs. William Andrews Clark, Robert visited me in an uncontrollable state of excitement. He had just visited Emil Herrmann, the Lord Duveen of violin dealers, who had a penthouse on West Fifty-seventh Street next to Carnegie Hall. Here, in a two-story-high cathedral-like studio with huge windows, Emil Herrmann sat among his fabulous collection of Stradivari and Guarnieri violins and cellos. Robert had gone to Herrmann for the simple reason that he needed some new strings and wanted to have his bow rehaired.

As one entered the Herrmann penthouse, there was an anteroom with glass cases containing strings and rosin, tuning forks and mutes and metronomes, and all the things that violinists buy. On the walls were centuries-old posters and concert programs of Nicolò Paganini, and framed photos of Yehudi Menuhin, Jascha Heifetz, and all the other masters of sheepgut and horsetail. While Robert was delving into his pocket to pay for his strings, Mr. Herrmann came out of the throne room and, seeing Robert, motioned him in. "I want to show you something fantastic," he almost whispered. He tiptoed to one of the big glass cases and pointed out a set of four priceless Stradivarius instruments, two violins, a viola, and a cello.

"All my life I have had my eyes on these instruments," said Mr. Herrmann. "At one time they all belonged to Paganini. After his death in 1840 they were sold individually by his illegitimate son, Baron Achille. They remained separated for more than a century. One day when I was quite young," reminisced Mr. Herrmann, "I saw the viola. It was the first of the four instruments I became acquainted with.

"Do you know the history of this viola?" inquired Emil Herrmann, his eyes shining behind the thick lenses of his gold-rimmed spectacles. Maas learned that this was the viola for which Hector Berlioz, the great French composer, had been commissioned by Paganini to write the celebrated "Harold in Italy," which is based on Lord Byron's *Childe Harold*. The truth about the commission was shrouded in mystery. Paganini was maniacally stingy, so it was unlikely that Paganini, himself a composer, would have paid another composer to write music he could have written himself. Some believe the explanation is that Berlioz was then a sick man in financial difficulties. A group of friends and admirers wanting to help him, but knowing his fierce pride, decided upon a subterfuge. What could have been more flattering to a man of Berlioz's spirit than to have the great Paganini come to him with a commission? The money was handed to Paganini. There is a sequel that supports this version. When Paganini saw the completed score of "Harold in Italy," he refused to play it, claiming that he had not been cast in a starring role and that the orchestra had been given too much importance.

"The first time I saw this viola," said Herrmann, "a vague project began to take shape in the back of my mind. One day—when, where, and how I did not know, of course—would it be possible to bring these four legendary instruments together again? To reassemble them, as they had been assembled and matched by Paganini? "A few years later I saw this violin." Herrmann picked up the instrument and turned it over to show the finely carved maple back and thick orange varnish. "This was Paganini's concert Strad. One hears a great deal about Paganini's Guarnieri, which the Italian government keeps enshrined in the museum in Genoa. But people forget that many famous violinists have at least two instruments. Menuhin for years had a Guarnieri companion to his Strad. So does Heifetz. Paganini's passion for instruments went further. He was a collector and a shrewd investor. This particular Strad," said Herrmann, giving it a shrewd investor's glance himself, "was made by Stradivari in 1727, when he was eighty-three years old. It is in perfect condition. Paganini bought it from Count Cozio di Salabue, who sold it to him in 1816." Herrmann walked over to a table and leafed through an enormous volume bound in rich blue Morocco leather.

"Here is ample documentation," he said, "the bill of sale from Count Salabue to Paganini." He turned another page. "A letter from Paganini," Herrmann said, and quoted from it, translating as he went along: "This violin has a tone as big as a double bass—never will I part with it as long as I live."

"This violin went through some strange peregrinations," continued Herrmann, turning to further documents in the impressive leather volume. "In 1893 it was sold to a Dutch concert violinist who took it with him to America, and, by the way, every time the violin was sold the price went up considerably," said Herrmann, talking more to himself than to Maas and making a careful mental note.

"Don't forget, Stradivarius, in his long life of ninety-three years and with the aid of his sons and assistants, made an estimated one thousand instruments, the vast majority of them violins, but also a small number of violas, cellos, and guitars. Every year the number of these instruments diminishes in almost predictable mathematical progression. In time of war they are destroyed by bombing. They perish in fires. In recent memory Jacques Thibaud and Ginette Neveu died with their instruments in plane crashes. Violins are irreparably damaged in automobile collisions. They are even stolen. In the course of little more than two centuries the number of surviving Strads has gone down from an estimated one thousand to an estimated five hundred, and of these only a small number are in perfect condition. How many will survive another century from now? How many in another five hundred years? And there will never be another Antonio Stradivarius!

"Think of the price of eggs," Mr. Herrmann continued, taking Maas completely by surprise. "A hundred years ago you could probably buy a dozen eggs for a penny. Throughout the economic history of modern man, the purchase value of money has gone down and down and down. That's another way of saying that the price of things has gone up and up and up. If that's true for eggs, which are produced just as well and plentifully today as a century ago, think how much truer it is for a Stradivarius!" Mr. Herrmann paused for better effect. "It's the best long-term investment in the world."

Mr. Herrmann had deliberately not mentioned the cello, and he must have known that Robert's hands were itching. "And here," he said innocently, "is the other violin, the one I would consider as the second violin in a quartet. It's a beautiful early Strad, made in 1680, when Stradivari was young and still under the influence of his master, Amati."

Maas was allowed a close look at the early Strad with its supremely elegant Amati outline. Robert could contain himself no longer. "Please, Mr. Herrmann, let me see the cello."

Did Herrmann have an inkling of our extraordinary project? Had someone, somehow, dropped a hint as to the identity of the mysterious patron, despite all the secrecy surrounding the plan? Emil Herrmann was reputed to have the sharpest nose in all New York. When a potential Strad buyer was still at home, struggling with embryonic impulses as yet deeply buried in his unconscious, Mr. Herrmann had already picked out his instrument for him and written up the bill of sale.

Mr. Herrmann turned his back to Robert for a moment and carefully took the cello out of the case. "Here is the cello," he said, superfluously. "It's the last of the four instruments I've acquired. I had to wait eleven years until the owner died, when I was fortunately able to buy it from his estate. It took me twenty-five years to bring these instruments together. Now they will never be separated again. Piatigorsky offered me a king's ransom for the cello. A well-known violinist wanted to buy the 1727 Paganini Strad. I've turned them both down. The four instruments will be sold together, or not at all. Of course," said Mr. Herrmann quizzically, "who has enough money to buy four Strads all at once? Certainly not an artist."

Robert took the cello in his hands and looked at it speechlessly. It was an incredible masterpiece, covered with fiery red varnish that intensified the beautiful natural grain and flame of the wood. "This cello," said Herrmann slowly, "was made by Stradivari in the year 1736, when he was ninety-two, one year before his death. There probably is no other instance in history of a genius being at the height of his creative powers at such an age. Stradivari took a great and justifiable pride in it, as you can see by looking at the label inside the instrument."

Maas peered through one of the two f-shaped slits in the belly of the cello and read the label on which Stradivari had proudly inscribed in his own handwriting in Latin, "Made in my ninety-third year."

Herrmann took a gold-mounted cello bow from the piano. It was a Tourte, the finest of bows, two hundred years old, worthy of the Strad that Robert now held in his hand. "Try it," suggested Herrmann. Robert did not have to be coaxed. He sat down, firmly planted the end peg of the cello on the floor, and drew the bow full-length, starting with the lowest string and producing a full-throated tone that vibrated throughout the cathedral-like sanctum. Robert looked up and exchanged a glance with Herrmann that required no words. For the next hour he explored the instrument from its lowest region to its upper most, trying a Bach sonata, snatches from Beethoven quartets, the Haydn concerto, even simple scales. At the end of the hour he returned the cello to Mr. Herrmann, and shook his head, saying, "Ahh, if I could only have a cello like that!" Pure wishful thinking.

The next day Robert and I visited Mrs. Clark. Soon the conversation drifted to the name we had to decide upon for the new quartet. This was no small matter. One name after another was proposed and rejected. Then Robert cannily mentioned the Paganini Strads. To my amazement he added, "Last night I had a fantastic dream. I dreamt we were playing a Beethoven quartet on the Paganini Strads. Fantastic!" It was indeed fantastic. Mrs. Clark jumped at the bait: "If you had those Paganini Strads, the name would be a natural. You'd be the Paganini Quartet. I want to see those instruments!"

The next day she made an appointment to see Emil Herrmann, took a casual look at the instruments—and wrote a check for the full amount. *Time* and other publications reported the purchase price as a quarter of a million dollars. Today the instruments must be worth a million. And that's how the Paganini Quartet got its name.

The responsibility of caring for a fragile instrument several times more valuable than a Rolls-Royce (and completely irreplaceable, of course) weighs heavily on one. In my first months with the fabulous "Paganini" Strad, I spent many a fitful night. My dreams were peopled with burglars, arsonists, and con men. Gradually, I learned to live with my new responsibility. And every day as I looked with renewed wonder at this remarkable wooden box, I became more and more fascinated by the image of the man who had created it more than two centuries ago: this mysterious figure, this genius whose creation had come to affect my life so deeply: Antonius Stradivarius. Who was he? How had he lived?

Antonius Stradivarius is, of course, the most famous string instrument-maker of all time. During the golden age of violinmaking, the seventeenth and eighteenth centuries, most of the great makers lived in Cremona. To string instrument lovers, the names of Guarnieri, Amati, Bergonzi, and others are as familiar as Stradivarius, and sometimes as highly prized and cherished. In almost every case these makers were members of a durable dynasty, handing down their superb craftsmanship from father to son. The descendants of the Gaglianos and Guadagninis, who were famous in the eighteenth century, are still active as violinmakers today, but not nearly as successfully as their ancestors.

Sometimes I wonder, what was the special magic of Stradivarius? For although a fine Stradivarius has a tone that is miraculously velvety and mellow, only a player of great skill can take advantage of its exquisite possibilities, and even he cannot do justice to it if he has been accustomed to playing an ordinary instrument. A Strad needs to be coaxed and cajoled. It wants to be treated like a beautiful woman. It has infinite nuances, and it gives the player a feeling of limitless depth. But to get the best out of a Strad may take a year of hard work and experimentation. And because a Strad is extremely sensitive to changes of weather and climate, it can turn into an instrument of torture for the traveling concert artist.

A wealthy English amateur once asked Jacques Thibaud to try out his Strad. The French violinist complied and commented, "What a marvelous sound!" "Yes," concurred the amateur, taking the instrument from Thibaud and unself-consciously drawing a few sour notes from it. "Now it *isn't* so marvelous," said Thibaud, never at a loss for words.

Among today's famous violinists, many prefer a Guarnerius del Gesu because of its greater power, so necessary in today's huge concert halls. Time and again, experiments have been conducted in the course of which a well-known violinist would alternately play on a Strad and various other instruments, including unknown contemporary violins. Almost invariably the experiments ended inconclusively or with Stradivarius losing out. Why? Mysterious factors may be involved. The mere knowledge that one is cradling a heavenly Stradivarius in one's arms makes one's adrenalin course more rapidly. Playing a Stradivarius is a form of self-hypnosis. Playing *four* of the most famous Stradivarius instruments simultaneously, as we did in the Paganini Quartet, was a veritable happening.

Did Stradivarius have a secret? Strange tales have been told about the varnish he used and the "filler" he applied in treating the wood. These "secrets," the legends say, Stradivarius took with him to the grave. Highly improbable. Stradivarius had five children, two of whom, Francesco and Omobono, followed in their father's footsteps. Their violins, until the master's death, bore the label *"sub disciplina Antonii Stradivarii."* They learned their craft from him and worked in his shop until his death. It is most unlikely that Stradivarius could or would have withheld any secrets from his own sons in these circumstances. The simple truth is that no man can will his genius to another.

Violinmakers all over the world have pried into Stradivarius' secrets and methods since the day he died. Precision instruments have been used to measure the thickness of the wood in his violins. This thickness, it was found, varies from less than one-tenth of an inch to perhaps one-sixth of an inch toward the center. Yet, such was the scientific precision of the mind that had conceived these frail instruments that for centuries they have withstood a string tension equivalent to more than sixty pounds. Now, using similar wood, Stradivarius' imitators build what they hope are duplicates. Are they? Not at all. For one thing, no two chunks of wood are ever identical in grain, character, or age.

Above all, no one has ever been able to imitate Stradivarius' marvelous varnish. This varnish, it must be clearly understood, is not used solely to beautify or preserve the instrument. It has an enormous influence on the tone, and more than anything else determines its characteristics. If Stradivarius had any secret to his varnishmaking method, it was the secret of infinite patience. For to make and apply a pure oil varnish must be a labor of love. Stradivarius brought infinite love and infinite care to his creations. In one of his two surviving letters the master complains of the difficulty of getting the varnish to dry, adding, "Without the strong heat of the sun, the violin cannot reach a state of perfection." His descendants and the ensuing generations would not wait for the agonizingly slow drying process of a pure oil varnish. They turned to alcohol-based varnishes, for a much faster and more economical drying time.

One may question whether the appearance of a

Stradivarius instrument was as beguiling on the day it was made as it is today. For Stradivarius had a partner of surpassing genius: Time, a partner rarely given his proper due. What we gaze at in ecstasy today is a mellowed instrument, with the exquisite imperfection of varnish that has been rubbed every day for two hundred and fifty years; rubbed by each succeeding owner five and six hours a day, as his fingers ran up and down the finger-board in every conceivable violinistic pattern, the hand itself moving back and forward on the belly and back of the instrument. Each day, when day was done, the entire violin was lovingly cleansed of the accumulated rosin dust of the bow, and rubbed and rubbed and rubbed with a soft cloth. There is little doubt that when the Stradivarius instruments first emerged from the shop, they must have had an appearance of excessive brilliance and perfection, like those of the best contemporary master.

Another major reason that it is so difficult to imitate Stradivarius is that Stradivarius never imitated himself. He experimented ceaselessly to produce ever greater instruments. And at the very end he reverted to the simplicity of his youth, thus closing the vast cycle of his creative life. Simplicity is indeed the final phase of complexity.

Anyone who has been present when a priceless Stradivarius has been taken apart in the repair shop of a master violinmaker, and who has seen the incredibly fragile pieces—the spruce top, the maple back—lying separately on the table, and then has watched all the pieces being reassembled with only a little glue, will no longer wonder that in the scant three centuries since Stradivarius created his masterpieces more than half have vanished from the earth.

To chronicle all the tragedies would fill volumes. In Berlin a famous Stradivarius was stolen from a violinmaker's shop. Only after committing the crime did the thief come face to face with reality: a stolen Strad is worthless; you can't sell it, except to a junk shop for perhaps ten dollars because only an expert would recognize and pay for a Strad. There are unlimited numbers of violins on the market, all bearing the identical label: "Antonius Stradivarius Cremonensis Faciebat Anno—" followed by the year, which may be anywhere from 1666 to 1737. Labels are cheap, and for every genuine Stradivarius, there are at least a thousand counterfeits. Strangely enough, there is no law against bogus Strads.

If, on the other hand, a thief takes the stolen Strad to an expert violin dealer, he will promptly land in jail. For almost every real Strad is catalogued, described, and pictured in standard reference works. And even if it were not, the expert immediately recognizes a Strad by its unique appearance. He spends his life studying them and ends up knowing them as if each were a personal friend. Obviously in the face of such odds only a lunatic would steal a Strad. Unfortunately, there are many lunatics: Strads continue to be stolen, and they rarely turn up again.

On only one occasion, to my knowledge, was there an attempt to steal the famous Paganini Strad. It happened in 1948, when the Paganini Quartet gave a concert in St. Paul. As I arrived at the stage door, a little man impeccably dressed in a black tuxedo received me courteously. "This way please," he said. "Here is your dressing room." He helped me with my coat and briefcase, then: "Now let's take a look at the stage lights." He summoned the electrician and together we decided on the lighting.

After we returned to the dressing room he pointed to the washroom at the other end of the passage, saying, "I know how careful you are with your Strad. I shall be glad to watch it while you leave the room."

Although I felt no distrust, out of habit I left the Strad

with one of my colleagues in another dressing room. The man in the tuxedo hovered over me until it was time to go on. After every number he stood in the wings, applauding and shouting "Bravo!" As we went on for the last number, he said to me, "Ah, Debussy, how magnificent." Those were the last words I heard him utter.

After the concert, when we began to put our instruments away, the cellist exclaimed sharply, "My bow is gone!" At this we all looked in our cases. The extra bows we always carried with us had disappeared.

"Please call your manager at once," I urged the committee surrounding us. As they seemed nonplussed, I added, "You know, the man in the tuxedo."

"The man in the tuxedo?" they queried. "We thought he was *your* manager!"

I raced over to the electrician. Yes, he had seen him walk out through the back door while we were playing the last number; he had walked out of our lives forever —with the bows, which he obviously had concealed under his overcoat, taking them as a consolation prize when he failed to pry me away from the Strad.

Of course, if one must snatch a Strad, the dressing room is without a doubt the ideal place, particularly at the end of a concert, when the sweat-soaked artists, haggard and bedeviled by autograph-hunters, are slightly *non compos mentis.* These are the only times when I must confess to real anxiety for the safety of my good companion. While I am signing autographs, my eyes dart back and forth from the programs to the violin. I am not so much afraid of thieves as of the curious. On one occasion a lady was just about to dig her fingernail into the varnish of the violin to test its composition. I snatched it from her with a frantic yelp. On another occasion I turned around to see three beefy stagehands clutching my Strad like a baseball bat. Innocent curiosity, but enough to account for many gray hairs.

In our time, despite plane and automobile crashes, the rate of destruction of Stradivari instruments is probably slowing down in inverse proportion to their astronomical increase in value. During his lifetime Stradivarius demanded the equivalent of $60 to $100 for a violin, an extremely high price compared to the prices of his rivals' instruments. Even then dukes and princesses collected his instruments. By the middle of the nineteenth century the price had gone up to about $1000. Today a first-class Strad costs several hundred thousand dollars, and they are exceedingly hard to come by. In 1971 a Stradivarius violin was auctioned at Sotheby's in London for $201,000, then, "a record" high. For, while the number of surviving instruments constantly diminishes, and their owners become increasingly reluctant to part with them, a whole new market has developed. Countries like Japan and previously so-called backward countries in Asia and Africa are getting used to Western music and want instruments to play on.

Of course, only a minority of these instruments, perhaps forty or fifty, are of the quality and immaculate condition of the "Paganini." Many of them have suffered the ravages of time and intemperate use. Also, for all his genius, Stradivarius was human and fallible. Not all of his instruments are of equal quality. Even the choice of wood varied, depending on Stradivarius' purse, the buyer's affluence, and on what was available.

What will happen to the market for Strads in the future? In the long run, it can only go up. The well-preserved ones will become increasingly rare because it is impossible to halt the attrition caused by destruction and damage. Today the owner of a Strad wraps his precious possession in costly silks and beds it in a form-fitting alligator case heavily lined with velvet. A violin thus protected is safer by far than a human being.

True Strad lovers are incurable romantics. They invent special names by which famous Strads are then known and identified. For example, there is the "Red Diamond," named for its magnificent red varnish. Some years ago its owner was caught in a sudden flood tide on Ocean Boulevard at Santa Monica near Los Angeles. To save his life and his "Red Diamond," he jumped out of his car and began wading. He barely escaped being drowned, but a vicious wave knocked the fiddle out of his hand and carried it out to sea. The next day, however, an appeased Neptune washed the "Red Diamond" ashore. The celebrated violin was in a pitiful state, warped beyond recognition. The twenty-four-hour immersion in salt water had bloated it into a shapeless mass. The glorious red varnish was replaced by a grayish-white film.

At first it seemed as if the "Red Diamond" was beyond rescue. Then a top violin surgeon went to work. He built a special tank, with gauges to regulate the temperature as well as the moisture content of the inside air. For a full month he kept the injured "Red Diamond" inside this tank. During the first two days and nights he never went to bed. The problem was to dry the bloated spruce top and maple back with such scientific precision that they would again match with the same miraculous perfection that Stradivarius had brought to the original creation. This problem was almost insoluble because spruce and maple shrink differently. It required the patience of a Job, but the "Red Diamond" was saved and continues to take its place among the proud creations of Antonius Stradivarius.

Other glamorous names for Strads have been borrowed from their original owners. Thus there is the "Duke of Alcantara," the "Duke of Cambridge," the "King Maximilian." No Stradivari owner is ever without one or more certificates—a Strad without papers is like a dog without a pedigree. These certificates were issued by such famous dealers as Herrmann, Caressa,

Hart, and Lachmann. But the most highly prized of all is the Hill certificate, for the confidence it inspires is magical and it is the first thing a prospective buyer asks for.

Sometimes not all parts of a violin are authentic. The design and sweep of a Stradivarius head, or "scroll," are instantly recognizable by the practiced eye. A few Strads have false scrolls, the original presumably having been destroyed. Although the scroll is purely ornamental and has nothing to do with the tone of the instrument, the violin expert or collector who owns such a fiddle goes about like a haunted man. The instrument is spoken of as if it had some fearful disease. The owner will roam the earth and poke his nose into fiddle shops until he discovers a genuine Strad scroll, the remnant of another violin that has been destroyed.

Sometimes more than the scroll may be missing—for instance, the whole top, known as the "belly." The famous "Bass of Spain" cello was a case in point, but with a special twist, for it was the discarded belly that was first discovered, roasting in the sun, cracked and damaged, in a Madrid shop window. Luigi Tarisio, an enthusiast famed in the violin trade a century ago, journeyed on foot from Paris to Madrid, bought the belly for a few dollars, and then spent months tracking down the remainder of the vanished instrument. When he found it, expert hands glued the original belly back to the cello. Today the "Bass of Spain" resides in San Jose, California, the proud possession of a prominent city official who rarely lets the instrument out of his sight. Collectors do not buy Strads simply for their tone: they cherish them as objects of art, similar to prized paintings, the equals of any Titian or Rembrandt. I have seen collectors look for hours at a Strad they intended to buy, and never ask to hear it.

Probably every surviving Stradivarius is accounted

for, whether it be in Europe, the United States, or Asia. Nonetheless, thousands of hopefuls continue to dream that the old fiddle inherited from a great-grandfather might turn out to be a genuine Stradivari worth a fortune. Rarely does a week go by without my receiving anxious "Stradivari" letters or visitors. Sometimes when I give them the sad news, they say, "But it is so *old.*" And I answer, "Yes, but everything that is *old* is not necessarily *good.*"

The most pathetic character I ever met was a man who held an enormous knotted handkerchief up to my face. "I have a genuine Stradivari here," he added.

"Not in that handkerchief," I said. "There couldn't be." But he nodded vigorously, and was down on his hands and knees untying the handkerchief. Inside it were perhaps a hundred pieces of wood, smashed fragments of what had been a violin. "You see," he said triumphantly, "I told you." Of all the people with "Strads" whom I had been forced to disappoint in the course of the years, none had seemed so pitiful. "Yes," I said, "perhaps it was a Strad."

And yet, after all these years, I go on answering the inquiries that pour in from people everywhere. Because in my heart I am just as hopeful as they. Because someday, somewhere, the miracle may happen.

8

The View from the Podium

RECIPE FOR A CHAMBER SYMPHONY

1. Take thirty-five well-seasoned musicians
2. Add Board members to taste
3. Mix (not too vigorously)
4. Keep at even temperature *(and never allow to boil over)*
5. When mixture is ready, drop in one (1) medium-sized manager
6. Keep well supplied with lettuce
7. Baste frequently until done

The first years of the Paganini Quartet were exciting, and there were thrilling occasions, such as playing the entire Beethoven Cycle at the extraordinary Teatro Colon in Buenos Aires, with every one of its three thousand seats filled, and with such marvelous acoustics that the softest *pianissimo* reached out to the last row. But man cannot live by thrills alone. There was also Podunk and Hackensack and thousands of miles of traveling through sleet and ice and fog. After the first fifteen years I began to experience a feeling of lassitude. The Quartet had had a great career, but it had also had more than its share of tragedy. Only two years after it was founded Robert

Maas had died in the middle of a concert featuring the world premiere of a new work dedicated to the memory of Alphonse Onnou, the Belgian violinist who had been Maas's lifelong friend and closest associate in the famed Pro Arte Quartet. This memorial concert took place in an atmosphere of heavy solemnity at Mills College in Oakland, where Onnou had been a familiar figure to many of us there. We finished playing the piece and left the stage for an intermission. Suddenly Maas collapsed and died. One woman wrote in demanding a refund because the last work on the program had not been performed.

After the shocking tragedy it seemed impossible to continue our series of summer concerts at Mills, but the head of the music department implored us to stay on. His life's work was at stake. So we stayed, and Victor Gottlieb, a brilliant young American cellist, agreed to take Maas's place for the remaining concerts.

Ten years later the violist of the Quartet, Charles Foidart, collapsed and died immediately after a concert at the University of Arizona in Tucson. We had played an encore at the end of the program, Haydn's variations on the Austrian national anthem. To my intense surprise, Foidart, who never indulged in histrionics, suddenly lifted his viola high and turned full face toward the audience as he played the noble variation for viola solo, an instrument rarely singled out in the classical quartet literature. It was the last thing he played. These tragedies and the other personnel changes that took place in the Quartet over the years made it imperative to restudy the entire quartet literature from scratch each time, a task of heroic magnitude. For each new player has a different style and personality that have to be broken in to match the style and interpretations of the Quartet as a whole.

Eventually, I found I had lost much of my enthusiasm

for rehearsing and traveling with the Quartet, and I had always promised myself that when this happened, I would frankly face the issue. One of the things I had admired·most about Maas was his remarkable ability to renew himself indefinitely. When he played a Beethoven quartet for the five hundredth time, he played it with the concentration, dedication, and freshness of his first performance. It was a quality I utterly lacked, and what originally had emanated from the depth of my being was now produced synthetically. As far as the listener was concerned, there was still that same dramatic *crescendo* leading to that same passionate climax, but as far as I was concerned, a slick computer system was taking over, with extraordinary efficiency. My bow would move closer to the bridge as planned, my left hand would vibrate more rapidly in order to produce that *crescendo* and the ensuing climax, but I was on automatic pilot, a mere onlooker, objectively observing a meticulously trained machine that had been perfected over the years. I was becoming restless. And after playing the Paganini Strad for twenty years with the Paganini Quartet, I also came to believe what I never would have believed at the beginning: violins, like human beings, become fatigued, exhausted, and sick. They lose their vitality and resilience like old and chronically ill people. When I propounded this thought to Desmond Hill, the head of the world's most distinguished violin firm in London, he by no means denied it. With cool scientific detachment he did question the reliability of my measurements and criteria. How could I be sure that my own hearing had not changed? Had I measured the thickness and quality of each set of strings when replacing them over the years? He suggested that a dozen other factors had to be taken into consideration. I listened to him but still trusted my own ears. Perhaps though, like a man who has wearied from an affair that has lasted too long, I was only trying to find a reason for ending my long association with the Paganini Quartet.

The final concert tour of the Paganini Quartet was one of the most successful. Although the audiences and critics were unaware of our secret decision to disband at the end of our twentieth year, they lavished praise and affection on us. As we read our reviews, it almost seemed as if the critics had a foreboding of our plan and were trying to dissuade us. "PAGANINI QUARTET AS GREAT AS EVER," announced one blazing headline.

But our minds were made up, especially mine. A great string quartet makes insatiable demands on its players. After twenty years of almost daily rehearsal, frequently five and six hours at a stretch, after giving some fifteen hundred concerts in every corner of the globe, I felt an overwhelming urge to start a new chapter in my musical life, to devote my major energies once again to solo appearances and to conducting.

In March 1966 we played our last concert, finishing with the Debussy quartet, the work that audiences around the world identified above all others with the Paganini Quartet. Our faithful manager, Chris Schang of Columbia Artists Management, had specially flown in from New York. After the concert we sat and reminisced sentimentally through most of the night. The next day I took the four Paganini Strads, which Mrs. Clark had decreed must never be separated, and placed them in the custody of the Corcoran Gallery in Washington, D. C. (which Senator Clark had favored with so many of his art treasures). Then I flew home.

How can I describe my feelings as I returned to Los Angeles, minus a string quartet? All of a sudden I was thrice divorced, after twenty years of bliss and bondage. An enormous burden fell from my shoulders. No longer would I have the moral responsibility for the livelihood of three other musicians and their families. No longer would I travel to the four corners of the world, separated from my family and home for many months on end. I was ready to enter a new phase of my career. Henceforth, I would divide my time between teaching, lecturing at various universities, writing articles, making solo appearances, and, above all, conducting the California Chamber Symphony. I had founded the orchestra some years before, but because of my activities with the quartet had been forced to treat it like a stepchild. Now I would devote my best energies to its activities. I looked forward to it with tremendous excitement.

Conductors are born, not made, they say. Nonsense. Conducting is a virus. It enters the blood insidiously, no one knows when, where, or how. In my own case, my interest in conducting first emerged when I studied with Artur Rodzinski at the Curtis Institute of Music. In part, you will recall, my efforts had been a ploy to ward off the specter of graduation from that musical Shangri-la. But there was more to my involvement than that, for my early associations in life had made a lasting impact on me. Ignaz Neumark, the Polish conductor who had introduced me to Carl Flesch when I was a student, had been responsible for an abrupt change in my fortunes. His image loomed larger than life, and he was the first conductor I had come to know. Even as a child I had attended his concerts. How unforgettable, those magical early impressions: the conductor winding his way through the orchestra as he appeared on the stage, swiftly stepping onto the conductor's podium, acknowledging the audience's applause, then turning to the orchestra, raising his magical little wand—and suddenly heavenly sounds were created by the unified efforts of one hundred men. But my early fascination with Neumark did not stem exclusively from his musicmaking. Hundreds of stories circulated about this colorful, lovable eccentric, who was one of the last of the great boulevardiers; the cafés of all Europe were his natural habitat. He was a composite of all the nomadic concert artists who had roamed and crisscrossed Europe for the past century. In the course of thirty years we had countless reunions: on the Champs-Élysées in Paris, the Marszalkowska in Warsaw, Unter den Linden in Berlin, the Karl Johansgate in Oslo, the Piazza San Marco in Venice. On one occasion, I received a card asking me to retrieve his slippers, left under his bed in room 203 of Stockholm's Grand Hotel; I mailed them to him in Madrid. With the exception of a few years, which I shall describe later, I never knew this perennial bachelor to have a private address. Most of the time he wandered from hotel to hotel or slept at the homes of friends. His waking hours were spent in the smoke-laden atmosphere of the café, occasionally interrupted by the symphony concerts he conducted.

Neumark must have looked upon each of these concerts primarily as a gateway to the next café, for he rarely mentioned them. I would receive one of his spidery little scribbles that said, "I'll be in Amsterdam next Friday— you'll find me at the Krasnapolski." That he was also conducting the famous Concertgebouw Orchestra I had to discover in the newspapers. The essential point was that he was homing for his old haunt, the Krasnapolski Café on the Dam. There was no need to mention the time, because aside from rehearsal and concert hours, which could easily be ascertained, Neumark, with one or more friends, was sure to be found at a marble-topped table inside the Krasnapolski, surrounded by piles of newspapers, coffee cups, ashtrays piled high with cigarette butts. There this amiable hypochondriac would sit, myopically peering through his thick lenses, chainsmoking and periodically asking the waiter, "Please shut the window—fresh air belongs outside."

The moment I arrived he would jump up, a beaming

smile spreading across the narrow olive-skinned face topped by dark curly hair. "Ah, Temianka. Have you heard the latest?"—the invariable prelude to the latest musical anecdote or choice bit of personal gossip. His tone was rich with promise, a promise that was never disappointed. Neumark was a one-man information center for the musical world. If the second bassoonist of the Warsaw Philharmonic had hit the conductor over the head after a heated argument about the introduction to the *Sorcerer's Apprentice*, resulting in the cancellation of the concert, Neumark knew it. If a concert agent in The Hague had been caught pocketing a double commission, he knew that too. If Rubinstein's take after his last Albert Hall recital exceeded £2000 or if the first chair of a certain orchestra was available because the concertmaster had run off with the conductor's wife, Neumark was fully informed.

I never caught Neumark studying an orchestral score. Year after year he was the assistant conductor of the summer concerts at the Dutch seaside resort of Scheveningen. Though his musical competence stopped short of inspiration, Neumark had gradually become a fixture in tiny, tolerant, provincial Holland. He was persuasive enough to cajole the management of the resort into engaging those soloists who excelled as raconteurs. That they could play was taken for granted. What mattered was the repertoire of new stories they would bring to the supper table after the concert.

On one occasion Neumark chose pianist Moriz Rosenthal, by this time well past his prime, who was legendary for his biting wit. During World War I he claimed that his rival Artur Schnabel had been rejected as unfit for military service. When telling the story, Rosenthal would stop at this point, confident that at least one of his listeners would inquire *why* Schnabel had been rejected. "Stiff wrists!" Rosenthal would snap triumphantly. He also was reported to have referred to a rival pianist's performance of Chopin's "Minute Waltz" as "the loveliest quarter hour of my life."

On the basis of these credentials Rosenthal was engaged to play in Scheveningen, and for weeks prior to his arrival, Neumark and his coterie awaited the great man in breathless anticipation. But at his very first performance Rosenthal, old, nearsighted, and vainglorious, stepped too far forward while acknowledging the plaudits of his audience, fell off the stage, and had to be carried to his hotel room. He had no opportunity to make a single poisonous remark or tell a single biting story. The supper that followed without him was like a wake, and the unspoken verdict was that Rosenthal had been grossly overpaid.

When during World War II the Germans overran most of Europe, Neumark barely escaped and reached New York destitute. The New World had little use for unknown European conductors, and Neumark spent the war years in desperate poverty, living on handouts from charitable organizations and his more fortunate musical colleagues. He became an old man overnight, nearly blind, vegetating in unrelieved melancholy. So it came as a surprise when at war's end Neumark was discovered still among the living. The loyal Dutch immediately invited him to return to Holland, this time not as an assistant conductor, but as a distinguished guest. As a Jew who had survived the Nazi terror, Neumark became something of a symbol to the good Dutch people, and his return to Holland was a nostalgic reminder of the "good old days." He was greeted with an unashamed outpouring of profound emotion. A beautiful, wealthy Dutch baroness, half his age, fell in love with him, and at the marriage ceremony the whole Residentie Orchestra, The Hague's celebrated symphony, went to the City Hall to play Mendelssohn's "Wedding March." The event was reported on the front pages of the Dutch press, with elaborate photo coverage. For several months Neumark's new fame rivaled Toscanini's, at least in Holland. Neumark was guest conducting everywhere, the toast of every Dutch town.

But time, the great healer, is also the great corroder. Little by little the postwar situation in little Holland returned to normal, and the bigger-than-life-size image of Neumark gradually began to shrink. When I visited him in the luxurious home of his beautiful baroness, in a lovely wooded area some thirty miles east of Amsterdam, the first flush of triumph had already passed. To one who knew him as well as I did, Neumark was visibly uncomfortable in the midst of so much comfort. After speaking German and Polish during all the years of his bachelorhood in Holland, he was now learning Dutch, resolutely and pathetically.

He was obviously in trouble. Along with the linguistic problems and the diminishing musical returns, the honeymoon was clearly coming to an end. My friend's lovely young baroness was engaged in an agonizing reappraisal of the whole situation. Neumark's concert engagements were now rather infrequent. He sat at home, contemplating his embroidered slippers, chain-smoking cigarettes, swamped in idle luxury and dreaming of the good old days when the smoke-filled cafés in Warsaw and Paris were his natural habitat. Ultimately the beautiful baroness divorced him, his contract with The Hague Orchestra was terminated, and Neumark spent the last years of his life gazing at the Atlantic Ocean, patronizing the boardwalk cafés of a French resort. From time to time I would receive a short note requesting a shipment of another carton of his favorite brand of American cigarettes, the same that had helped him survive his American exile.

His death was prominently reported in many European papers, and it was only then that I learned that he had been a disciple of the legendary Arthur Nikisch, in the eyes of many the greatest conductor who ever lived; and I read of distinguished achievements and honors that Neumark had never even mentioned in my presence. As I read the obituary I was filled with nostalgic memories.

After I was graduated from the Curtis Institute, thanks to Neumark, who had introduced me to Flesch, and had started my solo career in England, I became aware that the conductorial virus still coursed through my veins, feverishly and unchecked. I promptly founded my first chamber orchestra. In addition to conducting it, I frequently appeared as violin soloist, combining the functions of conductor and soloist in the best eighteenth-century style. My violin section consisted in large part of England's most famous café, pop, and jazz fiddlers, the Mantovanis of London. They were all studying with me: Albert Sandler, Louis Stevens, Issay Schlaen, then household names to the English. When I gave a recital in Bournemouth, I discovered that Sandler had played there the day before, drawing twice my audience and five times my fee. These café princes were superb fiddlers. My main problem was to keep them from schmaltzing up Mozart.

Running my English Chamber Orchestra was comparatively easy. The musician's union did not interfere, the critics were benign, and audiences flocked to our concerts. There was no need for gimmicks and highpowered promotional campaigns. Bach and Mozart were the irresistible magnets.

Things changed after I formed the California Chamber Symphony.

Until then I had led a quiet, uneventful life whenever I was in Los Angeles, making only occasional concert appearances there which were reviewed by the critics with unanimous benevolence. On two occasions they

I knew that if I stepped outside the chalk circle I would be instantly disqualified. So I stayed inside and won third prize at the Wieniawski Contest after Ginette Neveu and David Oistrakh.

The rehearsals of the Paganini Quartet in my studio were not always as smooth as this one. The potential for a long drawn out argument in a string quartet is beyond belief.

We had a loving reunion in London with David Oistrakh, his son Igor, and Yehudi Menuhin. An admirer had sent a violin made of flowers. I didn't care much for Oistrakh's playing that night, and Menuhin's fingering was abominable.

I had supper with Golda Meir at the King David Hotel in Jerusalem after Piatigorsky's concert. She was eating grapes, and he was obviously fasincated.

Isaac Stern didn't say it, but it was obvious that he was critical of my viola playing when we performed Mozart's *Symphonie Concertante* at one of our Allegro Balls.

Oistrakh was as solid as a rock—musically as well as physically. No matter how serious he looked, he was always good humored and considerate.

"I may as well take the next plane back to New York," said Benny Goodman, but I was determined to have the concert first.

Yehudi Menuhin and I must have played together every duet and string quartet ever written, always fighting for the honor of playing second fiddle.

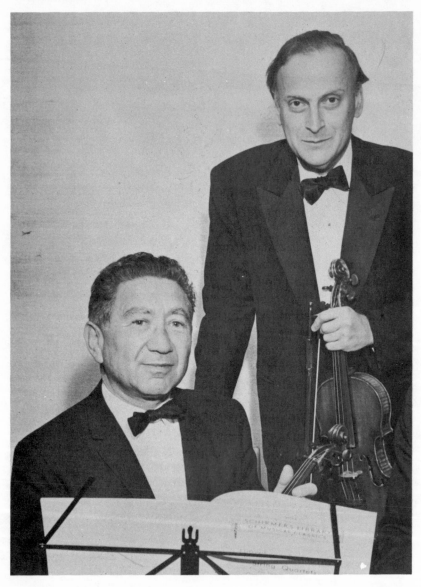

even invited me to be a guest columnist, stricken with amazement at the thought that a performing musician could actually write. All that changed after I reduced my activities with the Paganini Quartet and began concentrating on the California Chamber Symphony.

By dint of enormous effort I had given Los Angeles a chamber orchestra, which it had lacked until then, made up of thirty-five hand-picked virtuosos such as few cities anywhere in the world could boast. The first violin section alone consisted for the most part of former concertmasters of renowned Eastern orchestras, drawn to Los Angeles by the incredibly lucrative recording industry. The programs were of unusual interest, often featuring important works that had not previously been heard in Los Angeles. We brought leading composers and soloists from all over the world. Equally important, we provided live concerts for thousands of children whose cultural exposure had thus far been confined to *Mork and Mindy,* and *The Muppet Show.*

But the critics were unhappy because I was committing one unforgivable sin which brought down upon me the wrath of the professional opinionmakers: I was commenting from the stage on the music to be performed, sometimes going so far as to illustrate my commentary with a theme played by the orchestra or by myself on the violin. In so doing, I was violating convention and defying an unwritten but sacrosanct dictum: performers may have the agility of chimpanzees, but critics have a monopoly on all historical and musicological knowledge.

Long ago I reached the conclusion that printed program notes are rarely of any practical value. Most seem to start with the assumption that the average concertgoer has made a lifelong study of counterpoint. They are lavishly illustrated with undecipherable musical examples that the reader would not need if he knew half as much about the music as the commentator assumes.

.

But that's the least of it. There is usually no opportunity to read the program notes until one gets home after the concert, by which time it is too late.

Now it stands to reason that spoken program notes, accompanied by illustrations, can be far more informative to the layman than written notes. There is a piece by the contemporary German composer Paul Hindemith in which the second violins come in after the first violins, playing the same tune one beat later. This is like two actors reciting Hamlet's soliloquy at the same time, but one syllable apart. When I let the first and second violins take turns playing the theme, the audience was able to understand what went on.

There are two schools of thought about the relationship between the artist and the public. The one holds that there is a certain mystique about the artist that should be carefully nurtured and preserved. The artist who follows this precept makes every effort to remain aloof from "the people." Some of them will not even condescend to announce their encores, so that these are usually accompanied by the anxious whispering of one half of the audience asking the other half what the man is playing. According to that same school of thought, the artist who talks to his audience demeans himself and his profession. I am of the other school, and I had hoped the critics might have been more charitable about my delivering live program notes from the stage. A grievous miscalculation! If the critics already knew what I was telling the audience, it bored them. If they didn't, it infuriated them. I couldn't win. And they let me know it.

A conductor who wants to succeed in America has many other problems, I was soon to discover. He must please not only his audiences, but also his board of trustees, his orchestra players, his soloists, and—ah, yes —the Musician's Union. Don't get me wrong. I'm all in favor of the Musicians Union—that is, the American

Federation of Musicians. They're doing everything they can, according to their lights, to improve the lot of the musician. And undoubtedly Los Angeles has benefited from enlightened local leadership in recent years. On one hand, the union is immensely powerful: it calls strikes that paralyze the finest American symphony orchestras, imposing financial burdens that have put a number of them out of business. On the other hand, the union is powerless to prevent the recording and motion-picture industries from fleeing abroad, where recording pay scales are infinitely lower; or to prevent lavishly subsidized small and large foreign orchestras from touring the United States on their own terms and making it impossible for most American groups to compete in the American market.

Knowledgeable musicians rarely aspire to political power—they are too busy using their talents to make music. The Polish pianist Ignace Paderewski was one remarkable exception. When he became Prime Minister of Poland after World War I, Georges Clemenceau, the French Premier during the war, exclaimed, "What a comedown!" While a number of inferior musicians head for critics' jobs, a few others are ensconced among their betters on the boards of the Musician's Union, and in such other positions as various music associations have to offer on the local and national levels.

Sometimes their decisions are based on the political pressures to which they are undoubtedly subjected. For example, the Union has for years resisted the notion that one should be permitted to tape-record a rehearsal or concert purely for private purposes, concerned over possible unlawful commercial exploitation. To prevent this, taping was permitted only in the presence of a union official using a special machine designed to pepper the recording with beep signals that made it impossible to concentrate on the music. The fallacy of this precaution can be better understood when one reflects that any person intent upon dishonest exploitation cannot possibly be prevented from taping a broadcast, surreptitiously taping a live performance backstage or even from the auditorium, and fraudulently marketing existing recordings under false labels. On the other hand, no established concert artist would risk jeopardizing his entire career by this kind of practice. I tried to explain this to a now long defunct local board, without ever making a dent. Their credo seemed to be: "Don't confuse me with facts. My mind is made up."

Some years ago the Musician's Union adopted a new ruling. A clarinet player who plays both a B-flat and an A clarinet in the same concert (involving merely a quick switch in mouthpiece and no additional skills) must be paid 25 percent more. The same goes for other "doubling" instruments, such as trumpets and flutes. Anyone with a little imagination can easily see where all this is leading. Violinists will soon be demanding 50 percent more for plucking the strings in addition to bowing them, or for using a mute. Pianists may insist on a quota limiting the maximum number of notes to which the conductor is entitled, with premium rates for additional notes.

Players in the California Chamber Symphony are not on a year-round contractual basis. I pay them separately for each concert and the attendant rehearsals. I cannot afford it any other way; neither can they. They are in great demand in the recording industry, making far more money with rock 'n' roll records, TV programs, and motion pictures than any symphony orchestra could ever offer them. Some of them easily make $50,000 a year, and there are quite a few husband-and-wife teams who come close to doubling that figure. Compare these figures with the earnings of a symphony orchestra player. A decade ago, according to the Federation's official table

of wages, the members of the Los Angeles Philharmonic
had a guaranteed annual salary of $12,375. In Dallas that
figure was only $6845, not quite enough to live in the lap
of luxury; in Vancouver, $4050; in Honolulu, $3680; in
New Haven, $765. Fortunately, the orchestra players'
situation has improved enormously in recent years.

Of course, in order to earn $50,000 in Hollywood you
have to be part of that mysterious "inner circle"—those
who have personal connections with the powerful con-
tractors who have unlimited discretion as to who is to be
"called." The "call" is what all the musicians in the
industry are always waiting for. They used to sit within
grabbing distance of the phone twenty-four hours a day.
If they were not in, or their lines were busy, the call
went to the next player on the contractor's list. Shortly
after my arrival in Hollywood many years ago, when I
innocently asked to use the phone during a social visit to
a player's house, acute anxiety spread over his features.
"Make it short," he gurgled.

The commercial player is not concerned merely because he may lose a one-shot engagement. It could be a
long-term one, such as the popular *All in the Family* was,
assuring him a substantial annual income. The most successful players spend their days rushing from one recording studio to another, impartially playing rock 'n'
roll here, a Lawrence Welk-type show there, perhaps an
avant-garde session elsewhere, or jazz, or a hoedown.
The versatility of some of these players is remarkable.
They have been known to do as many as half a dozen
sessions in one day, to the point of collapse. Some of the
most prominent ones, such as Felix Slatkin and Mark
Levant, died of heart attacks in their forties.

Some of them end up losing all musical sensitivity.
The long and often deadly dull hours in the recording
studios take their toll. There the players sit, sometimes
doing nothing for long spells, counting their accumulat-

ing dollars while watching the clock intently (the Union has spelled out overtime payments to the second), while the harassed producer of the film or TV show is in an anxious huddle with directors, conductors, and backers, trying to solve all the unexpected problems that keep cropping up.

During these long waits the musicians never tire of their standard jokes. "What time is it?" one will say to the other, while both are staring at the big clock in front of them. "It's seventy-five dollars and fifty cents," the other will reply, calculating the accumulated overtime with lightning speed. Small wonder these business tycoons feel highly independent of symphony conductors. They are also very sensitive.

I lost one clarinetist and violist for not having shaken hands with them on the stage, after the West Coast premiere of Gian Carlo Menotti's *Triple Concerto a Tre*. I apologized and explained the physical impossibility of traipsing around the large stage to shake hands with all nine soloists who were involved, in addition to calling the composer out of the audience and shaking hands with him. But I was unable to placate them.

There is no doubt in my mind that an instrument is often responsible for imparting certain characteristics to its user. Violinists, like Mischa Elman, Fritz Kreisler, Yehudi Menuhin, have high-pitched voices, as if they were emulating their instruments' E strings. Those who play second violin, in orchestras or string quartets, often have deep-seated inferiority complexes. They go through life playing second fiddle, literally and figuratively. Violists are sometimes ornery, the mules of the music world—a cross between a violin and a cello and often a cross to their colleagues. Cellists are hams. They feel very secure, bestriding their instrument as if it were a horse. Bass players are melancholy, because the low, apocalyptic groans and grunts of their instruments seem to betide woe and catastrophe. Many trumpeters are brash and raucous. Caesar Petrillo, the notorious past president of the American Federation of Musicians, was a trumpeter. So were the last two presidents of the Los Angeles Musician's Union. It's hard to keep a trumpeter down. He wants to bulldoze his way through and be heard, the way he is when he blasts his way through the full orchestra. Besides, he only plays 10 percent of the time. Mostly he sits and counts bars, feeling unwanted while everyone else is playing. Have you ever looked at a trumpeter's orchestra part? It usually consists of one or two pages, while the first violins have heavy books on their stands.

The Los Angeles Union, with a membership of roughly twenty thousand, shares in the prosperity of its members. Since the initiation fee is now about $200 for each new member, the Los Angeles Union, over the years, must have taken in more than $2 million from that source alone. Of course, there are also the annual dues, plus deductions from the players' earnings. The saxophone alone has approximately twenty-five hundred addicts represented in the Los Angeles directory of the Musician's Union. Even such exotic instruments as the Washboard, Theremin, Electric Synthesis, Tin Whistle, Rothphone, Photoplayer, Saw, Jaw Harp, and Kadiddelhopper are separately represented and listed.

The problems I have with my orchestra at home are one thing. Going on tour with the California Chamber Symphony is something else again. The budget calls for a reduced orchestra, and not all of my top players can afford to sacrifice for weeks on end the princely incomes they earn in the Los Angeles recording studios. On one occasion my superb solo cellist, Willy Vandenburg, who also served as assistant conductor, remained loyal. For years he had served in that same capacity with the Phila-

delphia Orchestra under Leopold Stokowski, and with
the San Francisco Symphony and the Los Angeles Philharmonic. But his regular partner on the stand backed
out. I considered myself fortunate to sign up the solo
cellist of the Detroit Symphony, a Brazilian who did not
speak English.

The public is not aware of it, but cellists are the acknowledged comedians of any orchestra. The Paganini
Quartet's cellist, Robert Maas, who started out playing
in the summer orchestra in the Belgian seaside resort of
Ostend, on one occasion, shortly before a concert was to
start, removed all the screws that kept the big drum
attached to the drumstand. Since the orchestra was
seated on a series of semicircular risers resembling an
amphitheatre, and the drum was on the top riser, the
drummer's first mallet blow at the beginning of the concert sent it careening wildly. It picked up speed as it
thundered across the stage from riser to riser, missing
the conductor by inches and miraculously injuring no
one when it came roaring down the aisle, where it was
stopped by someone in the audience, probably a football
player.

Willy Vandenburg's proudest memory is the occasion
when the San Francisco Opera had a German guest conductor who wore hornrimmed spectacles and a huge
black beard. After the last rehearsal Willy collected modest dues from the whole orchestra for some undisclosed
purpose. When the conductor entered the pit that evening, resplendent in white tie and tails, he suddenly
stopped in his tracks, glued to the spot, holding on to the
railing to steady himself: every member of the orchestra
was wearing hornrimmed spectacles and a huge black
beard.

I made Willy promise that he would not indulge in
similar pranks during our tour, and he honored his
promise. His new pranks were completely different. The

pièce de résistance on our program in the smaller towns was Saint-Saëns' *Carnival of the Animals,* for two pianos, string quintet, flute, clarinet, and percussion instruments. It is a series of musical miniatures, humorous parodies on animals, from jackasses to roosters. We had a brilliant bass player, a recent immigrant from Hungary whose knowledge of English was only slightly superior to that of the Brazilian cellist. The first night, when Béla had finished his elephant solo, Willy fished in his pocket, turned around and threw him a handful of peanuts. When I objected, Willy devised a new strategy: he surreptitiously passed one single peanut from stand to stand until it reached the back of the orchestra where the bass player was located. Three or four peanuts later I finally discovered why the orchestra was in hysterics, uninspired by the bass player's brilliant performance.

Béla's playing was so remarkable that I gave him an opportunity to play one of his favorite solo pieces unaccompanied by the orchestra, a programmatic piece by a Hungarian composer describing life in the lonely *puszta,* the Hungarian equivalent of the Russian steppe. At one moment in the elaborate tone painting the composer depicts a deserted farmhouse where flies are buzzing around. (If this seems farfetched, remember that composers have a curious penchant for imitating the sounds of insects. The most famous is Rimsky-Korsakov's "Flight of the Bumblebee," but there are also the buzzings of the "Dragonfly" for cello by Popper and the violinistic "Bee" by Schubert (a namesake of the great Schubert). The favorite device of these composers is to use the extreme high register of a string instrument where the eternal rosin lies and where buzzing noises are produced with ease.)

The Hungarian composer was fully aware of the rich entomological possibilities in that high register, especially on the bass. At the approach of the fly episode, Béla

doubled over, the upper part of his body falling forward
until it almost seemed to hit the floor, in order to reach
the fly-producing region near the bridge. The effect he
achieved was extraordinary in its realism. Unfortunately, in that very moment Willy, a little Dutchman
with the agility of quicksilver, frantically started slapping his thighs, his ears, his hands, and sometimes even
his cello. The response he got from the orchestra was
overwhelming. Even after I made him stop his antics, the
mere memory made it impossible for anyone to keep a
straight face when Béla started playing that passage
thereafter.

There is one poetic number in the *Carnival* in which
a cuckoo, deep in the forest, is impersonated (imcuck-
ooed?) by a single clarinet monotonously reiterating the
philanderous cuckoo call, joined only by the two solo
pianos playing a serene melody, perhaps foreshadowing
that happy day when cuckoos will no longer lay their
eggs in other birds' nests. David Atkins, a serious bespec-
tacled young clarinetist, was supposed to deliver all his
cuckoo calls from one spot deep in the forest, namely,
backstage; but infected by the zany spirit that by this
time pervaded the orchestra, Atkins threw away the
script. The first gentle cuckoo calls emanated from the
backstage area all right, but then, suddenly, a clarinet
seemingly untouched by human hands appeared at the
far left side of the stage, extruding through the curtain
in an unexpected *fortissimo* call. Inexplicably, the next
call emerged from the opposite far right end of the stage.
Atkins had the agility of a gazelle. The audience must
have been thinking that I deployed an army of clarinet-
ists backstage. On one occasion Atkins' whole bespecta-
cled head and clarinet suddenly protruded over the top
of the curtain, high up near the ceiling. He was wearing
a red Turkish fez that he must have found in one of the
dressing rooms. I later learned that Atkins had borrowed

a high ladder for the occasion and practiced all afternoon doing dry runs until he got his timing perfect.

They are still talking about that concert in Napoleon, Ohio.

One night at three A.M., as I was sleeping the deep sleep of the exhausted in my motel room, I was awakened by the telephone. Willy, not sounding his usual ebullient self, was calling from a hospital. He and Béla, on their way back to the motel, were hit by a speeding car. I rushed over to the hospital. Willy was in fair condition with some broken ribs, but Béla was a pitiful sight. One heel was completely shattered, literally pulverized. Looking around the ill-equipped little hospital, I had misgivings. In the morning I called a physician friend in Chicago, some fifty miles away. By midafternoon he arrived at the hospital with a top orthopedist. After one look, they hurriedly removed Béla to a hospital in Chicago, where extensive surgery was promptly performed. I was informed by both doctors that a delay of a few more hours would have meant certain amputation, possibly death. Long after the tour was over, he recovered.

During the early part of the tour I had often invited the Brazilian cellist to play a solo, but I had always received a monosyllabic refusal. Now, after the accident, he was the only member left in the bass section, and I told him I was counting on him for the famous Swan solo in the *Carnival*. He smiled enigmatically.

Ten minutes before the concert began that evening, I received a message saying that he had suddenly been called away because his wife had had a heart attack. I was amazed, less by his defection than by the fact that he knew such a difficult word as "heart attack." The most complicated word I had heard him utter until then was "no," every time I asked him to play a solo.

Obviously it was too late to cancel the concert. All I

could do was substitute solos by the various outstanding virtuosos in the group, with the pianists alternating as soloists and accompanists. After the concert I was glued to the telephone until two in the morning, calling New York, Boston, Los Angeles, San Francisco, and I don't know how many other cities. Good cellists are unavailable on short notice. Finally I found one who could fly in for one concert only, the next evening. There was considerable suspense as the decimated orchestra awaited the next concert with an unrehearsed unknown cello soloist. All went relatively well. The orchestra generously applauded the cello soloist, who barely caught the next plane out, while I returned to making long-distance phone calls. Again I finally located a cellist who was free for the next concert only. And so it went, all week long. The daily change of solo cellists became a subject of intense fascination to every member of the orchestra. The basic question as to whether there would be one at all was a matter of ceaseless speculation. But they kept coming, young ones, old ones, pretty girls, sour-faced veterans, Americans, foreigners, Left-wingers, and Birchers.

No matter. What preoccupied everyone from morning to night was: How will the next one play the Swan? In the course of a week of seven one-night stands across half of the United States, I heard more different interpretations of that hackneyed but immortal piece than I had ever thought possible. Slow swans, fast swans, little swans, big swans, sloppy swans, immaculately clean ones, neurotic and erratic swans, passionate and phlegmatic ones, hysterical Russian swans, emotionally overwrought and academically correct Prussian swans. At the end of the week I never wanted to see or hear another swan.

Willy Vandenburg, his ribs on the mend, ultimately rejoined us before the tour came to an end. In recognition of his valor, I presented him with a lavish certificate in the style and terminology used by violin dealers when they authenticate Stradivari violins and other precious instruments. It read as follows:

CERTIFICATE BY
MESSRS. W. E. HILL & SONS
140 Bond Street
London W.1, England

We hereby certify that the Instrument submitted to us for examination, known as the "Willy Vandenburg" and bearing the label "Jacques Vandenburg, Fecit 1901, The Hague, Holland," is a genuine product of this master. Although unusually small, it is one of his finest and best preserved examples. The back is in one piece, except at the bottom, the belly bulges and is slightly warped, the neck is extremely short, the scroll finely cut. There is very little original varnish. The original tailpiece, though well-worn, is still adequate. The F-holes are large and characteristic of this master's work. There are few repairs. The present bridge is by Dr. W. J. Healy of San Francisco.

At the present time the instrument is owned by Mrs. Willy Vandenburg of Santa Cruz, California. Moderate use of this aging masterpiece is respectfully recommended, as it may crack under strain.

W. E. Hill and Sons

Measurements:
    From scroll to tailpiece: 61"
    Circumference: 62"

Some of our best musical jokes are saved for the Allegro Ball, the annual black-tie event that, in true American fashion, serves to replenish the empty coffers of the California Chamber Symphony in the absence of adequate government support. How resourceful an American musician has to be in order to go on making music! Especially conductors. When you finally walk out on the stage to conduct the orchestra, it is only the last link in a long chain of complex maneuvers that have preceded it. Take the Ball alone. The loving dedication of the devoted members of the board goes into the engraving of the invitations, the addressing and mailing, the planning of the menu, the floral decorations, the telephone campaign, and the seating of the guests, each one of whom clamors for the "best" table. The diplomatic plastic surgery required to restore all the noses that are out of joint —you wouldn't believe it. We finally solved the problem by assigning all the worst tables to the board of trustees and calling it the Diamond Circle. At one Allegro Ball, we performed Saint-Saëns' *Carnival of the Animals* as it has never been performed before. Five pianists, including Bronislaw Kaper, Gina Bachauer and conductor Zubin Mehta, competed for the two piano solos, exuberantly shoving each other off the bench to usurp piano power in the middle of a phrase. At one point, Zubin, who started out in life as an orchestral bass player, made a flying leap to capture the bull fiddle just in time for the famous Elephant solo, nosing out the regular bassist, Pete Mercurio. Pete had his revenge a couple of minutes later, and Zubin moved down to the xylophone and the chimes. Ogden Nash's enchanting verses, especially written for *Carnival,* were declaimed by an impressive body of stars headed by Anne Baxter and Cesar Romero, with a couple of musicians thrown in for good measure. No one who heard Piatigorsky recite the Kangaroo and the Cuckoo on that memorable night, in his rich Russian accent, will ever forget it.

I am happy to say we had a good rehearsal. Nonetheless, disaster struck. Just as we were about to start the performance that evening, one of the pianists announced with a smile, "I forgot my music." Panic spread among the performers as they realized the implications of the disaster. We were already on the stage, had acknowledged the applause of the expectant audience—and now, suddenly, nothing. At this point I remembered that I had an orchestral score of the piece, somewhere. While I went hunting for it, the audience had to be kept entertained, somehow. I entreated the guilty pianist to play a solo while I rushed out to get the music. Have you ever tried to persuade a virtuoso to give an unplanned, unpaid performance on the spur of the moment? If he is young and unknown, the customary snow job is to tell him it will help his career. If he is past that stage, you're up against it. I begged, cajoled, and exhorted. Finally, he condescended. The situation under control, I bolted and returned with the music just as he played the final chord of a Chopin Polonaise. The audience is convinced to this day that the whole thing was a carefully planned comedy routine. The pianist has never forgiven me. He feels I owe him a fee.

One of the most difficult aspects of a conductor's life is his relationship with soloists. When there is musical empathy between them, all is well. But sometimes they emerge from two different worlds and collide like meteors in space! One memorable concert involved Benny Goodman, who had specially flown in from New York to play the concert with me, making a sudden switch from the Rainbow Room to UCLA. We were scheduled to do the world premiere of an excellent new clarinet concerto by the English composer Malcolm Arnold, famed for his score for *The Bridge on the River Kwai.* I received the manuscript score of the concerto well in advance and had studied it carefully. The role of the orchestra was not merely to accompany. The score proclaimed a dialogue on equal terms between soloist and orchestra, clearly indicated by the composer, who fre-

quently marked the orchestra parts *ff* meaning *fortissimo,*
the standard indication in music for "exceedingly loud."
Furthermore, there were long stretches during which
the orchestra had the field to itself, giving the soloist a
chance to relax and count the house. Unfortunately
Benny seemed to feel that an orchestra should be seen
and not heard. Time and again he would interrupt the
rehearsal to address himself directly to the orchestra,
admonishing them to play as softly as possible. My repeated invitations that he look at my score to convince
himself of the *fortissimo* indicated by the composer were
swept aside. After a number of these interludes, Benny
threatened to leave unless I capitulated. "I may as well
take the next plane back to New York," he said at one
point. By this time the whole orchestra shared Benny's
wish for his speedy return journey to New York, but I
was determined to have the concert first, so I capitulated,
abjectly. From then on the orchestra did everything
Benny asked for—at the rehearsal. Benny was delighted.
Sometimes he turned around to make sure the orchestra
was still there, so unbelievably softly did they play.

That evening Benny came on stage beaming and smiling, waving at the audience almost two thousand strong.
The beginning went well enough. Then came an orchestral *tutti* (when everyone except the soloist plays), which
the orchestra had played that morning as delicately as a
Chopin nocturne. This time I gave a vigorous downbeat.
The orchestra responded—with an attack of indescriba-
ble fury. The King of Swing swung as he had never
swung before. He faced the orchestra as if stung by a
tarantula, frantically hissing and shushing through
clenched teeth, wildly flapping both arms, an operation
made somewhat cumbersome by the necessity of hanging on to his clarinet.

To no avail. The orchestra gave its all. Turning back
toward the audience, Benny compensated for the unex-

pected setback by taking liberties in the interpretation and tempo that had not been discussed or rehearsed. The end result was a most lively performance. The soloist was dealing with a group of virtuosi whose extensive experience in the recording industry had trained them for every possible emergency, whether the music be classical or commercial. Benny's performance had something of both. He is a born musician, with a natural feeling for a phrase, but without the self-imposed iron discipline that is so essential to the performance of "classical" music.

The audience roared with delight at the unconventional proceedings. We had to repeat the last movement of the Malcolm Arnold concerto. This time Benny Goodman went all out, making it clear that events until then had merely been a warmup. Using the lightbox at the edge of the stage as a footstool, he rested one raised foot on it and really started swinging. The orchestra, never to be shaken loose, swung with him. The result was a performance that left the audience cheering while the cavernous old auditorium itself seemed to be swaying slightly.

Guest conducting other orchestras is another activity of mine. For example: I am greeted at the Mexico City airport by a strikingly handsome, tall Peruvian with long dark hair. He looks like a descendant of the Inca kings and is deeply distressed: the soprano soloist who has been engaged upon my recommendation to perform in Shostakovich's Fourteenth Symphony has failed to arrive. The last signal received from her was a phone call two days earlier, announcing that she would arrive yesterday. When she didn't step off the first flight, he figured she had missed it and would arrive on the next one. So he stayed at the airport, distances in Mexico City being what they are, and patiently waited. She wasn't on that one either. By this time his Sunday was shot anyway, so he remained at the airport, desperately hoping that she would get there on the last plane. When she did not, a new theory took shape: of course—she would be traveling with me the next morning. But when I stepped off the plane unescorted, he really panicked. Where was our soprano? She had a key role in the new Shostakovich symphony. Since it would be impossible to replace her on short notice, the performance would have to be canceled if she did not show up.

We drive straight to the rehearsal hall, where the orchestra is waiting. I say nothing about the impending crisis; I shake hands with the concertmaster and begin to rehearse. At first the orchestra is restless, inattentive. Who is this new guy who has the gall to tell them what bowings to take? The ever-present latent hostility between the lions and the lion-tamer is definitely there, and nothing can be achieved in that atmosphere.

A conductor's success depends on his ability to win over his orchestra, for if he doesn't, all is lost. Every first rehearsal with a new orchestra is a debut, a test of strength. So I resort to my favorite device, I borrow the concertmaster's fiddle and demonstrate exactly how I want the phrase played. The whole orchestra applauds, and I am *in*. After all, the violin section is the largest in any orchestra. Now I have majority support. Every word I utter is listened to avidly. The battle is won.

After the rehearsal I rush to the hotel and register. I race to the phone in my room to solve the mystery of the missing soprano. No reply from her California home. I call her coach. (Every singer has one; the coach has the brain, most singers have only a voice.) The coach is cooperative and promises to undertake a massive one-man hunt for the soprano. I go to bed, exhausted. A loud shrill telephone ring awakens me at one A.M. from a deep sleep. My soprano is on the line, still in California. "I have no money for my plane ticket," she says. I reply, in a deadly voice, "If you are not here tomorrow, the Philharmonic Society will bring legal action against you, and I shall personally see to it that you are blackballed throughout the Western hemisphere for at least the rest of your natural life." The response is prompt. She will get on the next plane. I finally drop off to sleep, and again the strident summons of the telephone. Once more, now at three A.M., my soprano is on the line. She is filled with remorse and goodwill, and has just discovered there is an earlier plane she can catch by rising from her bed of repentance at five A.M.

She finally arrives, an impressive lady with long jet-black hair. She is carrying so much stuff that she can hardly squeeze through the door of the plane. In one hand is an enormous bottle of distilled water, in the other a ballooning package that turns out to contain twenty cans of tuna fish. She is surprised to find me ignorant of the fact that Mexican foods and liquids are full of germs lethal to Americans. But she isn't taking any chances.

My other vocal soloist, a French basso profundo, is a delight—would that all singers were so easygoing and cooperative. He arrived in Mexico City on time, knows his music, and is the jolliest fellow on earth. He is very modest about his beautiful voice, but inordinately proud of a peculiar capacity to imitate the noise of a vehicle in outer space. He does it without moving a muscle in his face, to the amazement and consternation of all who meet him for the first time. He stands there, smiling, and suddenly one hears *"beep, beep, beep,"* getting louder and louder and louder—absolutely frightening when it gets very close—and then, thank God, gradually receding and disappearing. A completely harmless creature, I say to myself, smiling happily because we have at least one singer of ideal disposition.

My Inca prince picks me up for the rehearsal the next

morning, looking pale and exhausted. It turns out he has just had a terrible argument with the basso profundo, who has informed him that unless he is paid immediately, he will take the next plane out. There is talk of instigating a lawsuit against the basso profundo and performing only those parts of the Shostakovich symphony in which he does not participate. Cooler counsels prevail, the basso profundo is paid, and he arrives at the rehearsal wreathed in smiles, imitating the sputnik. It is a happy moment in musical history.

Following this averted crisis, there is the unavoidable press conference. I find myself sitting on a couch with high Mexican dignitaries, the mayor, and members of the government, who are anxious to have it known that they are sponsoring one of the concerts, full of concern about the culture and well-being of Mexico's millions. I am asked to describe Shostakovich's new symphony. I rise to heights of eloquence, explaining that, following a serious illness, Shostakovich has dedicated this entire symphony to the subject of death. Everyone is profoundly moved. The journalists scribble furiously, the photographers pop flashbulbs, and the television cameras grind away. Everyone shakes hands and congratulates me. I can hardly wait to see the newspapers. There isn't a word about Shostakovich. It's all about the enlightened initiative of the government, its concern for the people, its support of the arts. Every paper misspells my name in a different way. Ah, well, the pictures are nice—one paper even has them in color. At one of the concerts a baby begins to cry, and all of a sudden we have three singers instead of two. In stereo. Nobody seems to be doing anything about the baby. At the end of the movement I walk off stage, stumbling over the television cables, and request that the third singer be removed. A whole squad of administrators and ushers moves into the auditorium and gently escorts the baby and its creators toward an exit. The concert resumes.

The next movement of the symphony is all about suicide. The soprano begins and gets so deeply involved in her emotions that she fails to notice that she is one bar behind the orchestra. If she would only look at my beat, I could easily straighten her out. I give her a look that spells murder, not suicide, but she does not notice. We go on for one full page until she does, and I am profoundly grateful that Shostakovich is not in the audience. When it is all over, the soprano and I shake hands, take a joint bow, and I manage a smile that is a triumph of hypocrisy.

9

The Mysterious Art of Conducting, or Speak Loudly and Carry a Small Stick

Conducting is undoubtedly the world's healthiest indoor activity. Most conductors live to a biblical old age. While executives, managers, and orchestra musicians die in their tracks in their forties or fifties, conductors remain young in their sprightly eighties. Evidently one wave of the stick is worth a thousand pushups. Toscanini conducted until he was eighty-seven and retained the physique of a young man. Bruno Walter, when he was past eighty, told me he felt no older than he had at forty; he conducted until his death at eighty-four. Leopold Stokowski was still conducting at eighty-nine, Sir Thomas Beecham until well into his eighties, Pierre Monteux until his death at eighty-nine. A conductor in his sixties is practically a spring chicken.

What makes conductors so indestructible? Is it the vigorous physical exercise of wagging a stick? That is only part of it. There are other factors, such as the daily ego gratification. What adulation! It is Maestro here, Mae-

stro there. What power! The lives of his orchestra players, and their families, are in his hands. He can hire and
fire at will. When Rodzinski became permanent director
of the New York Philharmonic, he began by dismissing
more than forty players. Furthermore, a conductor has
to solve so many problems that he has no time to grow
old. A conductor must be a diplomat, politician, a masterful organizer, public-relations wizard, and financial
expert. He must be able to wheedle money from wealthy
music lovers, and reconcile the opposing viewpoints of
feuding board members. He may have to favor soloists
and composers who are protégés or friends of prominent
supporters. He must make speeches for ladies' matinée
clubs, give interviews to the press, appear on radio and
television, dance at the symphony ball, fondle martinis
at cocktail parties, munch cookies at receptions, and
shake hands with five hundred people standing in line.
He must attend luncheons, dinners, and suppers. In his
spare time he must also study scores, audition orchestra
players, rehearse with orchestra and soloists and—oh yes
—conduct concerts. It is a distinct advantage if a conductor can also conduct.

Once upon a time there was a popular notion that an
artist needed time to meditate and think, leisure to rumi-
nate, to create that deliberate vacuum that encourages
the onrush of new creative ideas. Images pass through
the mind: Beethoven strolling through Vienna woods,
Gauguin sunning himself on the beaches of Tahiti, Toscanini resting on his private island in Italy, Paganini
forgetting his cares at the gambling tables. Is there a
conductor today who plays poker or roulette? If so, ten
to one he is fulfilling a social obligation or memorizing
a score. In fact, I knew one conductor who did both at
the same time: mechanically nodding to the talkative
lady on his left, he would lift food to his mouth with the
fork in one hand, drum the rhythm of a symphony on the

table with the fingers of the other, while absently humming the tune under cover of his mustache. During the shrimp cocktail he went through the first movement; the Scherzo went with the soup. It took two helpings of the main course to memorize the long Adagio; he skipped the dessert because a conductor has to consider what is left of his figure. He worked on the Finale during coffee and brandy. He was the great French conductor Pierre Monteux.

What has brought on this mania for conducting by heart? (A misnomer, by the way, because many who conduct from memory do so without heart.) It all started with Toscanini. Now I have no quarrel with a man conducting by heart when he has a photographic memory. The trouble is that some men who pretend to conduct "by heart" have no memories at all, relying on their orchestras like riders who rely on their horses to find the way back to the stable. One irate concertmaster when asked what the Maestro was conducting at the next concert, answered, "I don't know what he is going to conduct—but *we* are playing Beethoven's Fifth!" Dame Myra Hess, the famous English pianist, is reputed to have asked Beecham, "Sir Thomas, are you again going to conduct by heart?" "Certainly," said the conductor affably. "In that case," she said, "*I* am going to use my music." Once Otto Klemperer was interviewed by a journalist who wanted to know why he used a score when so many others conducted from memory. "Because," replied the German master majestically, "I can read music."

There is a vast difference between a soloist performing from memory and a conductor doing likewise. The soloist really must know every note—if he falters for one fraction of a second, the music stops catastrophically—for nothing makes the violin or piano go on by itself. But the conductor? Even if his mind wanders from Mozart's

"Jupiter" Symphony to "You Ain't Nothin' But a Houn' Dog," the imperturbable orchestra players continue reading the music in front of them. One conductor, the German Oscar Frid, once gave a violent beat, supposed to produce a *fortissimo* blast by the whole orchestra. He almost lost his balance as the cello section responded with an anemic little grunt. The maestro had simply skipped a bar, the one just before the triumphant C-major chord that begins the coda to the Overture of Weber's *Der Freischütz*. One day Richard Burgin, long-time concertmaster and associate conductor of the Boston Symphony, asked me which I found easier, playing the violin or conducting. "Let me think a minute," I said. "No, you don't have to think," answered Burgin. "I'll make it easy for you. Right now it is six in the evening. If I were to ask you to conduct the accompaniment to the Beethoven violin concerto tonight, would you accept?" "Of course," I said without a moment's hesitation. "Now," insisted Burgin, "if I were to ask you to *play* the violin concerto tonight, would you accept?" "Of course not," I said indignantly. "Well, there is your answer," said Burgin smugly.

A conductor with one strange idiosyncrasy (so the story goes) conducted the most complex modern scores from memory, to everyone's amazement. Again and again, during rehearsals and concerts, he would pull up his left sleeve, closely scrutinizing something concealed beneath it. The orchestra players were mystified, and the conductor's peculiar behavior became the subject of endless gossip and speculation. One day, in the middle of a performance, the conductor collapsed and fell to the floor. In a flash, the entire orchestra was on him, tugging at his left sleeve. There they found a tiny piece of paper taped to his shirt cuff. On it they read, "Violins to the left—cellos to the right."

By contrast, Dimitri Mitropoulos had such a phenomenal memory that he knew not only every note in the score, but even the printed rehearsal numbers. During rehearsals he would stop, put his hand to his forehead, think a moment, and say, "Eight bars before number thirty-seven please." Louis Krasner, who gave the premiere of Arnold Schönberg's excruciatingly difficult violin concerto, told me that he went with Mitropoulos to the first rehearsal with orchestra. Suddenly Krasner realized he had forgotten the orchestra score. He started to turn back. Mitropoulus waved him on. At the rehearsal he conducted the stupendously complex score from memory. There were frequent stops for corrections, customary at a first rehearsal. Krasner sometimes found it difficult to find his place in the middle of the piece. No matter, Mitropoulos sang it for him. Von Bülow, who championed Brahms's music, used to say there were two kinds of conductors—those who have the score in their head, and those who have their head in the score.

Have you ever seen what an orchestra score looks like? Take the score of a Mahler symphony, for instance. There is a stave of five parallel horizontal lines for each different instrument: the piccolo at the top, followed by the flutes, oboes, English horns, clarinet, bass clarinet, bassoon, contrabassoon, French horns, trumpets, trombones, tuba. Then the percussion instruments, of which there may be easily half a dozen or more: kettledrums, cymbals, woodblock, snaredrums, xylophone, triangle, bells, celesta. There may also be a piano, and perhaps two harps. Finally there are the first and second violins, the violas, cellos, and basses. Thus there may be from twenty to twenty-five staves (of five lines each), all of which the conductor is expected to scan simultaneously, which is comparable to reading all the lines of a page in a book at the same time. In addition, some of the staves are in a different key, because there are several transposing instruments, such as the clarinet and the French horn. Transposing is comparable to finding several lines in that book you are reading in a different language, say French, German, and Russian, all intermingled with your English. And the conductor still has to read them simultaneously.

Now you may ask, How does anyone know whether the conductor *really* reads all those twenty-five staves in the score at a glance? And what happens if he doesn't? Nothing. The orchestra plays on. Those conductors unable to see and hear are usually smart enough to let the orchestra read the piece through several times, confident that the players, without any guidance from the conductor, will solve most of his problems anyway.

What, then, is the real function of a conductor? Certainly not to memorize. The true function of the conductor is, first of all, to produce fusion and unity from the individual efforts of a hundred unreconstructed musicians. His first function is to bring all the sounds into focus, to balance the instruments so that no one section drowns out the other. The small group of brass players, left to their own murderous devices, could easily exterminate fifty men sawing away on their violins and cellos. The delicate flute, oboe, clarinet, and bassoon must be carefully poised and attuned. Kettledrums, cymbals, and other atomic weapons must be kept under strict control.

Is this enough to make music? Not yet. This is only creating the conditions that make it possible to produce great music. And here we begin to enter the mysterious realm of creative art. What matters is the conductor's command of the infinite spectrum of sounds, of tempi; the deliberate contrast between passion and serenity, between climax and languor, between speed and suspended motion; the masterful control of those megatons of vibration and volume that lie between the two extremes of an orchestral crescendo, and the judgment, taste, and experience to know how much or how little to use, because all that's in the score is the one word *"crescendo."* Even then, the conductor, knowing all these things, may still be unable to bring the music to life. For the real conductor must also be a master psychologist. He stands face to face with a hundred experienced musicians, many of whom are underpaid, cynical, and tired. They are frustrated Horowitzes and Heifetzes. They have played that Fifth Symphony a thousand times. "You know, I had an awful nightmare," said one orchestra player to another. "I dreamt I was sitting in the orchestra, playing the Fifth Symphony again." Said the other orchestra player sympathetically, "How dreadful." "But that wasn't the worst of it," said the first player. "When I woke up, I *was* sitting in the orchestra, playing the Fifth Symphony."

To arouse and inspire his men, the conductor has to be a combination of Svengali, Dale Carnegie, Billy Graham, and Genghis Khan. He hypnotizes, cajoles, exhorts, threatens, curses, apologizes. Every successful conductor has devised his own personal methods, which are particularly effective when the conductor has the power to hire and fire. If he is a guest conductor, he leans more heavily on Dale Carnegie. The more experienced start their first rehearsal with a new orchestra with an emotional appeal that would make a drill sergeant weep in his gin. "Gentlemen, without you I am nothing—I stand before you with humility—please help me." Sometimes this approach works wonders. The musicians cooperate so enthusiastically that the guest conductor is given a permanent appointment. He then promptly fires half the orchestra, as Rodzinski did.

Toscanini was a combination of Svengali and Genghis Khan. In one of his obituaries I read that his men *loved* him. I don't believe it. They certainly admired him, and he inspired and hypnotized them. But love never thrived on abuse and insults, certainly not among men. And

Toscanini excelled at abuse and insult. On one occasion, having hurled unprintable Italian insults at a player in front of the whole orchestra, Toscanini found the man waiting for him outside afterward. The player didn't know a word of Italian, but what he said to Toscanini in English would have made a sailor blush. Toscanini dismissed him with a lordly gesture, saying, "Is too late to apologiza!" On another occasion Toscanini stomped out of a recording session in a state of fury only a few minutes after it had begun, leaving the recording company the whopping bill for the orchestra. The following day, when Toscanini had cooled off, the recording director, without a word, played back to him what had been captured on tape. It began with a minute of music, suddenly interrupted by a torrent of such profanity that Toscanini blushed to the roots of his hair. He was deeply shaken, like anyone who found himself on the receiving end of a Toscanini tirade.

Fortunately, there was a lovable side to the old Maestro. When Bronislaw Huberman founded the Palestine Philharmonic (now the Israel Philharmonic) in the wake of Germany's regime of Nazi terror, Toscanini flew halfway around the world to conduct the opening concerts. He accepted no fee and insisted on paying his own expenses. When another great musician, Adolph Busch, was stricken by illness, Toscanini, then past eighty, jumped into his car and drove all day to reach his bedside.

Many legends circulated about Toscanini. One dreadful piece of nonsense that gained wide credence was that he, and he alone, carried out the precise intentions of the composers to the last microscopic flyspeck. Toscanini was supposed to have a direct pipeline to Mozart and Beethoven, and therein lay his greatness. What utter stupidity! When Toscanini conducted Ravel's "Bolero" in Europe, the composer was for once present in the flesh. And what did Ravel do? He ran out of the hall in anguish and fury, crying, "He murdered my 'Bolero.' The tempo was much too fast."

It would be a dull world if there were indeed just one correct way to interpret a great piece of music. All musicians would have to play everything with the deadly conformity of junior business executives. Gone would be the thrill of hearing a recording of the "Emperor" Concerto as played by Schnabel, then going to a concert to hear Rubinstein, Horowitz, Serkin, or Casadesus present an equally glorious but different conception of the same masterpiece. For herein lies precisely the challenge to the master interpreter: to divine the intentions of the composer behind the notes that tell only half the story. I have heard Furtwängler conduct certain works almost twice as slowly as Toscanini. But each made the music sound right in his own manner, each *compelled* you to accept his monumental convictions while you listened. Even more paradoxical, each interpreter might modify his own interpretation at the next performance, for the search for perfection in art is endless, and the definitive performance remains eternally unattainable.

Some conductors develop a "Father knows best" attitude toward their players that probes deep into their personal lives, particularly if the conductor has a strong-minded wife. Mrs. Monteux's concern knew no boundaries. At one time the baldheaded members of the San Francisco Symphony were ordered to wear hairpieces at all concerts. The following Friday afternoon the orchestra was unrecognizable: no longer did the brilliant lights of the giant chandeliers in San Francisco's stately opera house reflect on pates waxed and shining. An impenetrable jungle of luxuriant toupées filled the stage. Where venerable artists, ripe with years, had once joined in the common cause of music, a Mardi Gras crowd of Elvis Presleys seemed to have taken over. A sigh of horror went through the staid Friday-afternoon audience. Women tried to recognize their husbands, boys their fathers, pupils their teachers. Board members wandered disconsolately through the corridors. The experiment was abandoned.

Another time the New York Philharmonic had a paternalistic conductor whose wife attempted to instill some *esprit de corps* into the wives of the orchestra. She summoned all hundred of them to a meeting and made a beautiful little speech, exhorting the women to send their husbands off to rehearsal in the most cheerful possible spirit. The wife of the clarinetist rose to reply. "Madame Rodzinski," she said, "our husbands are cheerful enough *before* the rehearsal. The problem is, how do we make them cheerful *afterward?*"

It is impossible to be a great conductor without being a great musician. But every great musician is not necessarily a good conductor. Ravel, for instance, confined his conducting to vertical and horizontal motions of the right wrist, as if he were testing it for symptoms of arthritis. A metronome would have done just as well. Some of the world's most celebrated virtuosi have been dismal failures as conductors.

What does the special gift of conducting consist of? It is one of the hardest things in the world to analyze. A great conductor, in addition to being a great musician, is also a born actor. But experience is the great taskmaster. In Germany conductors rise through the ranks. They begin by coaching opera singers, then become assistant conductors in one of a hundred provincial opera houses, gradually being promoted to bigger cities and more important jobs until they end up, some of them, in Berlin or Vienna.

I don't believe that conducting can really be taught. Every conductor has to develop his own brand of body

English—a mysterious something that grows slowly and organically, and ultimately becomes the unself-conscious projection of the sum total of one man's knowledge, experience, insight, and judgment. Pretty gestures by themselves are meaningless. What a good conductor does not do is as important as what he does.

A number of great conductors started out quite differently. Monteux sawed away on his viola in the Opéra Comique in Paris until he was past forty. Others were born to wealth or married it, bought a baton and an orchestra, and began acquiring experience at the top. When Thomas Beecham first founded the London Philharmonic with the fortune amassed through his father's pharmaceutical products (Beecham's pills), it quickly became known as the London *Pill*harmonic orchestra. In time Sir Thomas became one of the world's great conductors.

Sir Thomas was also one of the world's greatest eccentrics. On a sunny day he thought nothing of hailing a passing cab on Oxford Street, throwing his fur coat inside, and instructing the cabbie to follow him while he took his morning walk.

When I first met Beecham, he said, "Temianka, Temianka. What an unusual name. Where were you born?" "In Scotland," I answered. "Well," retorted Sir Thomas, "shouldn't your name be Tam O'Shanter?"

The story was printed in *Punch*. There was only one thing wrong with it. Beecham never said it to me. He thought of it afterward, and good promoter that he was, made sure it got the widest circulation.

Serge Koussevitzky had begun as a fabulous double bass player and started his conducting career when his wealthy wife sponsored an orchestra for him. I went to one of his concerts when he was in his seventies with fellow conductor Fritz Reiner. "By Gad," said Reiner, in feigned astonishment, "he has learned to conduct!" That was a tribute of sorts, coming from the supreme virtuoso of the baton. Reiner himself suffered from periods of depression during which he would barely move the stick. During one such episode a trombone player, sitting way in the back of the orchestra, brought a pair of field glasses to the rehearsal which he trained on Reiner. "What are you doing?" screamed Reiner who was not noted for his angelic disposition. "I'm trying to see your beat," answered the trombonist, unshaken. It was his last frontal view of the great Hungarian conductor.

There is little danger that trombone players will have trouble observing Leonard Bernstein in action. Ever since his arrival on the scene, a whole new school of conducting has developed. Gone are the dignity, the serene command of a Bruno Walter or an Otto Klemperer, to say nothing of a Pierre Monteux, whose slightest gesture, merest glance, produced the most sensitive response from a hundred men and women. No, today's modern conductor is different. He crouches and snarls like a jaguar; he jumps three feet into the air like a kangaroo. He lunges with his baton deep into the orchestra, mimicking Douglas Fairbanks in *The Three Musketeers.* He impersonates Sam Snead, firmly grasping his baton with both hands, swinging and slicing, whacking an imaginary golfball. He is conductor, acrobat, and choreographer all in one. He is the symphonic Walter Mitty. Meanwhile the long-suffering orchestra continues to play the music, imperturbably.

Conducting, unfortunately, offers unique opportunities to the worst as well as the best. Rich amateurs can hire an orchestra for short or long periods, and so long as they conduct standard works that the orchestra has previously rehearsed and performed countless times under competent conductors, the orchestra will function fine—just so long as the amateur conductor is smart enough not to interfere.

No one can fake on the violin or piano, or give a vocal recital without adequate training. But anyone with a good arm can wave it. RCA Victor once sold record kits complete with conducting batons. It took more skill to make the batons than to use them.

The world is full of instant conductors. New York's onetime Mayor Fiorello La Guardia, England's Prime Minister Edward Heath, and comedian Danny Kaye are among the many amateurs who have conducted symphony orchestras. They never gave violin recitals.

When I made my conducting debut barely out of my adolescence, I anxiously asked George Szell—who was responsible for my engagement—for some last-minute advice. "Follow the orchestra," he said half-seriously.

Many years ago a man named Joseph Stransky captured the conductorship of the New York Philharmonic, with the aid of his wealthy wife. Orchestras, of course, are chronically in debt. According to the story that made the rounds at the time, Stransky was sentenced to die in the electric chair for having murdered his concertmaster. The executioner strapped him in, connected the electrodes, and applied an initial current of five thousand volts, enough to kill the most hardened criminals instantly. Stransky didn't react. The executioner tried again, this time doubling the voltage. Still no effect. They tried once more, this time using a twenty-five thousand-volt blast, enough to kill a herd of buffalo. Stransky smiled placidly.

An electrical engineer was called in. He examined first the chair, then the condemned man. Whereupon he turned to the executioner and gave his verdict: "It's really quite simple—this man is a non-conductor."

Such are the charitable stories musicians circulate about each other, especially about conductors.

What is the future of the mysterious art of conducting? We have come a long way since the time of Johann Sebastian Bach, who led his small orchestra while seated at the harpsichord or the organ, sometimes whacking a rolled-up piece of music on a chair or a music stand to keep the players together; or since the days of Jean-Baptiste Lully, who stamped his cane on the floor. The first of the great conductors, Felix Mendelssohn, kept a score in front of him because to perform from memory was considered "showing off." When he once forgot his music at a concert in London, he placed the wrong music on his piano rather than being accused of playing from memory. Now we have entered the electronic age. Many modern composers add prerecorded tapes to their compositions for orchestra, with amplifiers placed all around the auditorium. The volume of sound produced is frightening.

Sometimes, in my nightmares, I see conductors discarding the conductor's stand in favor of a master panel with a hundred buttons wired to every seat in the orchestra. Simultaneous electrical impulses will produce a perfection of orchestral ensemble without precedent in the annals of music. By increasing the current, the conductor can force recalcitrant players into line. Incorrigible members of the orchestra will be disposed of through an ejector mechanism. No more turning of pages, which reduces the orchestra's efficiency (because one player on every stand has to interrupt his playing every minute or so to engage in this operation). All the sheet music will be mechanically wound on drums, with, of course, the conductor regulating their speed. In those same nightmares I worry about unions continuing to reduce available rehearsal time, taxing the conductor's ingenuity to find shortcuts. I have absurd nocturnal visions of an immense horizontal pole with loops through which all the outside fiddlers pass their right arms, thus being forced to bow up and down with the concertmaster. The conductor, whether he knows his symphonies from memory or not, dispenses with score and music stand. Powerful projectors throw the score on the ceiling above the conductor, invisible to the audience. Thus the maestro is able to indulge in heavenward glances conveying his spiritual communication with the divine powers that inspire him. Finally, in the same dreadful nightmare, I see members of the audience arriving and leaving at will through individual trapdoors beneath each seat. Instead of paying when they enter, they are given something resembling a turnpike toll card and pay upon leaving, in accordance with the musical mileage consumed.

In my waking moments I view the future of the art of conducting more optimistically. Probably never before have there been so many highly trained, gifted young conductors. The availability of recordings and printed pocket scores of thousands of symphonic works provides the aspiring conductor with previously nonexistent opportunities. Such organizations as the American Symphony Orchestra League offer special practice orchestra seminars in which the fledgling conductor tries his hand under the supervision of a master. Motion-picture cameras and tape-recorders grind away while he is conducting. Afterward he views and hears what he has done. A master conductor analyzes his mistakes and gives him advice. Richard Lert was especially admired for his ability to help his young colleagues in these sessions. Once, when he was again complimented, I heard him speak the final word on the whole subject: "But of course"—he said with a slight air of impatience, as if it should be obvious to everybody—"every good conductor is first and foremost a teacher."

IO

The Music Critic, or
Murder in the Concert Hall

Don't believe everything I say in this chapter. Performers and critics are, after all, natural enemies. You see, I'm already exaggerating. Nonetheless, some of my best friends are critics. I chide them as unmercifully in private as they chide us in public. For instance, sometimes I ask them: What credentials do you bring to your profession that permits some of you to make such devastating judgments? How do most of you stay where you are? If a medical student is drummed out of the corps, he isn't named editor of the *AMA Journal*. If a law student fails the bar exams, he isn't put in charge of the *Law Review*. If a businessman goes bankrupt, he isn't rewarded with a column in *The Wall Street Journal*. But many an aspiring musician unable to make the grade gets a job as a music critic. I know one music critic who considers himself a composer. Nobody plays his music. Nevertheless, he has sat on a powerful West Coast paper for many years, in cantankerous judgment of all composers, conductors, and soloists. The vast majority of music critics would be forced to admit, however reluctantly, that they couldn't play a one-minute piece to save the lives of their families. Some studied musicology, which is to musical performance what anatomy is to open-heart surgery. Musicology is music history, theory, science, and research. Music performance is a different ball game. Knowing that Beethoven was born in 1770 and went deaf doesn't necessarily mean that you are equipped to pass judgment on a performance of his last string quartets. But I would not mind all this so much if some critics would not conceal their love of music so effectively.

Every profession has its built-in character distortions. A politician becomes verbose. A policeman becomes suspicious. If you say "Good morning" to a psychiatrist, he will wonder, "Now what does he mean by that?" The character distortions developed by many music critics are frustration and anger. Do they really have inferiority complexes? God knows. But I remember what one psychoanalyst told a patient after five years of intensive therapy, "You don't have an inferiority complex; you *are* inferior."

The most serious indictment of the critical profession is its simple failure to recognize true genius. From Beethoven to Bartók. Philip Hale, one of America's most influential critics, called Beethoven's Ninth Symphony "stupid and hopelessly vulgar music." This, mind you, as late as June 1899, when Beethoven had been dead for seventy-two years. "As a work of art, it is naught," pontificated *The New York Times*, referring to Bizet's *Carmen*. The London *Saturday Review* disposed of Brahms's majestic Fourth Symphony with: "There is no more intolerably dull symphony in the world." "Poison—rank poison," said the London *Musical World* of Wagner's *Lohengrin*. And of his masterpiece, *Die Meistersinger*, the *Berlin Montagszeitung* wrote, "A more horrendous *Katzenjammer* . . . could not be accomplished even if all the organ grinders of Berlin would have been locked up in

the circus, each playing a different waltz." Edward Han-
slick, the greatly feared and powerful music critic of the
Vienna *Neue Freie Presse*, charmingly evaluated one of the
greatest works of the nineteenth century thus: "Tchaikovsky's violin concerto gives us for the first time the
hideous notion that there can be music that stinks to the
ear." Beethoven, Bizet, Brahms, Wagner, Tchaikovsky!
What else is there to say?

Does anyone think that matters have improved since
those days? Bartók, commenting on the premiere of his
violin concerto, wrote to Joseph Szigeti on January 30,
1944:

> The critics, of course, remained true to themselves
> though they wrote a shade more kindly than usual. I
> would not even mention them but for the fact that one
> of them made an asinine remark to the effect that he did
> not think this work *would squeeze out* the concertos of
> Beethoven, Mendelssohn, Brahms. How is it possible to
> write such stupidities? Who but a candidate for a lunatic
> asylum would want to "squeeze out" these works?

We musicians are in the strange position of being publicly judged and sometimes victimized by our musical
inferiors, day after day, from the beginning to the end of
our careers. How devastating the effects of a music critic's onslaughts can be is proven by the fact that such
world-renowned conductors as Sir Thomas Beecham,
Sir John Barbirolli, and Rafael Kubelik were driven out
of (respectively) Seattle, New York, and Chicago by
critical persecution that took on the aspects of personal
vendettas. In each instance the critic escaped scot-free,
no matter how incensed the public was. For the freedom
of the press that every newspaper editor fiercely defends
becomes a privileged sanctuary or a sniper's paradise
when the critic is unprincipled.

It is useless for the performer to direct his protests to

the critic because the critic consigns most of these letters to the wastebasket. In those rare instances in which he allows them to be printed they will assuredly be followed by another letter representing the opposite viewpoint. Perhaps I have overlooked something, but I have never known a critic to apologize or admit he was wrong. When John Foster Dulles was Secretary of State, he was asked whether he had ever been wrong. Mr. Dulles thought long and hard. "Yes", he finally said, "once—many, many years ago. I *thought* I had made a wrong decision. Of course, it turned out that I had been right all along. But I was *wrong* to have *thought* that I was wrong." Mr. Dulles missed his calling. He should have been a music critic.

There are times when I view music critics more in sorrow than in anger. They are the butt of countless jibes on the part of performers, who give critics a wide berth, perhaps because they fear they will be accused of currying favor if they are observed to greet the hereditary enemy. Most musicians experience a sense of acute discomfort in their presence. The critics are no less self-conscious and are wary of expressing an unprinted opinion—I was almost going to say an unpaid one. Have you ever noticed their behavior at concerts? They cultivate a highly professional blank look throughout the proceedings, a look that may spell delirious enthusiasm, bottomless contempt, or complete mental vacuum. Of course they don't applaud. Only once did I know a critic effusive enough to come and embrace me backstage after a concert. Still very young, I was enormously impressed. "Boy, am I going to get a great review!" I naïvely exclaimed to my father. The next morning the critic, after a few encouraging words about my "future," tore me limb from limb.

Although critics usually have the last word because of the strategic position they hold, there are instances in which they came off second best. Max Reger, the composer, achieved the ultimate in German delicacy when he wrote the following letter, famous among musicians: "I am sitting in the smallest room of my house and have your criticism before me. Soon I shall have it behind me." Fritz Kreisler, who in the twenties and thirties was probably the most famous living violinist, was savagely attacked by the pontifical Ernest Newman of the London *Sunday Times* for having concealed the identity of his own original compositions behind the names of little-known old Italian masters. Newman was a first-class writer, but he was beaten at his own game in the superb exchange of letters published in the *Sunday Times*, in which Kreisler proved he could handle polished invective as brilliantly as a flying staccato. His definition of Newman as "that musician by the grace of *Grove's Music Dictionary*" left Newman crawling underneath his bookshelves.

The famous feud between the two men was sparked by Kreisler's revelation, at the age of sixty (in 1935), that it was he who was the author of many works hitherto programed as seventeenth- and eighteenth-century compositions, mostly under such obscure or forgotten names as Francoeur, Martini, Pugnani, *et al.* The enchanting little masterpieces had become vastly popular in the intervening years. They were played in concerts, cafés, and even churches throughout the world. At the insistence of his adoring audiences Kreisler had to play them in all his own concerts. To finish without such encores as "Caprice Viennois" or "Tambourin Chinois" would have been unthinkable.

Why had Kreisler originally published so many of these compositions under another name? His explanation was forthright and plausible: when young and unknown, "I found it impudent and tactless to repeat my name endlessly on the program." Kreisler's revelation delighted most of the musical world. There was an out-pouring of new admiration at the discovery that Kreisler, in addition to being a superb violinist, was the actual creator of so many musical gems. But Ernest Newman, the critic, did not share the general delight. He was not amused—in fact, he took it as a personal affront. Spitefully he wrote:

> I do not know if any comment has been made in the press on Kreisler's recent admission that certain works long regarded as being merely arranged by him are his own compositions. . . .
>
> Now if this news is true, the revelation is both welcome and regrettable. It is welcome to show how easy it is, and always was, to write this kind of music. The average concert goer no doubt feels that those hateful fellows the critics have had their ignorance shown up and been made to look foolish. . . .
>
> The simple truth is that a vast amount of seventeenth and eighteenth century music was merely the exploitation of formulae, the effective handling of which is within the scope of any ordinarily intelligent musician today. . . . In so far as Bach and Handel merely sat down in perfectly cold blood and ground out their morning's ration of music according-to-the-recipe they merely produced well-sounding stuff that anyone of any intelligence today could turn out by the handful. . . .

Having already stated three times that anyone, just anyone, could have done as well as Kreisler, Newman ran the argument into the ground. He repeated:

> Anyone with the least bit of music in him and the least knowledge of the period could produce this sort of thing any morning with the hand he did not require for shaving. . . .
>
> . . . the average music of that period is as easy to imitate as the average political speech of today. . . .
>
> As far as the merely musical point is concerned, then, there is nothing whatever in Kreisler's achievement. . . .

Kreisler, a gentle man of almost endless good humor and humility, was aroused. World-famous as he was, the *Sunday Times* could hardly refuse to publish his reply. It said in part:

> ... that inveterate grumbler Mr. Ernest Newman took up the gauntlets against me, ostensibly on behalf of musical ethics, but in reality in his own defence. He is hard put to explain why he, the musical augur par excellence, failed to nail down my transcriptions for the pastiches they were. There was really no necessity for Mr. Newman to worry, for the prestige of a critic with a sense of musical values is not in the least endangered because a piece, which he pronounced good, is found to have been written by another person than he thought. The name changes, the value remains.
>
> But Mr. Newman's pique is aroused. . . . He proceeds to tell an astonished world that there is a formula by which any ordinary intelligent modern musician can write in the style of any composer of the seventeenth or eighteenth century he chooses. . . .
>
> Of course, there is no such formula, as the eminent critic knows very well.

Mr. Newman did not give up. He replied to Kreisler's letter with a second, still more vehement attack, again laboring his proposal that "any ordinarily good musician" could have done as well as Kreisler. Then Kreisler had the final word. Calling Newman "a meritorious compiler of data from musical reference books," he wrote:

> I suggest that Mr. Newman be taken at his word and compelled to prove his simple-formula theory, by turning out *in clausura* a specified piece in antique style. (If, as an alleged second grade product by Bach or Handel, this piece succeeds in getting by the caretaker of Queen's Hall, I am prepared to make humble apologies.) Or are we expected to believe that this grandiloquent censor, who for years has been lecturing eminent composers,

instrumentalists and singers on their respective art, may in the end not be able to qualify as an "ordinary intelligent musician," according to the standard set up by himself?

Mr. Newman unable to meet that challenge, went down for the count.

I have two successful battles of my own to report. The first was against a critic in Tallinn, the capital of Estonia, one of the three small Baltic countries absorbed by Russia during World War II. It was my debut in Tallinn, and I was playing with a local accompanist who did a lamentable job. Throughout the concert he was about half a bar behind me. When he joined me after the cadenza in the Mendelssohn concerto, he suddenly started playing twice as fast. There was not the remotest possibility of my keeping up with him. I had to bring him to his senses somehow. There was no time to think. I excitedly began beating time with my foot. Everybody noticed, including the pianist, and we weathered the crisis. Except that the pianist's paramour, who was in the audience, became infuriated with me. As she was also the critic's wife, my outlook for a favorable notice and a brilliant Estonian career suddenly began to dim.

I know very little Estonian (only the word Estonia), so I could not tell what the next morning's paper was trying to do to me. That evening I played in another Estonian town. Backstage I found a letter with a yellow tulip attached to it, yellow being the color that symbolizes hatred. Inside the envelope was that morning's criticism accompanied by a translation. When I finished reading, I was stupefied. "Last night," stated the opening sentence, "we heard the worst violinist who ever appeared in Estonia—and we have heard many bad violinists." From there on the article gradually became unfriendly.

After recovering my composure I put the review in my pocket, picked up my fiddle and played the evening's concert. At the end a number of disappointed-looking musicians came backstage. One of them, acting as a spokesman, said, "We came because we read that review in this morning's paper." Then he added generously, "That critic is crazy. You are certainly not the worst violinist who ever played in Estonia!"

The next morning I called on the editor of the newspaper to demand a public retraction and apology. He flatly refused, stating that he had full confidence in the integrity of his staff and would in no circumstances interfere with their sacrosanct editorial freedom. At that time I was still a British subject, and a British passport carried tremendous prestige. When the editor made his brave statement, I rose, whipped out my passport, and began walking out of his office, declaring that I would have to talk with my ambassador. The editor jumped up, coaxed me back to my chair, and in a tone of voice several shades paler asked me to state my demands. We understood each other perfectly. On the front page of the next day's paper appeared:

> An apology by the editor.
> An apology by the critic, including the abject admission that I was *not* the worst violinist ever to have played in Estonia.
> An unbiased review of the concert by Estonia's leading violin teacher, whose wife evidently had no commitments to the accompanist.

My other successful joust with a critic occurred in Toledo, Ohio, after a concert with the Paganini Quartet. The hall was packed, the audience was enthusiastic. But the critic seemed not to have heard things the same way the audience did: his review the next day made me realize how innocuous tornadoes are, for even the worst tornado leaves *something* standing. This was total destruction, except for the closing sentence, which read, "Ah well, the coffee in the intermission was good."

I was determined to get even. But how? Anger defeats its own purpose. My strategy had to be different. I hit upon the sorrowful approach as I wrote my letter. Toledo, the new Athens of culture, was having its morale undermined day after day by a pocket-sized Joe McCarthy who could see nothing to praise in a community that had so generously clasped him to its bosom. The people of Toledo wanted to build—the critic wanted to destroy. Would the good people of Toledo allow evil to triumph?

It was a good letter. I checked it with a lawyer friend for possible libel and changed it here and there. The next problem was to get it published in the Toledo paper. Fortunately I had gotten the background on the local situation. There already was widespread resentment against the critic, and people were only waiting for the right moment to act. So at the bottom of my letter I listed the names of several prominent community leaders to whom I was sending copies. Sending copies is a powerful device; it is the best arm-twister developed since the invention of judo, and should be used only when absolutely necessary. It always works, and it worked this time. My letter was published. I'll never know exactly how much it contributed to the firing of the critic. But fired he was.

I know of only one instance in which a concert performer was awarded damages when he sued a music critic and his paper. An English critic had stated after a London concert by a singer named Steuart Wilson that he was "incompetent." Wilson sued and received £2000, then roughly $10,000.

I myself have never felt that there is anything unethical in maintaining personal relations with a critic. I knew the late Olin Downes, who was the musical pontiff of *The New York Times.* We shared the same passion for chess, and occasionally would play through half the night. Knowing his strong feelings on the subject of bribery, I trembled at the thought of losing a game, arousing his suspicions, and bringing disaster upon myself at my next New York concert. Downes once told me about the honest critic who had received a case of French champagne as a softening-up present from an unknown pianist about to make his debut. The champagne was too good to be returned, so the critic squared his conscience by starting his review: "I wish to express my warmest thanks to Mr. Ivory Keys for the case of champagne he so generously sent me this week; it was absolutely first rate. Unfortunately, the gentleman's debut last night was not in the same class. . . ."

Too few critics realize how much the performer, walking out on the stage to face his audience, gives of himself night after night. Or how inhuman it is to expect the same degree of perfection at all times. What sustains the artist, even the most famous and self-assured, under such pressure and tension is the encouragement he receives from the outside world: his audience, his colleagues, his friends, and the press. The point is beautifully illustrated by a little-known Heifetz story. Engaging a new secretary to accompany him on his tours, Jascha supposedly said, "You need not compliment me after my concerts. If I play well, I know it myself. If I don't, I shall only be disappointed if you flatter me." The young man took him at his word. Six concerts later, an angry Heifetz walked up to him. "What's the matter? You don't like music?" Dame Myra Hess, the least vainglorious of artists, said to me once, "I, and all of us performers, need encouragement all the time. I could not go on without it." It is this need for moral support that makes the artist sometimes hypersensitive to criticism.

I occasionally defend the critic's right to free speech. But I cannot defend his right to be vicious or witty at the artist's expense. A brass knuckle to the critic who obliterates the budding career of a young artist with a review of two sentences saying, "Mr. Ebenezer Schlivovitz gave a recital in Town Hall last night. Why?" Or, "Yesterday Miss Eileen Jones played Brahms in Carnegie Hall. Brahms lost." A singer who had a packed house, thanks to her social connections and fabulous wealth, received the following notice: "As was proved once again last night, money talks; but it can't sing." Carl Flesch told me that early in his career a critic wrote, "Mr. Flesch's tone bears a striking resemblance to that of a canary suffering from acute laryngitis." Zero Mostel once conducted a serious orchestra concert. The critic wrote, "It was obvious that Mr. Mostel knew the music forward and backward. Unfortunately, it was impossible to tell which way he was conducting it."

I know artists who become physically sick with rage and frustration when they are the butt of such jokes. Nothing kills like ridicule. Thoughtless people love it and elevate the malicious critic in their collective esteem. The public ought to remember that the performer brings a lifetime of devotion and talent to his work. Within the space of a few minutes the thoughtless critic rips through an evening's performance representing years of study, leaving a twisted heap of wreckage. Often the death sentence is meted out in a hasty scribble or a breathless phonecall, the result of an early deadline. I know of no other profession in which such conditions prevail. But unfortunately, so long as people will want to read in the paper how they ought to have liked the concert they heard the night before, the critic will be critical.

Once, only once, I actually wrote a concert review. Roger Wagner, the choral conductor, had written a three-minute spoof billed as "Roger Wagner's Mad Mod Madrigal Chorale." We gave its "first and positively last performance anywhere" at one of our annual fund-raising Allegro Balls. Opera diva Dorothy Kirsten, movie star Sam Jaffe, composer John Green ("Body and Soul"), and a number of others joined in the fun as humble members of the chorale. The local music critic took the role of basso profundo.

At the conclusion of the performance, we bowed to thunderous applause. Whereupon I announced that thanks to my very special connections with the *Los Angeles Times*, I had obtained an advance copy of the review of our performance. I proceeded to read it. Here it is:

ROGER WAGNER CONDUCTS FIRST AND LAST PERFORMANCE OF HIS MANGLED OPUS "NOW IS THE MONTH OF MAYHEM"

It was a frustrating experience for the well-turned-out audience that attended the Eleventh Annual Allegro Ball of the Chamber Symphony Society of California. High-powered press agentry had touted the world premiere of a new choral work by Roger Wagner, which, we were led to believe, was of a magnitude to rival, perhaps even displace, such long-established favorites as Bach's "St. Matthew Passion" and Handel's "Messiah."

It did nothing of the sort. We have long known that Mr. Wagner is not a pianist. Now we know that he is not a composer either. No kin, he, of Richard.

Mr. Wagner's composition is, to put it in the most charitable terms, eclectic. He has borrowed shamelessly from Bach, Handel, Beethoven, and Lawrence Welk. The acrid sensuality and subdued rhetoric of the opening section in F major, "Now is the Month of Maying," were nowhere in evidence, due to the catastrophic intonation of some of the singers, especially the sopranos, altos, tenors, and basses.

As far as this reviewer is concerned, the heartrending cry of anguish, "Ach, wie jauchze ich," was virtually inaudible. Nor is there cause for congratulations for Mr. Wagner's choice of his singers.

Among the few redeeming features one must mention the rendition by Madame Kirsten of an aria which to this reviewer seemed vaguely familiar. For some mysterious reason Mr. Wagner scowled as only Mr. Wagner can scowl, and Madame Kirsten was forced to abbreviate the unknown aria [which was the universally known "Un Bel Di" from *Madame Butterfly*], bringing it to a sudden close with an exquisite trill preceded by an apoggiatura on an inverted C-sharp-minor eleventh chord.

The only other high point of an otherwise depressing evening was the discovery of an extraordinary new basso profundo never before heard in these parts. His all too brief solo consisting of the one word "A-Round," was the climax of the evening. One may confidently predict a brilliant future for this magnificent artist whose voice and stage presence remind one of the late Ezio Pinza. His is a name to be remembered. Unfortunately, it was not listed in the program.

Of the other performers the less said the better. Hopelessly incompetent singers, masquerading under such names as Sam Jaffe, John Green, and Henri Temianka, made one grateful for the one truly impressive feature of Mr. Wagner's composition: its brevity. If the composer could be induced to cut it by another three minutes the work would be greatly improved.

Let it be said to the critic's eternal credit that he laughed as heartily as anybody. As a matter of fact, he expressed his amazement that I had been able to parody his style so perfectly, and begged to be given a copy of my review. Let's be fair to the critics. They can be as jolly as the rest of us—except when provoked by a concert.

Then they sometimes find the temptation irresistible to indulge in a recklessly snide remark, no matter how cruel, unfair, or ignorant. Anything for a bon mot. At one of my concerts the critic wrote about the harpsichordist: "Considering how little he played, he might have phoned it in." I thought it was a vicious remark, but not the critic. When I protested, he answered, "It was in my opinion a wholly permissible and good-natured bit of humor . . ." I doubt that would have been his reaction if he had been on the receiving end.

Luckily the influence of most critics is limited to the community in which they are active, with the exception of large cities like New York. A good or bad review in *The New York Times* can have nationwide repercussions. But the critic in Natchitoches, a community in Louisiana, while he may blight an artist's hopes of sweeping Natchitoches off its feet, is incapable of interfering with his right to have another fling in Nacogdoches (Texas) or even Upper Musquodoboit (Nova Scotia). This considerably brightens the picture.

Let's be fair: Even in our own time there are music critics bountifully equipped for their demanding assignment. Yohanan Boehm, the critic of the prestigious *Jerusalem Post*, started his career as a french horn player in an orchestra conducted by William Steinberg. He studied piano and cello, is a composer of considerable attainments, and conducts. But what impresses me most about him is his intense involvement in a national program for music for children throughout Israel. Would that all critics were so positive!

The ideal critic, the one who knows as much as or more than the performer, does exist. Robert Schumann, the nineteenth-century German composer, was one. He understood music criticism in its noblest and richest meaning. He founded his own musical publication, *Neue Bahnen (New Paths)*, and selflessly used it to spread the fame of others whose talents he discovered: Schubert, Chopin, Mendelssohn, Brahms. Critics like Schumann do not arise often. The ideal critic is not merely a fine musicologist, he is not merely a trained sensitive musician, he is not merely a warmhearted human being: he is all three at once. A really gifted and competent critic has a talent all his own, only to a limited extent dependent on his technical knowledge of the instrument played or the medium employed. It is a talent compounded of innate artistic sensibility, instrumental and musicological training, an ability to use words, and a broad human understanding and sympathy that will not deteriorate under the corroding influence of a chronic surfeit of music. A man whose sole job it is to find fault with others who are creative, without being creative himself, without having his own frailties exposed in return, is almost fated to become snide and destructive. Some years ago Mildred Norton, of the now defunct *Los Angeles Daily News*, turned over her music column for three weeks to various eminent musicians, asking each to write a column on music criticism. Many grievances were aired and a good time was had by all. If Miss Norton's example were emulated, a much healthier musical climate might result.

A real music critic ought to have the conscience and ability to study a new score before criticizing it. He ought to have studied an old score before boldly pitting his opinion about its interpretation against that of the performer who has spent years of devoted research on it. How many critics can read a score? How many *do* read a score? How many look at it before criticizing the performance in detail?

Precious few.

I have spent all my life in music, but were I asked to be a music critic, I would turn down the opportunity on the grounds of my own inadequacy. I don't think I would have the temerity to quibble with Richard Tucker's high C or Anna Moffo's chest notes, or Rubinstein's pedaling. How could I be sure that my own digestion or the day's frustrations were not affecting my mood and my listening? I know too well the sweat, blood, and tears that have gone into a performance. I know how the artist's nerves and upset stomach, an uncongenial piano, or a thousand other factors can influence his playing. Would I have the heart to strike him down for one inferior performance? Not I. I know too much about it from the other side of the footlights.

My faith in the critics suffered its severest jolt because of a recording I made. RCA Victor, on one particular occasion, had somehow, inexplicably, dropped the entire slow section from the Paganini Quartet's recording of the Scherzo of Ravel's quartet, some two minutes worth of music. When I heard the recording, I was horrified. Imagine the sight of an elephant without his trunk. Imagine hearing the "Hallelujah Chorus" on a piccolo. I frantically called RCA long-distance. To my dismay, I found that the record had been shipped out all over the country. I sat back, crushed. When the record reached the critics for review, they would pounce upon this abominable disfiguration, comparable to the destruction of Michelangelo's "Pietà." My colleagues and I waited, holding our breath. After some weeks the first review arrived, forwarded by a hawkeyed clipping service that faithfully sent us every article that mentioned the Paganini Quartet. We scanned it in an agony of suspense. There wasn't a word about the rape of the Scherzo. Evidently the critic had not noticed. Shortly afterward another review arrived from the clipping service—again, no mention of the hideous desecration. Gradually whole batches of reviews began to arrive, dozens and dozens of them. They came from every corner of the Western hemisphere, the most prestigious cosmopolitan newspapers and magazines, and insignificant little provincial organs. All had one thing in common: not one critic ever mentioned that the Ravel quartet had been disemboweled. Maybe every one of them heard what was wrong with the recording; maybe they were just grateful to get through with the job two minutes earlier. After all, making one's living listening day and night to other people making music must be tough. I sympathize with the critics—sometimes.

II

The Concert Manager

Once upon a time there was a beautiful little bird with golden wings. Although the beautiful little bird was captive in a big gilded cage, she was not unhappy, for she had a glorious vibrant voice. All day long she sang Carmen and Tosca and Madame Butterfly, and Mozart's Queen of the Night, all the while jumping hither and yon. At the bottom of the cage lay a big black mangy bird with a nasty expression on its beak. The big black mangy bird never said anything, but it ate most of the food.

One day the conductor of a famous opera company happened by and heard the beautiful little bird singing the "Bell Song" from *Lakmé*. He went up to her, lifted his hat, adjusted his opera cloak, and quoth, "Madame, will you do me the honor of singing Lakmé at our next performance?" Then he noticed the big black mangy bird at the bottom of the cage. Suppressing a grimace, he added, "Of course, that bird stays here."

But the beautiful little songbird replied, "I can't go without him. He always comes along."

The next day the conductor came back, this time with his whole executive committee, and they promised the beautiful little songbird all the most tempting roles in

Tosca, Lucia di Lammermoor, The Magic Flute, and even *My Fair Lady.* "But," they implored, "please leave that horrible mangy black bird here."

"I can't—I can't," replied the golden songbird. "He always comes along."

"But why can't you?" implored the committee. "Why does he have to come along?"

"Because," said the golden little songbird, "he is my manager."

The man who told me this story was that impish Irishman Freddie Schang, then President of Columbia Artists Management, Inc., in New York, the biggest management in the world. Today the mangy blackbird no longer is confined to a cage. He occupies and owns an aviary six stories high on West Fifty-seventh Street. No longer, except in the rarest cases, does the mangy bird go along with the performing songbird. Modern mass-production methods have irrevocably changed the relationship between artist and manager during the past fifty years. The basic difference is that in the old days the manager was an impresario who personally supervised every detail of an artist's life and career, hovering over him from the minute he received the morning press reviews along with his breakfast, to the moment when, having been cheered to exhaustion by his adoring public, he retired for the night.

Today the manager commutes to his office like every other businessman. On the wall behind him is a huge map, with hundreds of colored pins, each indicating a town and a concert society in which the manager has acquired a vested interest. More pins are in the desk drawers, ready to be brought out as additional communities are captured. High above the din, remote from the battlefield, the modern concert manager operates like a five-star general.

Managers come in all shapes and sizes. They range

from Freddie Schang to Sol Hurok, the Russian immigrant who bills his own name ahead of Artur Rubinstein's, and to Rudolf Bing, who ruthlessly kicked legendary songbirds like Helen Traubel and Lauritz Melchior out of the Met. At the other end of the spectrum there are such melancholy characters as Mr. Kolischer of the Moscow State Philharmonic, a downtrodden factotum with the dress and demeanor of a pallbearer. There is no telling what goes on behind the façade of those hard-driven promoters. One day, after a lifetime of successful guerrilla warfare inside and outside his organization, Schang suddenly began buying the whimsical paintings of an unknown artist named Paul Klee. No one had previously suspected Schang's interest in art, let alone the unusual form his aberration would take. By the time Klee had become famous, Schang had one of the most important and valuable collections in the world.

Kolischer collected on a more modest scale. He asked me to bring him a plain black leather briefcase upon my next visit to Moscow. As consumer goods have always been in short supply in Soviet Russia, I gladly obliged. But my eye happened to fall on a brown briefcase that was so beautiful, and so superior to the black ones, that I bought it instead. When I proudly presented it to Kolischer, his face fell, an unlikely feat for a man whose face was permanently etched in melancholy. "I can't accept it," he whispered. "They would notice that I have a new briefcase. I would lose my job."

Some managers emerged from early careers as unsuccessful musicians, others don't know the first thing about music and care less. One of the senior members of the Columbia organization moved up to sell Reddi-Whip. When I saw him again, he was in a state of euphoria. "Much easier to sell than those ornery musicians," he chuckled. Rudi Bing started out as a singer. When I first

met him after he had fled Hitler's Germany, he was
renting a small apartment across the courtyard from
mine in the same building. He was desperate. He had
been opera manager in Germany, where opera was an
institution and hundreds of towns had their own opera
house with a year-round schedule. In England there was
only one opera house, Covent Garden, which managed
to squeeze by on a schedule of a few months annually.
It was difficult to see how this penniless refugee was
going to make a living in England. I felt very sorry for
poor Rudi Bing and his Russian wife, Nina. We would
talk by phone while looking at each other across the
courtyard, and eventually we became friends. One evening I invited the Bings to a little party, where I introduced them to Wolfgang Reinhardt, son of the celebrated stage director Max Reinhardt and then a young
movie producer. Wolfgang went on to Hollywood and
six weeks later a rare telephone call interrupted the depressing quiet that usually hung over the Bing apartment. "Hollywood calling," said the operator. "Wrong
number," answered Bing automatically, and hung up. A
few minutes later the phone range again. "Hollywood
calling for Mr. Rudolf Bing," said the operator this time.
Wolfgang Reinhardt was on the line. He was assembling
his cast for a forthcoming movie production of *The Great
Waltz* and for the leading part he wanted a certain singer
named Miliza Korjus. Could Bing, with his background
in German opera, locate her and negotiate a contract?
Bing was offered a reverse sliding-scale commission. Unlike a regular commission, his reward would be in inverse proportion to the size of the contract. In other
words, the cheaper the singer, the more Bing would
make.

It was probably the easiest deal Bing ever made in all
the years of his brilliant career that was to follow. Gor-
geous Korjus jumped at the offer. Bing waited a full day

before he notified Reinhardt, so the latter would not underestimate Bing's persistence, brilliance, and diplomatic prowess. Bing pocketed $7000, an immense fortune for him at that depressing moment of his life. But an even more astonishing development was to follow soon thereafter. "With my luck," Bing laughed later, "a unique phenomenon happens, totally without precedent. An eccentric Englishman suddenly builds an opera house in the country. Who would ever dream of it?"

When in the mid-thirties Mr. John Christie founded the Glyndebourne Opera on his country estate near Lewes in the Sussex Downs, inspired by his wife's beautiful voice and her love of opera singing, it seemed to the world as though Don Quixote had come back to life. There was not enough interest in England to keep Covent Garden going for a full season. How could anyone be persuaded to take a two-hour train ride into the countryside to hear opera at Glyndebourne? The idea was preposterous. But the owlish Mr. Christie, who looked like Samuel Pickwick, went ahead. He engaged the famous Carl Ebert–Fritz Busch team, formerly stage director and conductor respectively of the Berlin Opera, then both voluntary exiles from Nazi Germany. He built an up-to-date miniature opera house and produced nothing but Mozart during the first season. Artistically Glyndebourne was a triumph from the start, and very soon men were dressing in white ties, tails, and top hats at two in the afternoon in order to drive or ride out into the country for a Mozart opera beginning at five. Today Glyndebourne is as much a British institution as afternoon tea. It was not long before Bing, who had been Ebert's assistant in Berlin, was brought to Glyndebourne to handle the business side of the Festival.

By 1938 Bing had already risen to a position of some eminence, and in March of that year the British government sent him to Prague as a cultural delegate along with a group of other delegates representing business and government. As Bing stepped into the limousine to go to the airport an employee handed him an envelope. "Would you be so kind as to give this passport to Sir Hugh Sealy? He'll be on the plane with you." Bing looked for Sir Hugh, a prominent member of Parliament, at the airport and in the plane. To no avail. The plane took off for Prague. Unlike the other delegates, though, Bing flew first to Vienna for a one-day visit with his parents.

That day turned out to be the fateful twelfth of March, 1938, the *Anschluss*, the rape of Austria. All avenues of escape were immediately cut off by the German armies. Refugees from the Nazi regime, needless to say, were in special danger. Bing made his way to the station, hid in a lavatory on the train and got as far as the Czech border. There, in the black of night, all passengers were ordered off the train and lined up by the Gestapo. It was almost his turn when Bing's hand happened to brush against something inside his greatcoat pocket: the forgotten diplomatic passport! Being the image of the traditional British diplomat, tall, lean, reserved, and soberly dressed, Bing played his role to perfection, speaking as little as possible and understanding not a word of German. He wore his black homburg and presented his diplomatic passport. They waved the distinguished British diplomat on and Bing's life was saved. When he arrived in Prague, Bing mailed the passport back to its rightful owner, expressing his gratitude and the hope that Sir Hugh did not object to having had his name used. "No objection at all," replied Sir Hugh, "provided you let *me* use *your* name next time I visit Glyndebourne."

Those who complained of Bing as a tough and ruthless taskmaster at the Met may find it hard to believe that we engaged in all kinds of adolescent pranks during our London days. I had a collapsible stovepipe hat which was *de rigueur* whenever I was invited to the theater or a formal supper. Having made this heavy investment, I could not resist buying a false beard, which had only cost me two-and-six, the equivalent then of about half a dollar. It was the best beard I have ever seen. One hung it over one's ears like a pair of spectacles, and it fit so snugly that it was almost impossible to tell it was a fraud. Bing and I had no end of infantile fun with it. At one party he announced that a most distinguished scientist from Moscow had just arrived in London and would join the guests shortly. In those days, the thirties, illusions about the Soviet paradise were rampant. Everybody hankered for news from that mysterious distant Shangri-la. A few minutes later the great Soviet scientist arrived, wearing my hat, my beard, and my spectacles. He spoke only Russian, doubletalk Russian at that, but Bing obligingly translated all his remarks to the audience. No one had realized until then that Bing had such an extraordinary command of Russian. Bing and I had rehearsed our act as meticulously as a production at the Met, maybe a lot more meticulously. We made a sensation. Questions were fired at us from every corner of the room. We fielded them—if I may say so with all due modesty—brilliantly. At another party, with different guests, we reversed our roles, and Bing became the important scientist, while I was the interpreter with the unexpected command of Russian. Bing looked a little bit like Abe Lincoln when he wore my hat and beard.

The most pathetic concert manager I ever dealt with was a man named Spilman, the local Sol Hurok of Lodz, Poland's second largest city. After the concert he came backstage, looking miserable. "We had a very bad house, I lost a lot of money," he moaned. "But we had a full house," I answered naïvely. "It was all papered," he said. "I can't pay you your fee." I stammered, "But I had a lot of expenses. I traveled a long way to come here." Whereupon Mr. Spilman proceeded to draw from his left pocket, agonizingly and slowly, a few bedraggled five- and ten-zloty bills. He spread them out before me, with a hangdog look, obviously expecting me to say something like, "Case dismissed." Instead, I just stood there frozen and shocked—I was awfully inexperienced. At least a minute must have passed in dead silence before Mr. Spilman dug again, this time into his right pocket. It seemed to be an even deeper pocket than the left one. He fished around in it for an unconscionable time, and finally came up with a few silver coins. It was terribly embarrassing. Ultimately I settled for less than half my fee. When I got back to Warsaw, my manager there apologized profusely for having forgotten to alert me in advance. "He tries that on every artist," he enlightened me, somewhat belatedly.

An inexperienced soloist assumes a manager has magical powers. If only his manager would "push" him, the soloist's career would be made. Unfortunately most managers prefer the line of least resistance. They "sell" what they don't have to push—namely, the established artist. Sometimes, when a manager has the exclusive management of an artist who is in great demand, he can practice an effective form of blackmail. He will let the client have the big-name artist only on condition that he simultaneously signs up a young unknown for a separate engagement. Milstein and Piatigorsky benefited from that strategy in the earliest phase of their careers, when their manager, Alexander Merovitch, used the already established Horowitz as a pacemaker. Luckily all four were intimate friends.

The hopeful young soloists are not entirely wrong: big management *can* have magic powers. It can make or break the young performer. Take Columbia Artists Management, still the biggest concert management in the United States, and its subsidiary, Community Concerts, Inc., which it owns and operates. Community Concerts operates a chain in many hundreds of towns throughout the United States and Canada. An educated guess would place the number at approximately one thousand. Some towns drop out every year and others are added. Community Concerts organizes a series of concerts in each of these towns, usually without competition. The system functions with extraordinary efficiency. The home office in New York employs a large pool of trained representatives, each of whom is assigned to spend a week in each of the communities in his territory. That week is proclaimed as Community Concerts Week. The field representative obtains the free use of some convenient space, like the lobby of the leading hotel, sets up headquarters there, and selects a number of local bigwigs and smallwigs who agree to act as a committee to spearhead the local campaign. Tickets for the annual subscription series, which may consist of anywhere from four to seven concerts, can be bought only by what is usually called subscription, but what they call membership. The cost of these "memberships" is remarkably reasonable, and any local citizen who manages to sell ten memberships receives his own free. There is always a big kickoff dinner, at which the field representatives and others give pep talks. The unsophisticated audiences that are lined up for these concerts are usually not told what artists will appear on the series, let alone what programs they will play, although sometimes the services of one prominent artist will be announced, to whet the audience's appetite. The concerts are planned to take place either in the local high-school auditorium, or if necessary in a movie theater, the rental for which is nominal.

Memberships can be bought and paid for only during the single week of the campaign, neither before nor after, and late applications are turned down even if the concert hall is not sold out. This clever gambit pays off in the long run. In many towns the series is sold out, and even oversold, during the campaign week—oversold because Community Concerts correctly estimates that 10 percent of any audience never shows up at any one time, either because of illness or conflicts with other events such as bridge tournaments or weddings. What this means is that twenty-two hundred memberships may be safely sold for an auditorium seating only two thousand. Of course, all twenty-two hundred are paid for in advance.

Now, with every last penny securely in the bank, Community Concerts proceeds to budget the artists for the forthcoming concerts. By what system? The brain trust in New York, really Columbia Artists Management, assigns its artists to various areas, in effect controlling the amount of work each artist will have. A local citizens' committee will ask for a certain artist, only to be told, if it suits the management, that he is "not available" in that area during that season. I discovered that Community Concert Associations within a radius of thirty to forty miles from my home in Los Angeles were repeatedly told that I was "not available." There was nothing personal or unfriendly in their having been refused my services. More likely Community Concerts had a contractual obligation to some group it had imported, and the only way to meet that obligation was to cajole certain communities into accepting these artists in place of the ones they had asked for. Alternatively, after booking an artist for a solo appearance with an orchestra in a big city, Columbia had to find Community engagements en route if the soloist was to have money left over after expenses. Thus the majority of the soloists are pawns on the gigantic Community Concert chessboard.

How restricted Community Concerts is in furthering the young artist's career is best proven by the fact that

Columbia Artists (or CAMI, as it is generally called by the insiders) as a matter of policy discourages an artist's reengagement in a Community town. When Van Cliburn began his career around 1954, long before the Moscow triumph that brought him world fame, CAMI provided him with a respectable number of Community engagements, at a modest three-digit-figure fee of course. By the fourth season he was already on his way down. Instead of the thirty engagements he had had two years earlier, he had three Community concerts in the fall in McAllen and Graham, Texas, and in Natchitoches, Louisiana; then, after a three-month break, two more Community concerts, in Norwalk, Ohio, and Coldwater, Michigan. Why? Because CAMI cannot really help to build the young artist's reputation in this assembly-line operation. Hundreds of other young artists, most of them equally meritorious and equally unrecognized, are standing in line, waiting for what they naively think is their chance for a career. What irony! Without Moscow's recognition and Khrushchev's personal blessing, Van Cliburn today might be an obscure teacher in a little Texas town, or a shirt salesman. It is an open secret that prior to the Moscow contest, he was profoundly discouraged and in an acute state of depression.

Columbia Artists charges a 20-percent commission for every engagement it delivers to one of its artists. It charges an additional fee for engagements arranged by Community Concerts. In order to avoid the appearance of charging a double commission, Columbia Artists calls this second commission the "differential." The way it works is: Community Concerts, Inc., in New York will offer a certain artist a fee of, say, $1000. There exists, however, a contractual agreement between the artist and Columbia that in reality he will receive only $750. The difference between the $750 and the $1000 is the so-called differential. But of course the artist does not receive $750.

Columbia Artists first deducts a commission for obtaining an engagement for him with Community Concerts, Inc. The artist therefore pays somewhere around 40 percent of his fee in commissions. This compares with a 10-percent commission paid to concert managers throughout Europe. Out of his net fee the artist is expected to pay his accompanist's fee, all transportation for himself and his accompanist, and hotel expenses.

Is it worth it? On one hand Community Concerts provides an additional income, work, and experience for a lot of young soloists, as well as older ones. It also brings good music to hundreds of communities that lack the knowhow to organize concerts without outside help. On the other hand the Community Concerts system often permits great career opportunities to be missed. For if there is a choice or conflict between a prestige appearance in a big city such as Chicago (known as a "straight" engagement), and a Community Concert in the sticks, the economics in the matter become decisive. The straight engagement in Chicago nets Columbia 20 percent, the Community Concert approximately twice as much. Community Concerts wins. The soloist anxiously trying to build his career is the loser. Of course, he rarely finds out. I happened to find out because someone in Chicago called me to spill the beans, but my anguished protests to Columbia were to no avail. The Community engagement in an obscure suburb of Chicago remained in force and I lost the prestige engagement because the Chicago Society would have me only on an exclusive basis.

Don't let me convey the impression that CAMI consists of an assortment of ogres. Many CAMI managers, in their own way, are deeply devoted to some of their artists. I enjoyed a close personal friendship with my own manager, Chris Schang, Freddie's son, who was one of CAMI's vice-presidents until his untimely death. In

charge of CAMI's Soviet artists, he learned to speak
fluent Russian, just as he had previously learned French;
he even learned to speak Chinese. The problem with a
powerful management combine like CAMI is that the
men and women in it become caught in a huge machine.
Management has become unmanageable. It's the story of
the sorcerer's apprentice. Forces are unchained that pro-
liferate in all directions, unchallenged and uncontrolled.

George Szell once made a comment that I have always
cherished. Columbia had offered me an exclusive contract following a successful New York appearance. I
asked Szell to look over the complicated contract before
I signed it. It was full of "whereases," "the artist agrees
to," and all kinds of mysterious clauses, one of which
pertained to the management's unrestricted control over
any future hypothetical technological breakthrough
such as George Orwell, Aldous Huxley, and Ray Bradbury had not even considered. Szell, peering through his
thick lenses, carefully looked over the contract without
saying a word. Then, turning to me, he commented,
"They've left you just enough freedom to draw your
bow across the strings." I signed anyway. What choice
did a young artist have?

The relationship between artists and managers is
rarely ideal. More often than not the artist will say, "My
manager doesn't lift a finger. I get all the engagements,
and he gets all the commissions." Would the artist be
better off without the manager? Of course not. An artist
without a manager has the status of an unwed mother.
Thousands of concert societies, colleges, and other organizations must be fed continuous information about
the artist's ceaseless triumphs, so that his name is kept
before the public. While this never-ending stream of
printed pulp may swiftly land in the wastebasket, it
nonetheless has a subliminal impact. Sooner or later the
field representative, as the flesh-peddling traveling sales-

man is euphemistically called, will move in for the kill, sustained by high- or low-pressure long-distance calls to the local organization from his big chief in New York. Big organizations like Columbia have large staffs that concentrate exclusively on graphic design, printing, and promotion. They vie with each other in inventing new attention-getting devices. Bartlett and Robertson, at one time a popular two-piano duo, were startled to find upon their arrival in the United States that the cover of their new brochure consisted of a huge red stoplight with the one word "Stop!" underneath it, just in case anyone overlooked the subtle meaning of the red light. As one opened the cover the red light gave way to an equally large green light. Underneath the green light was the helpful explanation "Go." Upon closer examination that word turned out to be part of a complete, actually grammatical sentence: "YOU CAN'T GO WRONG WITH BARTLETT AND ROBERTSON." To prove that you couldn't go wrong, this was followed by a chorus of praise from newspapers all over the world. I have occasionally been tempted to ask my manager to print a brochure in which my good reviews would be printed in one column and my bad ones in another, side by side. After all, every artist gets good and bad reviews. It would be refreshing to get the complete picture for a change.

"ENGAGE TEMIANKA AND FIND OUT FOR YOURSELF." Now *there* would be an attention-getter.

The world of the virtuoso also has its own trade magazine, *Musical America*. Aside from the regular monthly issues there is the annual booking issue, which looks like the Manhattan telephone directory. In it virtually every virtuoso before the public proclaims his availability, usually in an impressive full-page ad with his photograph (sometimes taken twenty years earlier), his latest reviews and recordings, and the necessary information about his

concert management, eagerly waiting to handle inquiries and proffered contracts. Anyone taking less than a
full page (which now costs about $600) is virtually de-
moting himself, announcing to all the world that he can't
afford a whole page. "Don't engage me," the ad screams
from the rooftop; "I'm a poor *schlemiel* who hasn't made
it."

The most celebrated artists, such as Rubinstein, who
don't need to advertise, usually do anyway. When you
are in their income-tax bracket, it is almost a free ad.
Several virtuosos, such as Horowitz, Gould, and Piatigorsky, don't want to play any more and have become
notorious for canceling engagements long after accepting them. One wag suggested that they jointly advertise
in Musical America as follows:

> HOROWITZ
> GOULD
> PIATIGORSKY
> *Available for a limited number of cancellations.*

One evening Sol Hurok was at my house during one
of our impromptu quartet sessions with Piatigorsky and
other friends. "Tell me, how do you do it?" Hurok whispered in my ear. "I can't get him to play!"

Big outfits like Columbia have a special traffic department that plans all transportation and hotels for the
artist. They figure out how you get from Duluth, Min-
nesota, to Birmingham, Alabama, just in time for the
concert the next night. Once I had already boarded the
bus to Las Vegas, Nevada, when a Western Union messenger brought me a telegram from Columbia in the nick
of time. The community concert that night was in Las
Vegas, New Mexico.

To this day the concept of concert management differs
vastly from one country to another. During all the years
I knew them Ibbs and Tillett, the biggest English agents,

who are more a clearinghouse than a management, did all of their business by surface mail, considering airmail an extravagance to be resorted to only in dire emergencies. American management, by contrast, uses long-distance phonecalls and telegrams routinely, charging them all to the artist. Mischa Elman, the *enfant terrible* of great violinists, once retaliated by sending his manager a collect telegram with the following urgent message:

> AM SITTING IN THE DINING ROOM OF MY HOTEL HAVING FRENCH ONION SOUP, WHOLEWHEAT TOAST, FILET MIGNON MEDIUM RARE, MIXED SALAD WITH THOUSAND ISLAND DRESSING, FRENCH APPLE PIE À LA MODE, COFFEE WITHOUT CREAM AND SUGAR. WEATHER MARVELOUS. HAVE SPLENDID ROOM WITH MAGNIFICENT VIEW. NOW HOW DO YOU LIKE TELEGRAMS COLLECT? YOURS CORDIALLY, MISCHA ELMAN.

One has the distinct impression that a firm like Ibbs and Tillett deliberately refrains from promoting its artists, as an ungentlemanly pursuit, alien to the British concept of good sportsmanship. They are confident that concert societies all over the British Isles will keep coming back year after year, as they have for the past seventy or eighty years, and in subdued tones make their decisions known. No contract is ever necessary. I never signed one with Ibbs and Tillett, because their word was as good as a contract. Signing contracts with Latin American concert management is not generally necessary either for another reason: they don't pay any attention to them; they like to improvise. Many an artist has found his tour annulled just as he was about to step on the plane. Signing contracts with Russian concert managers has other disadvantages. You can't take the money out of the country. At the end of my Russian concert tours I left weighed down with all kinds of furs, books, and enough plane and train tickets to see me through my European tours for the rest of the year.

Foreign correspondents besieged my concerts, not for the music, but because they knew I would let them have my rubles at black-market rates.

Some managers guard their artists the way a mother hen watches its young. Rulle Rasmussen, a grand old rogue and Norway's leading impresario, used to travel with his artists wherever they went. This could be embarrassing, as it was widely known that he was a gay liberator long before it became fashionable. There was a wonderful feeling of spontaneity about concertizing in Norway. Rulle was always on hand to observe the progress of a recital. When a rising tide of public approval indicated that all was going well, Rulle went to the box office and hung out a sign saying:

BECAUSE OF THE SENSATIONAL SUCCESS
ONE MORE POSITIVELY LAST PERFORMANCE
TOMORROW NIGHT

As people streamed out of the concert hall they would line up at the box office and the concert scheduled for the next evening was sold out in a matter of minutes. Compare that with our highly organized American concert life. Nowadays most orchestras and other concert societies engage their soloists a year and more in advance. By the beginning of any one year all bookings have been finalized for the following winter season. If you want to engage a Rubinstein or a Serkin, you probably have to book two or three years ahead of time.

In Japan the system is quite different again. There an artist is likely to be booked by one of the newspaper conglomerates or the labor unions. The rivalry among the newspapers is so fierce that what one of them sponsors is blithely ignored by the others. When I went to the Osaka Festival with the Paganini Quartet, the Boston Symphony appeared there too, both of us sponsored by the owners of the *Asahi Shimbun*. As far as the two other major newspaper chains were concerned, *Mainichi* and *Yomiuri*, we had never set foot on Japanese soil. Even stranger were the experiences of the artists engaged by Japanese labor unions. The members, for a nominal payment of about twenty-five cents a month, were entitled to the concerts as a membership dividend. In the case of Ro'on, with a membership of more than a hundred thousand, some artists repeated the same concert every night for a month before completing their contract.

In Russia concert managers double as secret agents. Maybe not all, but certainly the one who traveled with me who was in the employ of the State Philharmonic. Individual enterprise is obviously discouraged. He met me at the railway station the day our tour started out of Moscow. To be precise, he picked me up at my hotel three hours before the train left. He had an acute anxiety complex about getting to railway stations on time. I learned why. Approaching the platform, we had to climb over hundreds of bodies surrounded by thousands of pieces of luggage and teakettles. Those were the unfortunate masses competing for whatever transportation was available. When the train finally arrived, there were mob scenes worthy of Sergei Eisenstein, the Russian film director. My concert manager participated in the mass assaults from sheer habit, until I pointed out to him that we could afford to sit back until everyone else was exhausted, and then take our reserved seats in the so-called "international" car. There is a limit to Communism, after all.

Jacob Tolshinsky was his name. He was a little man, badly dressed as most Russians are, and his total luggage for the month's tour consisted of a sausage-shaped container about half the size of a shopping bag. It was obvious that he was not thinking in such extravagant terms as a change of suit or shoes. He was exquisitely attentive. When the dinner hour approached, he insisted on going to the dining car ahead of me so that I would not suffer the frustrations of waiting for food and drink to be served. Waiters may be slow the world over, but when a Russian waiter disappears for an hour after taking your order, you have the nagging fear that he has been carted off by the Secret Police. Mr. Tolshinsky took care of everything. When he came back to escort me to the dining car, my table was all set for me, graced with a carafe of the finest vodka, mountains of fresh Beluga caviar, fragrant black Russian bread, butter, thick black pepper, and plump juicy lemons. A feast for kings. Foreign tourists usually complain about the food in Russia. They just don't know what to order. Stick to the aforementioned dishes, plus such soups as borscht and shchi (unpronounceable but exceedingly edible), smoked salmon, sturgeon, sausage, and, to top it off, ice cream, and you will be all right. The trick is to have a Russian concert manager, alias secret agent, to order your food in advance. When we checked into our first hotel, I found a bunch of fresh violets on my bedside table, courtesy of Mr. Tolshinsky. The honeymoon lasted for two weeks, during which he brought me a fresh bunch of violets every morning. Then it grew on me that I had no privacy except in my room. Whenever I went to a restaurant, a theater, a museum, or my own concert, Mr. Tolshinsky was always by my side. He arranged everything to perfection: the best seats, the best restaurants, and cabs, regardless of the prevailing scarcity. The only thing I couldn't have was privacy. In Kiev, one glorious spring morning, I succeeded in going off on my own. Even Mr. Tolshinsky sometimes had to go to the bathroom. I crossed the river, visited the magnificent medieval Ladra monastery, and relaxed in the luscious apple orchards, all white with blossoms.

When I returned to the hotel for lunch, Mr. Tolshinsky was waiting outside. His face was white with tension. He followed me to my room where, at the climax of a Dostoevskyan scene, he revealed that he was a member of the Secret Police, assigned to guard me. My escapade could cost him his job. I tried to appease him, but from that moment on Mr. Tolshinsky was a changed man. In fact, never before or since have I seen anyone change so irreversibly. He felt that he had failed and went into a deep depression from which he never recovered for the rest of the tour. Gone forever were the bouquets of fresh violets. He hung around stony-faced, a shadow of his former self. He had been the ideal concert manager, personal representative, and secretary. Now nothing functioned any more. Cabs failed to appear, room reservations failed to materialize, trains were missed. All my efforts to console him failed. The whole universe had been reduced to a single hopeless *nichevo*. Ultimately his depressing presence became intolerable. I phoned the Philharmonic in Moscow and declared I would cancel the rest of the tour unless they recalled Mr. Tolshinsky. They did.

The next day I found a woman waiting for me in the lobby. She looked as if she might have been a champion wrestler twenty-five years earlier. Moscow had sent her to replace Mr. Tolshinsky. As we boarded the train that evening I opened the door to my sleeping compartment and bade her goodnight. She wedged her way in and explained, "I sleep here too." I had heard that sleeping compartments on Russian trains were coed. Total strangers were thrown together in the course of an overnight journey. I had had fantasies about it, but the reality turned out to be different. Making the best of a bad bargain, I modestly undressed in the washroom and climbed into my upper berth. The next morning I awoke with a rude shock to the vision of the massive reclining figure below. She was not in the least embarrassed. "I dreamed you wanted to make love to me during the night," she said, "but I told you: 'Better not.' " Better not. I began to feel more relaxed about the whole thing. At least she wasn't depressed. One can't have everything.

Sometimes, in moments of euphoria, I try to imagine what the ideal manager would be like. He would have immense power, almost unlimited outlets, and unexpected cultural curiosity, like my friend Freddie Schang. He would be attentive to my slightest whim and personal need, like Mr. Tolshinsky at his best. He would be gentlemanly, with the most scrupulous sense of integrity, like Ibbs and Tillett in London. He would be a true friend and brother-in-arms, like Alexander Merovitch was when he first helped Horowitz, Milstein, and Piatigorsky make their careers. He would be able to organize concerts and sell them out on a day's notice, like Rulle Rasmussen in Norway, making it all seem like fun and spontaneous. When you find that manager, be sure to let me know. I'm waiting.

12

The Accompanist

In my career as a soloist I have discovered that no function in the peculiar world of music is more peculiar than that of the accompanist. Without an accompanist violinists, cellists, or singers could not give recitals—which creates a basic problem for the soloist: he must have another person on the stage to carry out an indispensable function, but he must not fall into the trap of having to share the applause and recognition of the public. Out of this dilemma has developed the concept that if accompanists must be seen, they should not be heard, or heard only as remotely as the tinkling of a distant bell. Better yet, the accompanist, if possible, should not be seen at all. For this reason the soloist stands in front of him during the concert, and after each piece discreetly drops him off backstage before taking his curtain calls alone.

For exactly the same reasons posters and advertisements announcing the recital of a soloist frequently leave out the name of the accompanist altogether, and the lettering in which his efforts are acknowledged on the house program are borrowed from the bottom line of an optometrist's chart. Even the critics reserve but a single sentence for the accompanist at the very end of

their rave reviews for the soloist. This sentence usually
góes: "Mr. John Faintly was at the piano." Or, if the
critic happens to be an exuberant and humane sort of
fellow, he may say, "Mr. Robert Ghostly was the able
accompanist."

In all the annals of the concert world I have known
only one artist, a fellow violinist, who found a way to
dispense with accompanists. He specialized in recitals
consisting of Paganini's twenty-four Caprices for the
Violin Unaccompanied, or Bach's six Solo Sonatas for
Violin. His remaining repertoire consisted of unaccompanied music by Reger and Rust, a German composer of
the past. In most of his concerts a dull somnolence would
gradually creep over the scattered audience. This particular violinist also had the strange habit of walking off the
stage as he was playing the final bars of a composition.
Once, when he finished with the Bach Chaconne, the
concluding chords barely reached the audience from the
dressing room.

If anyone in this vale of tears still innocently believes
that justice and democracy prevail in our society, let him
examine the status of the accompanist, the martyr of the
world of music, the unsung musical hero of our time.
Accompanists like Franz Rupp, Artur Balsam, Leon
Pommer, Adolph Baller, Harry Kaufman, and Ivor
Newton are or were superb artists in their own right, far
superior to some of the soloists with whom they appeared, and the equal of the best of them. The trumpet-
ings of the publicity agent and managers have made the
public believe that the star is the thing. But nine times
out of ten, what is called a violin recital is actually a
sonata recital, not for violin and piano, mind you, but for
piano and violin. For that is what Beethoven and Mozart
wrote on the title pages of their sonatas: "Sonatas for
Piano and Violin" because the piano part was the most
important. In many instances the accompanist, offstage,

is his soloist's coach, mentor, and teacher, particularly where singers are concerned. What you believe to be the soloist's convincing interpretation of a song or aria is often the result of months of painstaking work and inspiration on the part of the accompanist.

How indispensable an accompanist really is was never brought home to me so forcefully as the memorable night when my accompanist excused himself bashfully toward the end of the intermission, saying he would be right back. The electrician had already flashed the house lights, the audience had returned to their seats, and I stood in the wings with my violin, ready to go on again. There I stood and waited, unable to play a single note until my accompanist returned—and return he did not. After a few anxious minutes during which an impatient audience began to applaud, whistle, and stamp its feet, I made my way toward the dressing room and up a flight of stairs rather far from the stage. As I got close I heard a violent banging and screams: "Let me out! Let me out!" The racket emanated from the far end of the dressing room where the washroom was. Apparently something had happened to the lock while my pianist was inside, and he was imprisoned, cramped inside the narrow confines of the little washroom. "Get me out of here," he shouted desperately.

Something had to be done immediately. By now there was a furious cannonade of foot-stamping emerging from the auditorium that I could hear as far away as the washroom. The electrician ran into the hall to find some of the ladies of the concert committee. Soon they trooped backstage, the *whole* committee, wearing their bright little hats, and assembled around the table in the dressing room, to the accompaniment of what appeared to be a roaring bull in a pen. There was a good deal of nervous giggling when the crisis was explained. It was a hurried conference, in which, from his private location, the accompanist participated in tones of extreme urgency. The accompanist, a heavyset man, was becoming exasperated. The ladies scurried off in all directions to find a locksmith, while I morosely descended toward the stage in a state of numb despair. If my pianist could not get out of the washroom, no more concert. It was right then that I recognized that the accompanist is the fiddler's best friend. Suddenly there was a splintering crash. I turned around, raced up the stairs, and found the accompanist lying on the floor of the dressing room. With a strength born of despair he had lunged against the door with all of his two hundred and fifty pounds and crashed through it. His left arm was semiparalyzed for days afterward, but that night we went out on stage and somehow finished the concert.

The ideal accompanist must be a great pianist and musician without being aware of it. If he is, he breaks out of his cocoon and ultimately becomes a famous soloist, like Rudolf Serkin. A certain element of passivity in his nature is almost indispensable if he is to endure the lifetime of frustration imposed on him by the partners whose achievements he shares without sharing their triumphs and fortunes. Conversely, a famous soloist who occasionally stoops to accompany is likely to pull the whole blanket over to his side. Josef Hofmann, the Titan of the Piano, once generously tried to help an excellent but lesser-known violinist by officiating at the piano. He accomplished the exact opposite, for the gasping audience concentrated exclusively on the thunderous piano *tutti* that shook the walls of the small auditorium. Accompanying took on a new dimension that evening. The true accompanist is a self-effacing, devoted companion, a Sir Walter Raleigh forever spreading his cloak over musical puddles.

I vividly recall one accompanist whose own self-effacement was more than compensated for by his mother's hero worship of her balding bachelor son. She followed us from city to city. Night after night she sat in the front row, center, frozen in a state of hypnosis, training a pair of powerful field glasses on her beloved son's hands and face. She totally ignored me, the soloist. The audience, in turn, was engrossed in watching the mother. Ultimately I got another accompanist, with the crystal-clear understanding that he had no relatives with field glasses.

I once interviewed an accompanist who began by playing a Liszt rhapsody and a Chopin ballade, very ably indeed. Then we played some pieces together. A stocky fellow with a ruddy open face, he looked at me candidly and said, "If you engage me you will have much more than an accompanist. I can be useful to you in many ways. I will carry your bags, and if you are ever in trouble, I am very strong. Look. . . ." And before I could say another word he dove underneath my grand piano and lifted it on his back. "Do you have an old telephone book?" he asked, incongruously, I thought. I found a discarded Classified Directory of Los Angeles, a huge volume. He looked at me with a childlike smile and tore the book in two without apparent effort. Then, continuing to smile, he tore it in four. Sensing an unresolved doubt in my mind, he added, "I am also the world judo champion. There are three different ways in which I can kill somebody without leaving a mark. And, by the way, I compose and orchestrate. I'll be glad to arrange your music. In my spare time I do engraving." At this point I sneezed. My visitor said, "Lie down on that couch. I am a trained masseur. A good massage is the best cure for a cold."

I did not engage him. No soloist should hire an accompanist who can kill him without leaving a mark.

In the years immediately preceding World War II the German authorities encouraged the Jews to form their own cultural organizations, since they were no longer permitted to attend "Aryan" events. There was a diabolical method in all this: it made it easier to register all Jews for purposes of later deportation and extermination. In 1935 I gave a series of fifteen concerts for these Jewish organizations in Western Germany and—hard as it may be to believe—rarely have I encountered so much joy and carefree laughter. Here were people, many of whom had been until recently among the most privileged, affluent citizens of a progressive, democratic republic. Now life had become a nightmare. Jews hardly dared appear in the street.

It was in these circumstances that I appeared in Germany with my pianist accompanist, the brilliant Franz Osborn, son of the art historian. The concerts usually took place in synagogues and went routinely enough. Occasionally a rock would come crashing through a window while we were playing, and in the Orthodox synagogues the incredibly mobile Osborn had a tough time keeping the *yarmulke* on his head. In the course of the impassioned Franck sonata it went sailing into the air time and again, to be retrieved by the page turner crawling underneath the piano, or myself during a piano solo passage, or the agile Osborn himself catching the flying *yarmulke* in midair with his left hand while sacrificing a bass note. After the concert was over our real life began. Barred from restaurants, hotels, and nightclubs, we repaired to the beautiful, civilized homes of our hosts, who were later to be robbed of their homes and their last possessions. There the pent-up tension and despair gave way to unbridled relief, good-fellowship, and exuberance. As a comedian at the piano, Osborn was in a class with Victor Borge. He would do parodies on *Carmen* and *Madame Butterfly* that had everyone in hysterics. Supper was lavish, and the Jews, who always have been at their best when life was at its worst, laughed at themselves and their misery. I cannot remember a night that we did not stay up carousing until four in the morning, and never did music have a more magical effect on people demoralized by their impending doom.

Some years later Osborn, now graduated to solo stature, visited the U.S. for the first time and wangled a ticket to the Met on the day of his arrival. Desperately lonely, as one can only be in a big and unknown city, he peered at the milling throngs, in the forlorn hope of running into a friend. In the intermission, sauntering again through the endless lobbies, he suddenly recognized somebody. With outstretched arms he flung himself upon the approaching figure. "How have you been?" he exclaimed excitedly, pumping the man's hand and slapping him on the back. "My God—how long is it since we last saw each other?" "Only a couple of hours ago," stuttered the man, "when you left your hat and coat in the cloakroom."

One of my most cherished memories of my Russian tours was my friendship with a Russian accompanist, who spoke the most marvelous self-taught French. He had read Corneille, Rabelais, Racine, and Montaigne with the aid of a dictionary. The result was charming and bewildering. He sounded like a French aristocrat brought back to life after three hundred years in a deep freeze.

He was one reason that, from the very beginning of my career, I have had such a high regard for accompanists as truly civilized human beings. Another reason was my first Russian accompanist, Alexei Belenki, a champion chess player. The noble game of chess is as dangerous and addictive as heroin. From day to day, during our concert tour, we became more and more deeply immersed. Finally we had to set the alarm clock for seven thirty P.M., allowing us exactly one hour to get ready and reach the concert hall in the nick of time.

During intermission at the concert we would gravely

discuss the strategy employed in the preceding game. Then, our heads full of knights, pawns, kings, and queens, we would return to the platform to finish the concert. Our one deadly fear was that we might be cornered by an official supper invitation at the conclusion of the concert. I developed more headaches and incipient influenzas during those few weeks than at any time before or since. As soon as the performance was concluded we would rush back to my hotel room and even before taking off our overcoats survey the game as we had left it earlier that evening. Then, once again deeply immersed in the game, we would ring for the waiter and without consulting the menu or looking up, order supper.

A large percentage of the Russian population considers chess the national game. During our long train trips our compartment was literally jammed to the ceiling with kibitzers, at least four or five of them jostling each other in the upper berth, while the train conductor brought glasses of hot tea with lemon at all hours of the day and night. But there were also those who saved money by fetching their own boiling water at each train stop. Whenever we reached a station, even at three in the morning, there would be a mass exodus of men, women, and children—dressed in nightshirts, pajamas, underwear, and stocking caps and armed with kettles and teapots—running as if possessed to the end of the platform where boiling water was dispensed free of charge. Anyone who has ever witnessed this scene would agree that the Charge of the Light Brigade was anticlimactic.

On one occasion Belenki and I were about to begin a recital at the magnificent Philharmonic Auditorium in Leningrad when Fritz Stiedry and Oscar Frid, two prominent conductors, came to the green room to wish me good luck. I felt flattered that they had come to my concert. Of course they did not actually use the words "good luck"—that is considered bad luck in our profession, as it is in the theater. Superstition and tradition demand that you either say *"Merde"* or *"Hals und Beinbruch,"* ("Break your neck and leg"). So Stiedry and Frid said *"Hals und Beinbruch"* and were just about to take their seats in the auditorium when they noticed a chessboard in a corner. Belenki and I went out on the stage to play our opening number. When we returned to our greenroom, Stiedry and Frid, seated at the chessboard, briefly glanced up and gave me a baleful look. I was disturbing them! I swiftly retreated and stood shivering in the drafty backstage area until it was time to play the next number. Stiedry and Frid never heard one note of the whole concert, but they did congratulate me afterward.

I know at least one accompanist, Gerald Moore, who by a unique process of alchemy has converted the frustrations of his profession into pure gold. He wrote a book called *The Unashamed Accompanist*, made a recording by the same title, and gave platform presentations lampooning accompanists and soloists with a wit that kept his audiences in stitches. Like every true accompanist, he had a sixth sense, an uncanny intuition of what the soloist was about to do almost before the soloist himself was aware of it. This gift nearly made rehearsals superfluous. We played many concerts together across the length and breadth of England. After a while we would spend most of our rehearsal time swapping stories.

Another fine accompanist was Harry Kaufman, a brilliant pianist who also appeared successfully as a soloist. On one occasion, when he accompanied a beautiful and gifted young violinist for whom I had admiration unlimited, I joined them on the stage to turn pages for Kaufman. In a momentary fit of nervousness, my beautiful friend came in right in the middle of a piano *tutti*, a good page or more too soon. Without batting an eyelash,

Harry retrieved her so fast that the hand was quicker than the ear. Things went smoothly for a while; then, as I turned a couple of loose pages too impetuously, half of the music sailed away and landed underneath the nine-foot concert grand. While I crawled on hands and knees beneath the piano in full view of the audience, Harry continued calmly, capably, imperturbably, with nary a lost chord. An eternity passed, it seemed to me, before I emerged from down under, clutching the music.

I faced a unique situation when I first met Alec Templeton, the inimitable blind pianist and humorist. I don't think musical Braille existed at that time. In any event, Alec depended on his fabulous memory to play a piece of music after he had heard it only once or at most twice. We spent part of the summer at the Bohemian Grove north of San Francisco, twenty-seven hundred private acres of giant redwood trees. It was an enchanting summer stag paradise for multimillionaire "Bohemians" and tycoons (Alec and I were there by special invitation and probably the only real Bohemians or democrats). The members of the Bohemian Club, which included Herbert Hoover, Jean Hersholt, and many other notables, were determined to preserve the rustic character of our environment, for which reason only gaslight was allowed in the camp. Our large redwood living room was built around a gigantic redwood tree, with an opening in the big canvas roof to let the tree through. Near the tree stood a Steinway grand, and in the corner of the room a bar with a white-jacketed bartender. It was all very rustic. Because everyone knows that bars and Steinways existed in the gaslight era, and besides, they are made of lumber. Alec and I made music from morning until night, and experienced a never-ending delight in adding more and more pieces from my repertoire to his. That inexplicable sixth sense of the true accompanist was keener in Alec than in anyone I had ever met—for although Alec could not see me, he never failed to come in on the split second when I began to play. It was uncanny.

Alec's parodies on Wagnerian and Italian opera were the funniest I have ever heard. His imitations of Hitler's rantings and ravings were frighteningly real, even though he did not speak a word of German. Satirical verses on anyone he met spouted forth spontaneously. Sometimes he would start a set of Handel variations with the utmost seriousness and then, suddenly changing gears, start swinging, to the utter delight of his listeners. On one occasion during our stay at the Bohemian Grove we gave a Templetonian interpretation of the Beethoven violin concerto. The performance had been announced with great fanfare, so everyone was surprised when Alec came out on stage alone. He reassured the audience, explained that there was a long introduction to the work to be played by the piano alone, and that undoubtedly my arrival was imminent. He would therefore start the introduction in my absence. Alec began, and as he went on and on with the interminable introduction, the suspense mounted in the audience. What if the soloist did not make it? Of course, I was hiding backstage, biding my time. As Alec came to the end of the *tutti*, I entered, playing each note of the famous octave introduction accompanied by a rhythmical step toward the front of the stage. When I got to the end of the passage, I took a synchronized bow, launched into a wild cadenza, modulated to a popular Viennese tune that resembled the Beethoven concerto, and then Alec came in, ending that piece in the most improbable jazz version. Alec carried these things off superbly.

A few days later the gag almost ended in disaster. I had been misinformed about the starting time of a formal concert in San Francisco and was late. Alec, who had a delightfully childlike quality about him, was convinced I wanted to repeat the Beethoven stunt. He had to be

forcibly prevented from going out on the stage and playing the Beethoven introduction by himself. It would
have been a catastrophe.

Once I was a guest on his enormously popular NBC
radio network show, *Alec Templeton Time*. He was to accompany me in the Scherzo-Tarantelle by Wieniawski,
a virtuoso piece in which the piano alone plays an introduction lasting a few seconds prior to the violinist's entry. Alec was running the show from his seat at the
piano. When my turn came, Alec announced what we
were going to play and plunged right into the piece, not
realizing that I was still a good twenty feet from the
microphone. I sprinted toward the mike, raising my
fiddle and playing while running. No one except those
in the studio realized what happened. As I finally arrived
at the mike, listeners throughout the country must have
marveled at the most extraordinary *crescendo* ever produced by a single violin.

I was often Alec's houseguest. He collected music
boxes, of which there were about forty, ingeniously concealed in the most unexpected places. There was no way
of using toilet paper without being treated to a performance of "Three Blind Mice." Lifting the toilet seat
produced "I Cover the Waterfront." Before going out for
the evening the ritual required setting off all forty music
boxes, and then amidst the maddening, incoherent noise,
slamming the front door behind us.

Alec's great love of good music became his undoing,
for instead of being content with his immense success as
an entertainer, he adopted a new format, playing classical music throughout the first half of the program, and
giving his audiences what they wanted only after intermission. The scheme didn't work. As a serious pianist he
was no Rubinstein, and even if he had been, I don't think
audiences are capable of digesting a double image. They
want either to laugh or revere and develop schizophrenia
when expected to do both.

At the end of one of our stays at the Bohemian Grove I was given a souvenir book with autographs from the various Bohemians whom I had befriended. The drawings and dedications range from Edgar Bergen and Charlie McCarthy to Jean Hersholt, John Charles Thomas, Irvin Cobb, and Herbert Hoover. Alec wrote the following lines, which he often recited at the end of a concert, accompanying himself at the piano.

Oh the comfort, the inexpressible comfort
Of feeling safe with a person;
Having neither to weigh thoughts nor measure words
But pouring them all out just as they are,
Chaff and grain together;
Certain that a faithful hand will take them and sift them
Keep what is worth keeping
And with a breath of kindness
Blow the rest away.

13

The Modern Composers —
Are They Noteworthy?

The most frustrated people on the face of this earth today are composers—composers of concert music, that is. Few people want to perform their compositions, and even fewer want to listen to them. There are of course a few conspicuous exceptions, which only serve to prove the rule. Benjamin Britten is virtually a British national hero; Dimitri Shostakovich is a Russian institution; Aaron Copland is referred to as the "Dean" of American composers, and Leonard Bernstein is music's Fair-Haired Boy turned gray. But for every Bernstein and Britten there are a thousand others who spend their lives covering stacks of music paper with those curious symbols that look like telegraph poles in distress, without much hope that a single page will ever be performed during their lifetime or thereafter. A good painting throbs with life the moment it is completed, a good book can be read by anyone who is not illiterate. But a musical composition is nothing but a mass of dead paper, incomprehensible even to a performer, until he has studied and played it. And play it most of them won't, if the work is "modern," a euphemism for music in which the audience is unable to detect a single appealing melody or a friendly harmony.

What has brought on this sad state of affairs? In the eighteenth and nineteenth centuries composers had no such problem. They wrote to entertain, as did Vivaldi, Haydn, and Mozart, or they wrote to uplift in their religious music, as did Bach in his church services and Handel in his oratorios. Entertainment and religion have always been popular. Music was meant to be enjoyed, not endured. In our own time most composers of concert music have ceased to be concerned with entertainment. The ones who do entertain are the movie composers. Their music is played a great deal, so they ride around in Rolls-Royces, sail their yachts, and visit world capitals. The composers of "serious" music sit in their garrets and eat their hearts out; some make a living as college professors. Even so famous a composer as Stravinsky had a thin time of it for many years. George Gershwin supposedly wanted to study with Stravinsky. He wired: "WOULD LIKE TO TAKE LESSONS WITH YOU. HOW MUCH DO YOU CHARGE? SINCERELY, GEORGE GERSHWIN." He got a telegram in reply: "HOW MUCH DO YOU EARN? SINCERELY, IGOR STRAVINSKY." Gershwin wired back: "EARNING $100,000 ANNUALLY. SINCERELY, GEORGE GERSHWIN." Stravinsky replied: "WOULD LIKE TO TAKE LESSONS WITH YOU. SINCERELY, IGOR STRAVINSKY."

My own first close contact with a composer of world renown occurred when I scheduled a performance of Ralph Vaughan Williams' violin concerto with my own Chamber Orchestra in London and invited him to conduct, with myself as soloist. Vaughan Williams is known to the world at large as the man who put "Greensleeves" on the map. To informed music lovers he is the composer who, reaching back to England's medieval church modes, projected the ageless face and tradition of England through his symphonies and other major works, as no other composer has done since Purcell. I braced myself for a long and arduous solo rehearsal. Vaughan Williams arrived, a big man, with a handsome, serene face. For some inexplicable reason I thought he looked like a village pharmacist. I tuned my violin, Vaughan Williams sat down at the piano, and we began.

Vaughan Williams did not have a single word to say about the first movement. Everything was fine and dandy. So we continued. I played the slow movement, again without interruption. And again, if I was to believe the composer, I had been infallible in my understanding of his music. To my relief he stopped me at the beginning of the last movement. "Much faster," he said. "Thank God!" I thought," I am human after all." We began again and went straight through the last movement. What I had expected to be a three-hour rehearsal was over in twenty minutes. We spent the rest of the afternoon chatting, over good English tea and scones.

Not even Beethoven, meticulous as he was, succeeded in making his intentions for tempi absolutely clear. A composer will write *allegro*, which originally meant gay, but has ended up simply conveying the composer's wish for a fast pace. How fast? It is true that the invention of the metronome by Beethoven's contemporary Johann Nepomuk Maelzel has made it possible to pinpoint the precise rate of speed, but metronomes prior to the electronic age were rarely accurate, and in any event composers change their minds, like ordinary human beings. The eminent violin pedagogue Max Rostal wrote to Bartók for a clarification on one tempo marking in his first string quartet, which he had written some years before. In reply he got a five-page letter in which Bartók proceeded to disavow practically every tempo marking he had originally indicated throughout the work. This was fine for Rostal, but where does it leave all the other performers who meticulously follow the indications in the printed score, convinced that they are being faithful to the composer's intentions? As I was to discover in the years ahead, most composers are strangely indifferent, not to say resolutely opposed, to the painstaking, meticulous preparation required for the best possible performance of their music. It must be that they are unwilling to squander their energies except on the creative process itself. Or perhaps they are so completely immersed in their own mental concept of their music that they don't listen critically to the actual sounds produced by the performer.

If Vaughan Williams exhibited none of the usual frustrations of composers, he did try to conduct, and for this I was to blame. At one rehearsal he tried, time and again, to cue the orchestra after my violin cadenza, always unsuccessfully. We were rehearsing in a room where there was no podium. Trying desperately to bring the orchestra in together, he would take several steps backward, then sprint forward as I reached the end of the cadenza, and bring his arms down with enormous vigor. But he always started sprinting too soon or too late, so that he either missed his entrance or barged right into the middle of my cadenza. Finally he turned and said to the orchestra, in the most disarming fashion, "Ladies and gentlemen, please don't look at me. Look at the soloist."

Some time after my concert with Vaughan Williams, I received a telephone call from a beautiful young blond pianist, Betty Humby, who later left her clergyman husband to live with Sir Thomas Beecham, whom she ultimately married. She wanted me to meet a brilliant but unknown young composer-pianist, Benjamin Britten. We were introduced and he proceeded to write a suite for Betty and me, of which we gave the first performance in London. I must confess to my chagrin that I did not instantly recognize in that early composition the genius who later skyrocketed to world fame with his *War Requiem*, his operas, and an enormous number of other works. Perhaps I was preoccupied with a problem that was to recur again and again in my career when dealing with composers. After the performer, sharing the composer's self-confidence, announces with much fanfare the forthcoming world premiere of a composition still in the fetal stage, he then proceeds to spend a fortune on hall rental, promotion, and advertising, making a last-minute retreat unthinkable. No sooner has the first public announcement appeared than the composer begins to experience symptoms of irregularity in the course of a pregnancy that until then has gone swimmingly. It had happened to Britten, and to make a long story short, I received the music from him only two days before the performance. As if to justify the delay, Britten had peppered the piece with fiendishly difficult passages. Taking my first peek at the completed score, I saw barbed-wire entanglements winding their way from beginning to end. To complicate matters further, I had a longstanding commitment to give a concert somewhere in Lancashire the day before the London premiere. I reserved an entire compartment on the train and spent six hours practicing Britten's piece while traveling north to the concert, six more hours traveling back to London, and then I practiced about ten hours nonstop on the day of the premiere itself.

The premiere went surprisingly well. Performers are able to summon massive reserves of adrenalin when disaster seems imminent. Britten joined us on the stage afterward, warmly shook hands, and shared in the applause.

If my experience with Benjamin Britten seemed unusual at the time, it was tame compared with my subsequent association with Serge Prokofiev, the Russian composer whose *Peter and the Wolf* made oboes

sound like ducks and bassoons like grandfathers. Prokofiev was the only composer in the Soviet Union granted
the extraordinary privilege of dividing his residence between Moscow and Paris. At the time the Ministry of
Cultural Relations had scheduled our joint appearance at
a private reception, Prokofiev and I were both staying at
the Metropole Hotel, at that time the best hotel in Moscow, a rating earned by virtue of the fact that it was
occasionally possible to borrow a plug from the cham-
bermaid when one wanted to take a bath. A national
bathtub-plug crisis hovered over Soviet Russia in those
days that still has not been solved.

Since cabs were also at a premium, VOKS, the Ministry of Culture, had asked that we remain in our room
until the limousine called for us at eight o'clock. No one
came to fetch us at eight o'clock, and no one had arrived
by eight-thirty. I became nervous and phoned Prokofiev's room. He called my attention to the fact that this
was Russia and assured me that there was nothing to be
concerned about. Another half hour passed and my telephone rang. It was Prokofiev. He seemed to have forgotten that this was Russia, and now he too was concerned.
All efforts to reach the Ministry of Culture by telephone
failed. In a country where equality was the order of the
day, the telephone system functioned no better than au-
tomobiles and bathtubs. There was no alternative but to
wait, and wait we did.

When the limousine finally called for us at about ten
P.M., we rushed to the auditorium, but the distinguished
invited audience, after waiting for two hours, had ad-
journed to the adjoining banquet hall where our arrival
was greeted in stony silence. The guests did not realize
that Prokofiev and I were not culprits but victims. I
hastily unpacked my violin and we played Prokofiev's
music to a somewhat less than responsive audience.
Then I headed straight for the remaining caviar, stur-

geon, smoked salmon, and vodka, Russia's greatest contribution to culture at that moment as far as I was concerned. Prokofiev, infuriated, demanded to be taken back to his hotel immediately.

My problem with Darius Milhaud, the most famous contemporary French composer, was of a different nature. Like so many other composers, he did not like to rehearse. Mrs. Elizabeth Sprague Coolidge, in celebration of her eightieth birthday, had invited Milhaud and me to give one concert in Boston and another in New York. I called on Milhaud at Mills College in Oakland, California, where he lived, and together we played the program through once. Then I took off my jacket in order to settle down to a serious rehearsal. Milhaud looked at me with amazement. "What's the matter?" he asked (in French, naturally). I explained. An incredulous look spread over his usually impassive features. I was utterly unable to persuade him to rehearse. He thought everything was fine, in fact perfect. With the aid of his cane he got up from the piano (he was not yet completely crippled in those days), and slowly moved away from it with an air of ill-concealed distaste. Perhaps I should mention that Milhaud by his own testimony had never taken a piano lesson. He had just "picked it up," and it is questionable whether we could have given a perfect performance even if we had rehearsed until doomsday. As a matter of fact, for not having taken piano lessons and being handicapped increasingly by arthritis, he did astonishingly well. I had to admire the agility with which he somehow faked his way across the keyboard.

Finally, in a spirit of compromise, Milhaud agreed to go over the program with me once again just before the concert, in Boston. We both stayed at what was then the lovely old Copley Plaza. Milhaud received me affably, and countering my proposal that we rehearse immediately, suggested that we first have a drink downstairs.

We went to the Carousel Room and sat on the rotating platform that made a slow but complete circle every eight minutes. I inconspicuously timed it on my stop-watch the first time around, in order to be able to keep track of the time without appearing overly anxious. When we had gone around three times, I suggested again that we rehearse. The concert was only two hours away, and what was worse, one piece had been added to the program which I had never played through with Milhaud. I had never even seen or heard the piano part.

To my relief, Milhaud agreed. Having whittled the remaining time for rehearsing to about twenty minutes (we still had to dress for the concert), he was civilized enough to prefer compromise to total victory. We had just time enough to play through the piece I had never heard with piano, and I was appalled to discover that Milhaud had employed his favorite device of polytonal-ity, which meant that while the violin was playing in one key, the piano was playing in another. It was totally unexpected (and I have never liked polytonality any-way).

I am glad we had the Boston concert first, although the New York concert was no better. The audience was one of the most distinguished for which I have ever played. Everyone had come to pay homage to Mrs. Coolidge on her eightieth birthday. Pianists Horowitz, Rubinstein, and Serkin were sitting in the front row. This did not seem to faze Milhaud in the least; he did not think of himself as a pianist. Afterward Mischa Elman came up to me and in his high-pitched voice squeaked, "I don't understand that music." With great difficulty I restrained myself from saying, "Neither do I."

But this reply would not have applied to the best of Milhaud's music, which I love. A few years later I participated in the world premiere of his String Quartets Nos. 14 and 15, at Mills College which was another strange affair. The Budapest String Quartet played the Quartet No. 14, after which the Paganini Quartet played Quartet No. 15. Then the Budapesters and the Paganinis came out on stage together and we simultaneously played both quartets. Lost in the maze of sound, I asked Milhaud at the rehearsal which part should be predominant. All he said was, "I want to hear everything." As a composer Milhaud was always listening to the whole score, polyphonically. As a performer one has a duty to guide the listener, highlighting melodies and developments in such a manner as to make the music, if possible, comprehensible at first hearing. Whenever Milhaud was present at a performance of his music, the audience reacted with extraordinary enthusiasm. The same composition, played in his absence, evoked a tepid response. Yet Milhaud, when he attended a concert, sat quietly in his wheelchair in the back of the auditorium. Having experienced this phenomenon time and again, I am forced to believe that Milhaud exuded an invisible, powerful magnetism.

An experience of an entirely different kind awaited me in the case of Alberto Ginastera, today the most prominent living Latin American composer, world-famous for his operas *Don Rodrigo* and *Bomarzo*, the latter banned in Argentina, the composer's homeland. About 1955 a charming young Brazilian pianist, Marisa Regules, brought me the manuscript of Ginastera's first string quartet. The name of the composer was at that time unknown to me. As a performer I receive manuscripts from hopeful composers in an almost continuous stream, making it impossible to do them justice. Thus, I laid the Ginastera aside until, perhaps two years later, one of my quartet colleagues called my attention to it. We began to rehearse the composition, which turned out to be music of dazzling brilliance, and that rarest of rarities among latter-day string quartets, a real audience piece. We played it everywhere, in America, Canada, the Orient, Europe, and ultimately in Buenos Aires, where we met the composer.

Ginastera was already familiar with our interpretation of his work, through the recording we had made of it. A warm friendship developed between us. Then in 1962 I read of the world premiere of a new work by Ginastera called *Cantata Para América Mágica*, based on pre-Columbian legends and Maya, Aztec, and Inca poetry. The piece was not exactly in a conventional medium since it was written for fifty-three percussion instruments and a dramatic soprano. I immediately decided to do the West Coast premiere. Little did I know what lay in store for me. The demands of the piece were ferocious. Some of the percussion instruments had to be specially made, others imported, still others rented. Two of them I dug up in the garden, because Ginastera specifically asked that two rocks be banged together at one dramatic climax.

As a matter of sensible budgetary planning I normally try to use approximately the same orchestration for all the works to be presented in the course of one evening, but that consideration had to go by the board in this instance. So I came up with a program that would be unconventional all the way through. I would start with a concerto by Vivaldi for four violins, then have four grand pianos moved on stage to repeat the same work in the pianistic transcription by Bach, both works accompanied by a string orchestra. The Ginastera, after the intermission, would provide the desired bone-shattering contrast and climax.

The next problem to be solved was to find a dramatic soprano who could cope with the part. It required a voice of tremendous range, almost, if not quite, matching Feodor Chaliapin's in the bass and Lily Pons's in the treble.

It also required dramatic power and projection, and a rhythm of steel. After auditioning large numbers of sopranos—short ones, tall ones, fat ones, thin ones—I came to the conclusion that there was only one solution to this extraordinary problem: import the singer who had been discovered and trained by Ginastera himself for the world premiere. She lived in Uruguay, and its proximity to Argentina made me think how much more meaningful the event would be if Ginastera could be present.

At this point I dimly began to realize the forces I was setting in motion, and it seemed ridiculous to put all this effort into one performance that would evaporate, so to speak, with nothing to show for it. I wrote to the head of Columbia Records, pointing out that it would be "unthinkable" not to record the work immediately following the performance. Perhaps never again could all the necessary forces be marshaled. He promptly wrote back to say that Columbia Records would never think of doing the unthinkable or failing to do the thinkable, and a contract was negotiated.

When all the instruments were installed on the large stage at Royce Hall, the view to the unaccustomed eye was not unlike something that future astronauts might find on Mars or Jupiter. Mounted on square and rectangular risers of varying heights, scattered across the stage, were assorted kettledrums of every imaginable size; small, medium, and large Indian drums; side drums, tenor drums, and bass drums; metallic sistrums (a kind of rattle); six Mexican wood drums; suspended cymbals of every size, clashing cymbals, and cowbells; various tomtoms, bongos, bells, triangles, and reco-recos (hollowed wooden cylinders rubbed with wooden sticks); claves (wooden cylinders that are struck together), gourds, and chocalhos (hollowed metallic cylinders filled with dried seeds and shaken); and, of course, maracas, sleighbells, and triangles. Finally such ordinary, everyday instruments as xylophones, marimbas, a glocken-spiel, a celesta, and two nine-foot grand pianos whose lids had been removed. There could not be many so-pranos with the power to compete with this diabolical explosion of decibels.

My next problem was quite serious. When I had en-gaged the best marimba player in town, by telephone, I had not noticed that she was pregnant. When rehearsals started, it was impossible to overlook the fact. Although she assured me that she could safely accept the engage-ment, a few days before the performance she informed me that the doctor had miscalculated: her baby could appear at any moment. It was too late to get another marimba player because the part was excruciatingly complicated. All we could do was pray. I was particu-larly alarmed because of an extraordinary coincidence. In his program notes on the closing number of the can-tata, "Song of the Prophecy," Ginastera had written, literally, "This is the climax. It symbolizes the end of the primitive world and the beginning of a new order in America. The walls of the auditorium will tremble and shake. As the ancient Greeks said when commenting on the terrific impact of their classical tragedies: *Pregnant women gave birth before their time* and people trembled, seized by cosmic terror [emphasis added]."

I was already seized by cosmic terror. And I trembled when at the dress rehearsal and at the concert the marimba player turned up with her obstetician and nurse and requested that seats be provided for them in the front row center. I could not make up my mind as to whether I should conduct the piece fast in order to gain time, or slowly in order to keep excitement to a minimum.

Compared with the crisis on the marimba front, mat-ters with Ginastera himself had so far gone relatively smoothly. He refused to fly, he never traveled without his wife, and he had broken his arm. When I met them at Union Station at the end of a long sea and train journey, they were beaming and smiling.

Mayor Sam Yorty had proclaimed Latin American Weekend for Los Angeles. There was a banquet at the Ambassador Hotel, and a champagne party in the magnificent setting of the pre-Columbian treasures of the Stendahl Gallery. At the intermission of the concert Ginastera and I were presented with a resolution on behalf of the City of Los Angeles. The bewildered official delegated to make the presentation, blinking into the spotlights, extolled me as the greatest living composer and did not seem to know what to make of the fellow standing next to me—Ginastera.

A few days earlier the dramatic soprano from Montevideo had arrived. She looked the part. When she stood on the stage, both feet firmly planted wide apart, her voice was heard above the din of all fifty-three percussion instruments.

The concert went beautifully. The walls in the auditorium trembled and shook during the great climax, but, thank God, not a single pregnant woman gave birth before her time, and I can testify to that because I watched the situation with an anxious eye all evening.

The next day we began our Columbia recording of the cantata. We all remained in a state of heightened anxiety, with the marimba player still hanging on. What would happen if she broke loose in the middle of the recording? Columbia Records had gone to a great deal of trouble and expense. Top executives had flown in from New York. But trouble, as it so often does, came from an entirely different and unexpected corner. The soprano had, in all innocence, written to her husband in Montevideo about a delightful young man she had met at our house, and how beautiful the ocean was at Santa Monica under a full moon at midnight. Her husband, like a good Latin

American putting one and one together, took the next plane to Los Angeles and insisted that she leave this city of debauchery immediately. She did. I always thought things might have gone differently if she had just not mentioned the full moon.

Now here was the situation. We had finished the cantata, but this was only one side of the record. The agreement was that the soprano was to do another work by the Brazilian Heitor Villa-Lobos on the other side, because it is an unwritten law in the recording industry that the two sides of a record must be matched on a geographical basis. If I see the Debussy quartet on one side of a record, I don't have to turn it over to know that the Ravel quartet has to be on the other side. If, God forbid, a Beethoven or Mozart quartet were to be there instead, it would be a calamity too horrible to contemplate. The soprano had started on the Villa-Lobos, but it remained unfinished. The recording in its present state was about as useful as an automobile without wheels. The crisis was ultimately solved by substituting a Latin American work for percussion instruments alone. The recording session was completed, the players went home, and the marimba player had her baby the following day. All was for the best in the best of all possible worlds.

Composers, even the most celebrated, suffer deep frustrations that range from the pathetic to the comical. I have indelible memories of a visit with Arnold Schönberg, the genius who revolutionized music in the twentieth century with his twelve-tone system. He complained bitterly that his violin concerto was not being performed and begged me to play it. I was embarrassed to have to admit that no orchestra management was likely to agree to a performance. Perhaps he knew what I did not further explain: the name Schönberg spelled bad news at the box office, and the cost of extra rehearsals, indispensable for the preparation of so difficult a new work, would be considered prohibitive. My reply to Schönberg was followed by a depressed silence. Then he said, "Couldn't you play it with piano, in a recital?" It must be difficult for a layman to understand what a humiliating compromise Schönberg was ready to accept. To perform with piano a work that was intended to be played with orchestra is like settling for an inferior black-and-white reproduction of a rich oil painting. Schönberg, sensing my hesitation, then said, "Couldn't you play one single movement?" I rarely have felt so depressed. And I couldn't do it. It would have been meaningless. After Schönberg's death, Mitropoulos was able to achieve what had been impossible during his lifetime. Twelve rehearsals were required before the concerto was performed by violinist Louis Krasner with the Minneapolis Symphony Orchestra.

Artur Schnabel, one of the most profound musicians of his time, who rarely played anything except classical music in his own concerts, composed abstruse, violently modern music of the kind that neither he nor anyone else performed in those days. It was a strange paradox. I learned how frustrated Schnabel felt when he wrote to congratulate me on my engagement to play the Beethoven Violin and Piano Sonata Cycle in Washington under Mrs. Coolidge's auspices. Schnabel's letter was in German (in longhand), and I translate it as faithfully as possible:

> If you could, in passing but urgently, communicate to that angel of chamber music, Mrs. Elizabeth Sprague Coolidge, that I have composed five string quartets and various other works in related categories, all of which I am prepared to dedicate to her (even a sixth string quartet, or anything else that she would want to "commission"), you could do me (and perhaps also her?) a great favor. Evidently she has not heard of my activities until now.

There was bitterness and frustration in every sentence. Schnabel was a man of uncompromising candor and integrity, and people either loved or hated him. I was in the first category, even if I did not always agree with him. He never gave any encores and never played sweet little nothings after intermission as was the custom in those days. Schnabel summed it up very neatly, saying sarcastically, "In the concerts of other performers only the first half is boring. In my concerts the second half is also boring." He was a great believer in "the line of most resistance," a phrase which he frequently used to emphasize artistic integrity. He also used to compare the recitals of other pianists with the day in the life of a tourist in Paris. "First they visit the cathedral, then they go on to the museum, and they end up in the bawdy house," he would say with a twinkle in his eye.

I met Aram Khatchaturian, the Russian composer famed for his "Sabre Dance" purely by chance. On one of my visits to Buenos Aires I discovered that the room next to mine was occupied by him. Khatchaturian, who spoke no Spanish, was lonely, and even though my Russian was primitive, I was an attentive listener. He never probed too deeply into how much I understood. At two and three in the morning, when I returned to my hotel, I would find him pacing up and down the hall in front of our rooms, wearing striped pajamas, his mop of black hair falling over his dark Armenian countenance, waiting for my return.

One morning he invited me to accompany him to his orchestra rehearsal, where I witnessed the most comical kind of frustration. I saw Khatchaturian's temperature gradually rise to the boiling point while rehearsing the orchestra in Buenos Aires because he was unable to get them to play one of his own compositions the way he wanted it. Finally he exploded in a torrent of fruity Russian abuse, some of which I understood. When he came to the end of his long tirade, he turned to the score, shouting in Russian, "Twenty," indicating the bar number at which the orchestra was to resume playing. Then he expectantly turned to the Spanish-Russian interpreter, waiting for him to translate his entire speech. The interpreter slowly rose from his chair, said languidly, *"Veinte,"* and sat down again.

One of the earliest concerts of the Paganini Quartet in San Francisco was attended by Ernst Bloch, the composer whose "Schelomo" Rhapsody for cello has become one of the great classics of the repertoire. The Paganini Quartet at that point was like a pair of new shoes, not yet broken in, rigid, uncomfortable in some of its interpretations. Bloch wrote me a letter after the concert which I have cherished ever since. The stature of the man was revealed in the manner of his criticism, uncompromising integrity combined with heartwarming encouragement. To me the letter was an object lesson in how to criticize constructively. Here it is, exactly as written by Bloch:

> I really wish I could see you and have a heart to heart talk with you. You and your confreres are too great artists that I may allow myself to confer "compliments" upon you . . . the quintet? Yes and no . . . to be frank . . . Schumann, superb, Beethoven??? My impression is that with the stupendous technique you all have and displayed and the perfect musicality also, your quartet could still do *much more,* if. . . .
>
> It is this "if" that I would like to discuss with you. And you will understand that I do not write in such a way to *many people!* I see the *tremendous possibilities* of your Ensemble and I would like to see them grow and be fulfilled.
>
> With warm friendly feelings, I am,
>
> > Sincerely yours,
> > Ernst Bloch

Shortly afterward we had lunch together. He was a fascinating conversationalist, with an endless fund of stories, and he looked like a Biblical prophet with his black beard and burning dark eyes. No description of Bloch could be more powerful than the famous quotation from his own writing:

> It is the Jewish soul that interests me, the complex, glowing agitated soul that I feel vibrating throughout the Bible: the freshness and naïveté of the Patriarchs, the violence of the Prophets, the Jews' savage love of justice, the despair of Ecclesiastes, the sorrow and immensity of the Book of Job, the sensuality of the Song of Songs. It is all this that I strive to hear myself and translate in my music—the sacred emotion of the race that slumbers deep in our soul.

He told me a pathetic story at lunch. He had received a letter from an unknown admirer in England, expressing a glowing passion for his unjustly neglected music and proclaiming the intention of singlehandedly organizing a Bloch Festival at Queen's Hall in London. From the ensuing correspondence with the unknown admirer, and letters from others, Bloch was deeply moved to learn that the organizer was a poor musician who had actually sold his own violin in order to raise the necessary funds to finance the festival. When, sometime later, Bloch returned for a visit to his native Switzerland, he gratefully invited this ardent fan to be his houseguest for a week. Within minutes after the man's arrival Bloch knew he had made a ghastly mistake: the man babbled on like a broken record; his worship of Bloch was so great that it was intolerable. Besides, Bloch liked to do most of the talking, and for once he was backed into a corner.

If my own experience is any guide, it would seem that the greater a composer is, the less room there is for vanity and conceit. And vice versa. When, as a friendly tribute, I invited Carlos Chavez to guest-conduct his Symphony for Strings with my orchestra, after I had done most of the rehearsing, he eagerly took all the bows by himself. When Roy Harris failed to finish a promised piano concerto in time for the scheduled world premiere, he ingeniously announced to the press that he was withdrawing the piece because I wasn't paying him enough. By contrast, when in 1970, I wrote to Shostakovich—whom I had met some years before—requesting the privilege of presenting the West Coast premiere of his new Fourteenth Symphony, he replied expressing "My gratitude for your interest in my music." Shostakovich had given his heart and soul to this masterpiece dealing throughout with the subject of Death, with which he had come face to face during a recent illness. Preparing and performing the work turned out to be a tremendous experience. French poems by Guillaume Apollinaire, Spanish ones by Federico García Lorca, and German ones by Rainer Maria Rilke had all been translated into Russian, and set to music in that language. Now, with the music matching the Russian syllables, it was not possible to sing the poems in the languages in which they had been written. So my Greek soprano and my American basso profundo, who had a major part in this song cycle that Shostakovich called a symphony, had to learn the texts in Russian. I had the texts printed in English in the program. Furthermore, since an audience unfamiliar with the work and with Russian could not possibly tell where one of the eleven movements ended and the next one started, I resorted to an unconventional device: I prepared a set of cardboards numbered from one to eleven, and had them displayed one at a time as the symphony unfolded.

I am a great believer in making unfamiliar music as clear as possible to an audience, and I think it is the lack of such concern that is often responsible for the audience's inability to understand and to respond. For example, when I conducted Stravinsky's *Pulcinella Suite*, based on old tunes by the eighteenth-century Pergolesi and his contemporaries, I first illustrated the work by playing the themes in their original Baroque version and instrumentation. When the orchestra then performed the suite, for once a lay audience was able to comprehend fully what Stravinsky had done with these themes, applying his blazing orchestral colors, savage rhythms, and biting harmony. If the modern composers of concert music, with their bewildering variety of new musical idioms and devices, want to be comprehended and supported by the populace, they should make the effort to establish the necessary means of communication. Unfortunately, many of today's composers and their interpreters act as if it were a disgrace to be understood. They are the isolated members of a small club, talking to each other in esoteric symbols.

After the Shostakovich premiere I sent the composer a tape-recording of our performance, with an accompanying letter. His reply, in the form of a two-page letter crowded with musical illustration, is an historic document, graphic and dramatic evidence of Shostakovich's unbelievable grasp of every smallest detail, and the deep conviction behind it. "Dear Maestro," he began. "In general the performance is wonderful—and I'd like to thank you warmly." He thoughtfully and in detail thanked both soloists and the members of the orchestra. "If you ever perform again my Fourteenth Symphony please note the following remarks:

> In two bell beats before 47 the fermata is too long. Pause before 81 too long, please almost attacca. Christina Krooskos sings beautifully the sixth part, but from 84 till 86 it must be more hysterical.

Thus he continued for two long pages.

I had conducted the West Coast premiere from a Xeroxed copy of the symphony manuscript. Just before

I performed the symphony again the following year I received a large package in the mail. There were Russian stamps on the wrapping, and in the upper-left-hand corner I was able to decipher the Russian writing: Moscow. I opened the package in great excitement: there was the printed score of Shostakovich's Fourteenth Symphony, clothbound. On the flyleaf, in Russian, in his unmistakable handwriting, it said: "To Henri Temianka with my profound gratitude and cordial good wishes. Dmitri Shostakovich."

14

Coda

Because my whole life has revolved around music, I have rarely been bored. How could I be? Other people may tick off the minutes standing in line for a plane that is delayed. They may get irritated, restless, even lonely. We musicians need to be alone, and the company of the elect is ours whenever we choose: Beethoven, Mozart, Bach, Schubert, and all the others. Their music goes around in our heads while others are killing time. A virtuoso carries a whole library in his head. His work is never done. There is always a phrase that needs improving—a section that must be memorized more securely.

How could I be bored when the world is full of fascinating places and people? In the course of my work I have known thousands of people around the globe, and, being gregarious, have loved knowing them. A traveling virtuoso becomes a linguist by force of circumstances. I have discovered that each new language opens up a breathtaking new world, filled with other sounds and customs. A musician's sense of touch and hearing are highly trained and developed. This seems to stimulate his other senses as well. How else is one to explain the musician's uninhibited joy in good food, his sybaritic love of all the pleasures of life?

I rarely look back, because there is always so much to look forward to. After a lifetime of pursuing music with the utmost intensity, I have yet even to hear most of Bach's 295 Cantatas, Schubert's 600 Songs, Haydn's 104 Symphonies, and most of the vast output of all the other Godgiven geniuses, from Palestrina to Bartók. All I know is the tip of the iceberg. Only a small corner of the veil has been lifted. I always look forward to the next thrilling encounter with unknown music. Even at the end of one's career one is only at the very beginning of a voyage of discovery. President Kennedy was fond of quoting the Greek philosopher who said that happiness was "using one's full powers along lines of excellence." If that is really the definition of happiness, then musicians are among the happiest people in the world.

Index